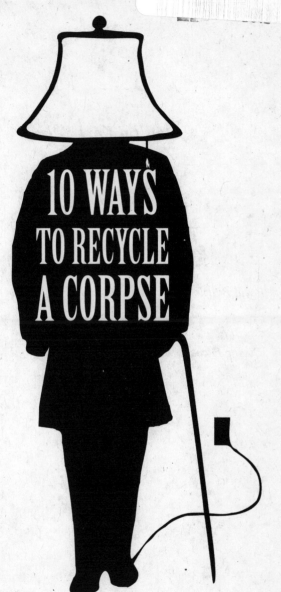

10 WAYS
TO RECYCLE
A CORPSE

Also by Karl Shaw

Gross

Gross 2: This Time It's Personal

The Mammoth Book of Eccentrics

The Mammoth Book of Tasteless Lists

Royal Babylon: The Alarming History of European Royalty

5 People Who Died During Sex

*Curing Hiccups with Small Fires: A Delightful Miscellany
of Great British Eccentrics*

100 More Dreadfully Distasteful Lists

10 WAYS TO RECYCLE A CORPSE

KARL SHAW

THREE RIVERS PRESS • NEW YORK

Library of Congress Cataloging-in-Publication Data
Shaw, Karl.
10 ways to recycle a corpse and 100 more dreadfully distasteful lists/
by Karl Shaw.—1st ed. p. cm.
Includes bibliographical references.
1. Curiosities and wonders. I. Title.
AG243.S48 2011
031.02—dc22
2011004414

ISBN 978-0-307-72040-5
eISBN 978-0-307-72041-2

Printed in the United States of America

Book design by Maria Elias
Illustrations used throughout this book are courtesy of *Graphics World
Instant Archive Art,* copyright © The Graphic Communications Centre
Ltd., 1981; *Humorous Victorian Spot Illustrations,* copyright © Dover
Publications Inc., 1985; *3,800 Early Advertising Cuts,* copyright © Dover
Publications Inc., 1991; *Big Book of Old-Time Spot Illustrations,* copyright
© Dover Publications Inc., 2001.
Cover design by Kyle Kolker
Cover photograph by © Underwood Photo Archives/SuperStock

10 9 8 7 6 5 4 3 2 1

First Edition

For Shona, Robert & Charlie

CONTENTS

Chapter Three
MEDICAL MISCELLANY

Chapter Four
WIZARDS OF ODD

CHAPTER FIVE
COURTING THE MUSE

CHAPTER SIX
SAINTS & SINNERS

CHAPTER SEVEN
MAD, BAD & DANGEROUS TO KNOW

CHAPTER EIGHT
AD NAUSEUM

Chapter Nine
LAST RITES

"A little bad taste is like a nice dash of paprika."

—Dorothy Parker

INTRODUCTION

Welcome to the follow-up to *5 People Who Died During Sex and 100 More Terribly Tasteless Lists,* another collection of grisly historical and contemporary facts and incidents.

The fact that Three Rivers Press wanted me to compile another one of these is testament to the public's thirst for morbid trivia and anecdote. This isn't a phenomenon of the twenty-first century. I'm sure there were once cavemen sitting around boring their friends with facts about the size of mammoths' testicles.

I'm sometimes asked how (and, not unreasonably, why) these lists come together. Some are gobbets of the past recycled—or dredged—from books I have previously written about royalty, dictators, scientists, eccentrics, and general historical oddities. I'll come across a story about, for example, some minor royal who kicked his valet to death (see *10 Milestones in Bad Juvenile Behavior*) then I might have a eureka moment when I think, *Didn't I read somewhere about a Russian duke who amused himself by kicking Hussars to death*—so I follow it up and fashion a list (or not, as is so often the case).

Some people might point out that trivia books strip meaning from knowledge, providing us with information but the not the context we need to apply it—and of course they would be absolutely right. The purpose is to titillate and entertain, so if you're not curious to know why Jack Nicholson asks his houseguests to piss in his garden or which African community punishes adulterous couples by feeding them to crocodiles, this book probably isn't for you.

As I write this I am up against a deadline, ruing a few lists that got away. So for now I have abandoned my search for more people who had sex with roadkill (there were one or two, believe it or not), famous people run over by cabs (the only two certainties in life—death and taxis), and relatives of the British royal family who supported Hitler, including Princess Michael's father, who was a member of the SS, although, according to the official palace explanation, only an "honorary" one. Sadly, I'm also giving up on my quest to verify a couple more royal "facts," including the identity of Prince Philip's relative who owned the biggest collection of sadomasochistic porn in Europe, allegedly.

I'm also left with this frustrating folder on my laptop called "facts with no home." For example, did you know that the Dead Sea Scrolls were written by a Jewish sect that was so holy its members didn't believe in defecating on the Sabbath? I've also had to abandon a list with the working title "God's Mysterious Ways" (Christians with tender sensibilities look away now) after learning the tantalizing fact that in Ezekiel 4:12–15 God offers a cookery tip to Ezekiel, suggesting he uses human excrement as fuel to cook bread, rather than the usual animal dung mixed with straw. (When Ezekiel protests, God generously allows him to use cow dung instead.) Did you know that He hates baldness? The Old Testament contains countless references as to how God will make Israel's enemies lose their hair and, in Revelation, at the end of the world God will render select groups of evil people bald.

I am grateful to several kind readers who have drawn my attention to errors in my previous book, despite the meticulous skills Three Rivers Press brought to bear on the unenviable process of editing, and I have tried in good faith to ensure that everything in this book, as far as possible, is accurate, although of course some of these "facts" are open to debate and interpretation. So, if you're ever on a TV quiz show and rely on this book to incorrectly answer a question about Chairman Mao's sanitary arrangements (an arcane subject I am now something of an expert on) or what Frank Zappa smeared on his friend's bedroom window, it's someone else's fault.

FOOD FOR THOUGHT

10 Extreme Food Fads

∫ 1 ∫ THE BEAN DIET

The Ancient Greek Pythagoras and his followers were among the earliest vegetarians, but it had nothing to do with healthy eating or compassion for animals. According to Pythagoras, vegetarianism was the only way to ensure you were not eating your grandmother or another relative, whose soul could have migrated to your neighbor's pig. The great mathematician was said to be so passionate about his diet that he met his death defending a bean field.

∫ 2 ∫ THE YOGURT DIET

The Russian biologist Ilya Metchnikoff, winner of Nobel Prize for Medicine in 1908, was a depressive who twice attempted suicide. His second attempt was with a large dose of morphine, which only succeeded in causing him to throw up and sit around in a catatonic state. While pondering the futility of life and the certainty of death, Metchnikoff was puzzled by the longevity of peasants in the backwoods of Bulgaria, many of whom lived to be more than a hundred. He decided that it was because they ate lots of yogurt. To test his theory he binged on untold gallons of the stuff, meanwhile boasting extensively about its life-extending properties. He died six years later at the age of seventy-one, leaving behind just a handful of fellow yogurt enthusiasts.

∫ 3 ∫ THE FRUIT-AND-VEGETABLE-FREE DIET

In 1770 English physician William Stark set out to find a cure for scurvy by subjecting himself to a series of dietary regimes.

Stark, a healthy six-footer, meticulously recorded the measurements of everything he ate, the prevailing weather conditions, and the weight of all his daily excretions. After spending thirty-one days on a diet of bread and water, which made him "dull and listless," he moved on to dietary experiments with olive oil, milk, roasted goose, boiled beef, fat, figs, and veal. After seven months of living exclusively on honey puddings and Cheshire cheese, he died of scurvy at the age of twenty-nine. He had considered testing fresh fruits and vegetables but never got around to it.

∫ 4 ∫ THE GRAHAM DIET

Advocated in the 1930s by the US Presbyterian minister Sylvester Graham, who taught that the consumption of meat and dairy products stimulated excessive sexual desire and "bad habits," including masturbation, which he regarded as an evil that inevitably led to blindness and insanity. The Graham diet consisted mainly of fresh fruits and vegetables, whole wheat, and high-fiber foods, especially the graham cracker, which was so bland and tasteless it earned him the nickname "Dr. Sawdust." He developed a band of dedicated supporters across the United States, but his diet soon lost popularity when devotees became too weak to stand up, and the remainder lost faith when their mentor dropped dead at the age of fifty-seven.

∫ 5 ∫ THE PEOPLE DIET

Montezuma II, the last Aztec ruler in Mexico, was famed for his gluttony. On a typical night he liked to eat chicken, turkey, songbirds, doves, ducks, rabbits, pheasants, partridges, quail, plus an adolescent boy or two, followed by tortillas and hot chocolate.

ʃ 6 ʃ THE "I'LL HAVE A GATOR SANDWICH AND MAKE IT SNAPPY" DIET

The actor Steve McQueen, in the last stages of cancer, lived on a diet largely comprising boiled alligator skin and apricot pits, washed down with urine, as was prescribed by his Mexican doctors.

ʃ 7 ʃ THE BOOGER DIET

According to Austrian medical expert Professor Dr. Friedrich Bischinger, picking your nose with your fingers and eating your boogers is a great way of strengthening the body's immune system. Dr. Bischinger describes mucophagy—the act of eating one's own extracted mucus—as "making great sense medically and a perfectly natural thing to do." The doctor also noted that children happily eat their own boogers, but by the time they become adults they have stopped under pressure from society.

ʃ 8 ʃ THE MILK DIET

The ninth president of the United States, William Henry Harrison, ate only cheese and milk products. His term, the shortest in the history of the presidency, lasted thirty days, eleven hours, and thirty minutes. The inventor Thomas Edison spent his last few years consuming nothing more than a pint of milk once every three hours.

/ 9 / THE TAPEWORM DIET

Tapeworms are parasites living in the intestine of human hosts, consuming the host's food. As a result, people with tapeworms are hungry all the time but still able to remain thin, no matter how much they eat. Advertisements for "tapeworm pills" first emerged in the 1920s and since then a number of famous women, including the opera singer Maria Callas, are alleged to have tried this eating plan. An urban myth circulated during the early eighties that a US diet company was offering a "miracle diet pill," and women who took it lost such an alarming amount of weight in a very short time that doctors decided to look into it. When they opened a bottle of these mysterious pills to investigate the contents, they were greeted by the head of a tapeworm.

/ 1 0 / THE FLETCHER DIET

Arguably the most revolting diet in history was an idea put forward by an American, Horace Fletcher in the 1900s. He was an athlete who had become so fat he was refused life insurance, prompting him to invent his own diet regime. After just four months he had shed more than forty pounds. Basically, on Fletcher's diet you can eat anything and as much of it as you like, but everything, including liquids, has to be chewed at least thirty-two times (or about one hundred times a minute) before tilting the head backward to allow the masticated food to slide down one's throat, accompanied by huge amounts of saliva. Hasty eating, Fletcher believed, resulted in undigested food clogging up the system, which led to constipation and the colon becoming a dangerous cesspool of bacteria (it was an era obsessed by the evils of constipation). People who gave

"Fletcherising," a try, including John D. Rockefeller and Mark Twain, found that they ate less because the chewing took so long, thus diminishing the desire to eat, not to mention the will to live. Fletcher died of bronchitis, aged sixty-nine.

Blood, Sweat, and Takeaways
12 SURPRISE FILLINGS*

404 B.C.: The great plague of Athens, probably caused by contaminated cereals, leads to the defeat of the Athenians in the Peloponnesian War.**

---

* Although it is widely assumed that modern-day food is relatively less natural than it used to be, mealtimes in the nineteenth century were a far more risky, and often lethal, activity. Catering standards were never more lax than in Queen Victoria's day, when deliberate food adulteration, with no laws to prevent it, grew to horrific proportions as food suppliers cheerfully ripped off and poisoned their customers at the same time. Some of the most common frauds included the use of ground stone instead of flour, fake cheese colored with red lead, baked horse offal in coffee, lead chromate in mustard, and iron bars baked in loaves to increase their weight. People died after eating green blancmange colored with copper sulphate and buns colored with arsenic. Fifteen people died after buying sweets that were found to be laced with white arsenic. Beer drinking was possibly the most dangerous activity of all: In one year there were over one hundred breweries convicted for contaminating beer with poisonous substances, including sulphuric acid, which was added to "harden" new beer and iron sulphate, added to give it a good frothy head.
** In the Middle Ages, illnesses resulting from contaminated food were often attributed to the wrath of God or malevolent spirits. The infectious disease ergot, often found in contaminated rye, induced a spasmodic muscle condition, which the Church named "Saint Anthony's Fire" and interpreted as retribution by God on heretics. In seventeenth-century America the hallucinogenic symptoms of moldy grain were thought by Puritans to be signs of witchcraft.

1861: *Mrs. Beeton's Book of Cookery and Household Management,* regarded as the housewife's cookery bible, contains several potentially lethal recipes, including one for mayonnaise made with raw eggs. Mrs. Beeton will go to her grave at age twenty-eight knowing nothing of salmonella.

1983: In August, the *Times* of London reports that a man living in West Germany found a human finger in his bread roll. In 2004 a man found part of a thumb in his sandwich, and in 2005 a whole finger was discovered in some frozen custard.

1992: A unique case of food contamination occurs in October, when nine people complain that Linda McCartney's famous brand of vegetarian pies had been "spiked" with steak and kidney.

1992: An American bread company is taken to court after a woman in Los Angeles finds a used condom in a large loaf.

1997: A British couple from Carlisle, Northumbria, find a six-inch bloodstained hypodermic needle inside a half-eaten loaf of bread purchased from a local supermarket.

1997: Dalvin Stokes sues a cafeteria in Winter Haven, Florida, after finding a condom in his sweet potato pie.

2000: An intact human head turns up inside a large cod for sale in a fishmonger's store in Queensland, Australia. Police determine that the head belonged to a thirty-nine-year-old trawler fisherman missing after falling overboard about thirty-one miles out a few days earlier.

2005: A human penis turns up in a bottle of ketchup in Stockholm, Sweden. Housewife Viktoria Ed, who discovered the organ while putting the sauce on bread rolls for her husband, Stefan, and their children, Madeleine and Simon, described it as "medium size." The Godegaarden brand ketchup was made in Turkey and distributed in Sweden by the company Axfood. Ed commented, "I will never buy this brand again, it's finished."

2008: A woman from Wisconsin tries to extort money from an expensive restaurant by putting a rat in her lunch. Debbie Miller, forty-three, threatened to alert the media unless The Seasons gave her $500,000. Instead of paying up, the owners turned it over to investigators, who smelled a rat when they determined that it had in fact been cooked in a microwave: The restaurant doesn't use microwaves. Miller is later found guilty of planting the rodent.

2008: Two UK shopowners are fined for selling chocolate cake that had been sprinkled with human feces. A customer alerted the authorities after sampling the foul-smelling *gateaux* and noticing that it didn't taste or smell "quite right." Saeed Hasmi and Jan Yadgari, who ran the Italiano Pizzeria in Roath, Cardiff, were fined £1,500 for selling food unfit for human consumption.

2009: A cook from New Jersey is found guilty of putting hair in the bagel sandwich of a police officer who had given him a ticket. The officer had ticketed the cook when he failed to pull over for a traffic violation. Police asked the local press not to report the incident for fear of copycat crimes, but the paper published the story anyway.

Gluttons for Punishment
12 MORE FOOD-RELATED DEATHS

488 B.C.: Anacreon, Greek poet and composer of drinking songs, chokes to death on a grape stone.

230 B.C.: The Roman senator Fabius chokes to death on a single goat hair that had inadvertently found its way into the milk he was drinking.

A.D. 30: Claudius Drusus, eldest son of the Roman Emperor Claudius, chokes after playfully tossing a pear into the air and then catching it in his mouth.

1589: The Duke of Brunswick is reported to have "burst asunder" at Rostock after eating a giant platter of strawberries.

1723: The Earl of Harold, Lord of the Bedchamber to King George II, chokes to death after swallowing an ear of barley.

1751: The French philosopher Julien Offray de La Mettrie dies after a feast given in his honor, at which he tries to show off by setting a new world record for eating pheasant paté with truffles.

1771: Adolf Frederick, king of Sweden, expires from digestive problems after dining on lobster, caviar, sauerkraut, smoked herring, and Champagne, topped off with fourteen servings of his favorite dessert: a traditional Swedish pastry served in a bowl of hot milk. He is remembered by Swedish schoolchildren as "the king who ate himself to death."

1872: Mark Twain employs a researcher, Washington newspaper man J. H. Riley, to prospect for diamonds in South Africa and gather material that Twain could use in a book. The venture is aborted when the researcher dies from blood poisoning after accidentally stabbing himself in the mouth with a fork after a stranger knocked his elbow in a restaurant.

1919: In Boston a giant tank at the Purity Distilling Company spills 2.3 million gallons of molasses, sending a fifteen-foot high wave of the brown goo traveling at 35 mph toward a street full of people. Twenty-one people die and 150 are injured.

1926: Stuntman Bobby Leach, the second person ever to go over Niagara Falls in a barrel, dies after slipping on an orange peel he just discarded. His broken leg has to be amputated, which led to the onset of gangrene that ultimately killed him.

1975: The Japanese actor Bandō Mitsugorō VIII dies after ordering four portions of the deadly delicacy fugu kimo (puffer fish livers) in a restaurant in Kyoto, claiming he was immune to the poison. When ingested, the toxin in fugu paralyzes nerves and muscles, which in some cases leads to respiratory failure and death. The chef of the restaurant, in awe of the prestigious artist known as Japan's "living national treasure," felt he could not refuse the request and subsequently lost his license.

2009: Twenty-two-year-old Vincent Smith II, a factory worker at the Cocoa Services Inc. plant in New Jersey, dies after falling into a vat of melted chocolate. He was loading chunks of raw chocolate into the vat to be melted when he slipped and fell into the vat, where he was knocked unconscious by a rotating paddle and subsequently drowned.

Your Eatin' Heart
12 ACTS OF CANNIBALISM

1820: The whaling ship *Essex* is sunk by a whale, and Captain Pollard and several of his crew survive a long ordeal at sea by resorting to cannibalism. Several years later Pollard was asked by a relative of one of the lost sailors if the captain remembered the man. He replied: "Remember him? Hell, son, I ate him."

1845: Sir John Franklin made a doomed attempt to traverse the Northwest Passage in the ships HMS *Erebus* and HMS *Terror*. His 128 officers and men were last seen near Baffin Island, two months after sailing from London with enough canned food to last five years. Unfortunately, the canning process was defective and the food became contaminated with lead. Those who survived by eating their colleagues died of scurvy.

1846: Lewis Keseberg is one of eighty-seven men, women, and children who set out on a two-thousand–mile trek west, looking for a new life in California, in a wagon train led by Illinois farmer George Donner and his family. The expedition was badly planned and ill-prepared, with insufficient provisions to survive the harsh winter. Of the original party, only forty-seven made it to the end of the trail, having survived by eating their dead companions. Some of the survivors struck a less than penitent attitude about their terrible dilemma. Keseberg cheerfully confessed to a preference for human liver, lights (lungs), and brain soup. In an emotional tribute to George Donner's wife Tamsen, he noted, "she was the healthiest woman I ever ate." Years later Keseberg became wealthy by opening a steakhouse.

1877: Lakota Sioux Chief Rain in the Face is the tactical genius behind the ambush of General Custer at the Battle of the Little Big Horn. Afterward he admits that he had cut out Custer's heart and eaten it. He said he didn't much like the taste of human flesh, he just wanted revenge.

1910: The Mexican artist Diego Rivera, noted for his murals and for his relationship with the painter Frida Kahlo, conducts an experiment with fellow students in an anatomy art class. For two months they live on nothing but the meat of human corpses purchased from the city morgue. According to Rivera's autobiography, "everyone's health improved."

1931: In the interest of research, allegedly, the American travel writer and *New York Times* journalist William Buehler Seabrook cooks and eats a chunk of human meat from the body of a recently deceased accident victim, obtained from a hospital intern in France. Seabrook, a friend of the occultist Aleister Crowley noted, "It was like good, fully developed veal, not young, but not yet beef. It was very definitely like that, and it was not like any other meat I had ever tasted. It was so nearly like good, fully developed veal that I think no person with a palate of ordinary, normal sensitiveness could distinguish it from veal."

1950: The politician Victor Biaka-Boda, a former witch doctor representing the Ivory Coast in the French Senate, tours his country to communicate with his constituents and find out about their concerns, one of which was a food shortage. They ate him.

1989: John Weber, a twenty-five-year-old factory worker from Wisconsin is convicted for the murder of his wife's seventeen-year-old sister. During his trial Weber confessed that he made a pâté from his sister-in-law's leg.

1992: The Milwaukee cannibal Jeffrey Dahmer admits to killing and eating seventeen young men and boys. Police raided his apartment and found severed heads in the fridge, skulls in his filing cabinet, and body parts in a kettle, but were puzzled by the discovery of a human heart in the deep freezer. Dahmer explained, "I was saving it for later."

2002: The West Coast rapper Big Lurch is convicted of murdering Tynisha Ysais in her apartment and eating parts of her face and lungs while high on PCP.

2004: Armin Meiwes, a forty-two-year-old computer expert from Germany, is sentenced to just eight and half years for killing, then frying and eating, a man he met over the Internet after his lawyer successfully argued that the victim had been "a consenting dinner date." Meiwes said later that his victim's penis tasted of pork and that he planned to list his "recipes" in his forthcoming autobiography and was looking forward to seeing his story made into a film starring Hugh Grant and Brad Pitt. German filmmaker Rosa von Praunheim began work on his movie based on the convicted cannibal with the working title *Your Heart in My Brain*. Plans for the film were shelved in

2006 when a retrial was ordered after a German prosecutor appealed Meiwes's sentence and he was convicted of murder and sentenced to life imprisonment. Since entering prison, it has been reported that Meiwes has become a vegetarian.

2009: The US rapper Eve is reported to have dumped her African boyfriend Teodorin Obiang, the son of Equatorial Guinean dictator Teodoro Obiang Nguema Mbasogo, after hearing allegations that his dictator father is a cannibal. Obiang wooed the star by lavishing her with luxury gifts, but twenty-seven-year-old Eve promptly ended the affair after Severo Moto Nsa, the leader of the government in exile, said "He (Mbasogo) has just devoured a police commissioner. I say devoured, as this commissioner was buried without his testicles and brain."

A Wee Drop of the Amber Nectar
10 PEOPLE WHO DRANK THEIR OWN URINE*

1. Hippocrates, Greek physician and namesake of the Hippocratic oath, believed that urine boosted the body's immune system.
2. When Ferdinand Magellan's fleet of five set out to circumnavigate the globe in 1519, each ship sailed with "50 casks of water, fresh and pure." It wasn't enough. Finding themselves in uncharted waters and out of water eighteen months into the voyage, they were forced to drink their own wee. Wrote Magellan, "It was surprisingly

* "Drink waters out of thine own cistern." —Book of Proverbs

not unsavory, having no worse a taste than a flagon most foul with rancid port, as many I have tasted before."

3. In 1978 India's Prime Minister Morarji Desai surprised US TV correspondent Dan Rather of *60 Minutes* by praising the benefits of urine drinking. Desai went on to explain how pee could help bridge the health care gap afflicting India's poor. Desai, a lifelong practitioner of "urine therapy," drank a pint of piss every day and lived to the age of 99.

4. The British actress Sarah Miles has drunk her own urine for over thirty years. "It tastes like good beer. You take it mid-flow every evening and morning. You just swig it down. It tastes fine."

5. Keith Richards drank his own urine in the 1970s as part of a failed detox cure.

6. Jim Morrison began drinking his own pee while on an LSD-induced spiritual quest in the Mojave Desert.

7. John Lennon also drank his own urine: All we are saying is give piss a chance. When Lennon was shot dead in 1980, his killer Mark Chapman was holding a copy of the book *The Catcher in the Rye* . . .

8. . . . whose author J. D. Salinger also drank his own wee.

9. Mexican boxing champ Juan Manuel Marquez ends his workouts by urinating into a cup and then knocking it back in one.

10. The actor Will Ferrell drank his own piss in 2009 while filming an episode of TV show *Man vs. Wild* with the survival expert Bear Grylls. The drink was paired with a meal of reindeer eyeballs.

5 People Who Drank Someone Else's Urine

1. In 2001 Holly Jones, a forty-six-year-old employee of Robinson Aviation in Whitestown, New York, was sent to prison for thirty days after surveillance cameras caught her urinating in the office coffee pot. Her fellow employees became suspicious when a "strong odor" was reported emanating from the coffee machine. Jones was said to be angry about being passed over for a promotion.

2. In 2000 a doctor from Show Low, Arizona, was charged with pederasty and drinking the urine samples of teenage boys. He persuaded his patients that vitamins in their urine would keep him healthy and youthful.

3. An Indonesian maid, Yuliana Tukiran, twenty-one, was jailed for ten weeks in Singapore for lacing her employers' coffee and tea with her urine. She told police that she was unhappy in her job and that pissing in her boss's beverage would somehow speed up her return to Indonesia.

4. David Shippentower, a forty-six-year-old member of the Confederated Tribes of the Umatilla Indian Reservation in Oregon, beat his friend Leonard Strong to death after his mate handed him a beer can filled with urine. The two of them had already knocked back a dozen or so cans of beer when Strong handed him the can as a prank. In 2003 Shippentower pleaded guilty to involuntary manslaughter and was sentenced to one year in jail.

5. In 1991 film director Mike Nichols was forced to drink urine after upsetting crew members on the set of *Regarding Henry*. The actor John Leguizamo recalled that Nichols

kept complaining that his cappuccino "tastes like piss" during shooting, so they decided to get even by urinating into the director's personal espresso machine. Leguizamo claimed the unsuspecting director drank the brew then commented, "Now that's a cup of coffee!"

8 Dictators' Diets

1. Joseph Stalin's bad-tempered paranoia was exacerbated by badly fitting false teeth and sore gums. He was quite fond of bananas, one of the few foods he could enjoy without discomfort. A Politburo member once presented Stalin with a crate of bananas, which, to Uncle Joe's fury, were discovered to be underripe. Stalin immediately sacked his trade minister and had the ship's captain responsible for importing the bananas arrested.

2. Benito Mussolini was convinced that Italy's lack of fighting spirit was the result of eating pasta. The Roman legions, *Il Duce* reasoned, had survived on a diet of stodgy barley porridge and conquered the known world, while his own soldiers struggled even to defeat Albania on a diet of spaghetti. According to the fascist leader, flaccid tagliatelle was symbolic of the Italian male's lost virility.

3. Jean-Bedel Bokassa, president of the Central African Republic, ordered the murder of one of his cabinet ministers then served him to his colleagues for dinner. Only after the meal was over did he reveal the ingredients to his guests. At the trial following his overthrow by French troops in 1979, Bokassa's French chef told how, whenever his employer needing cheering up, he would

order a slice off the leader of the opposition, whose stuffed carcass was kept in Bokassa's extra-large deep-freeze.

4. As a communist guerrilla fighter, dictator Enver Hoxha was forced to eat boiled gravel for three years. He made up for it when he became president of Albania: To ensure the conservation of supplies of his favorite dish, Hoxha made it illegal to fish for red-speckled trout; the penalty for catching one was fifteen years' hard labor.

5. Because his teeth were so rotten, in his later years Chairman Mao lived almost exclusively on stewed bamboo and stir-fried lettuce. Mao never ate fish for dinner: He routinely took strong sleeping pills before his evening meal and would often fall asleep mid-chew. His aides were expected to remove the food from his mouth: Fish bones could have been fatal.

6. The Libyan leader Colonel Muammar Gaddafi regularly flies planeloads of camels to international conferences then parks them on the hotel lawns. It is the only way he can guarantee a supply of fresh camel milk. In 2007, when the British prime minister Tony Blair visited Tripoli, he was advised by the foreign office: "If you are offered camel's milk, refuse as it causes uncontrollable farting."

7. The favorite dish of North Korea's Dear Leader Kim Jong-il is roast donkey eaten with silver chopsticks. In North Korea this delicacy is known as "celestial cow," out of respect to Kim Jong-il's late father, Kim Il-sung, who did not eat donkey.

8. According to Saddam Hussein's captors, his favorite breakfast cereal was Raisin Bran Crunch; his least favorite was Froot Loops. His favorite snack food was Cheetos, and when those ran out, Saddam would "get grumpy."

CHAPTER TWO
STRANGE BEDFELLOWS

The Love That Cannot Speak Its Name
5 PEOPLE WHO SLEPT WITH CORPSES

1. In 1886 a twenty-six-year-old Frenchman, Henri Blot, was arrested for raping several exhumed female cadavers. He was caught red-handed when a guard working in the Saint-Quen cemetery in Paris found Blot lying exhausted next to the corpse of a recently ravished ballerina. In court Blot said, "Every man to his own taste. Mine is for corpses."

2. The eccentric Welsh baronet Sir John Pryce (1748–1761) married three times. After the deaths of the first two wives he had his ex spouses embalmed and kept in his bedroom, one on each side of the marital bed. His third wife took umbrage at the idea of sharing her bedroom with two other women, especially decomposing ones, and refused to marry him until they were removed. After the death of the third Lady Pryce he invited a faith healer, Bridget Bostock, known as the "Cheshire Pythoness," to bring her back to life. The attempt was unsuccessful. Sir John dropped dead suddenly while contemplating a fourth marriage.

3. In 1849 Francois Bertrand, a twenty-five-year old sergeant in the French army, was convicted on fifteen counts of necrophilia after he dug up fresh cadavers with his bare hands from the grounds of Pere Lachaise and Montparnasse Cemeteries in Paris and sex with them. Bertrand admitted that his passion for young female corpses was so intense that he once swam across freezing lake in the dead of winter to get to a cemetery. On another occasion he was shot in the leg by a booby-trapped grave, yet still had the stamina to dig up and have sex with the

corpse. Forensic evidence showed that many of his victims, whose bodies were invariably hacked to pieces and left strewn around the cemetery, had been chewed upon.

4. Henrietta Churchill, Duchess of Marlborough, lost her mind after the death of her lover, the English playwright William Congreve, in 1792. She had his death mask attached to a life-sized dummy and spent the rest of her life treating it as though it was a real person. She held long conversations with the dummy, expected her servants to treat it like a real, live lord and called doctors in to examine it when it became "ill." Every night she undressed it and shared her bed, and eventually her coffin, with the dummy.

5. In 1926 a Key West, Florida, doctor, Carl van Cassel, fell in love with a young, beautiful tuberculosis patient, Maria Elena Oyoz. His feelings for his patient however were not returned. When she died he resolved to see much more of her in future. He talked the girl's family into having the body exhumed and placed in a mausoleum he had specially built for her so he could visit her every day. Locals became suspicious of his frequent trips to the cemetery and rumors spread that he was insane, so he kidnapped her corpse and took it home. He dressed her in a wedding gown, placed her death mask on her face, and covered the entire body with strong-smelling perfumes and wax to keep the flesh and bones from falling apart. He topped off his project by giving her glass eyes and a wig made of her own hair. Meanwhile he began a physical relationship with the corpse that was denied him while she was living. After holding the girl's body hostage for almost eight years, van Cassell's gruesome secret was discovered by Miss Oyoz's

sister, and he was arrested. In 1931 a court in Key West failed to convict van Cassel of necrophilia because it was not a crime in the state of Florida. When released, van Cassel calmly inquired if he could have the girl's body back. The court, horrified by the prospect of him resuming his sexual relations with the late Miss Oyoz, declined and ordered her reburial in a secret, unmarked grave.

10 Famous Collectors of Pornography

/ 1 / SAMUEL PEPYS

Pepys's massive "secret" diary recorded his love life in such graphic detail that some parts of it were considered unfit for publication; the full, unexpurgated details remained censored until 1970. Pepys was also an avid consumer of erotic literature, including the 1650s porn classic *L'Ecole des Filles* (*Girls School*), which Pepys described as "the most bawdy, lewd book that ever I saw."

/ 2 / REMBRANDT

As well as collecting porn, the bulb-nosed old Dutch master also executed a number of lesser-celebrated pornographic works, including *A Woman Making Water and Defecating* and an etching of a monk copulating with a milkmaid.

/ 3 / HERBERT SPENCER ASHBEE

The outwardly respectable Victorian gentleman and bibliographer secretly amassed a huge stash of porn running to thousands of volumes in several languages. He also wrote some of his own under the pseudonym Pisanus Fraxi. Ashbee willed his entire collection of books to the British Museum on condition that they kept everything. The trustees, desperate to hang on to some of the highly collectible, more conventional items, reneged on the deal and destroyed most of Ashbee's smutty literature.

/ 4 / RICHARD FRANCIS BURTON

Unlike the other great Victorian explorers, Burton also liked to explore native sexual practices, which he recorded during his various trips to Africa, India, and the Middle East, in minutely graphic detail. The British public was not quite yet ready to learn about such customs as genital mutilation, birth control, harems, and aphrodisiacs. Burton's frank translations of Eastern pornography shocked Victorian England to the core. His translation of the *Kama Sutra* was published anonymously in 1886. It would take the average couple three and a half years to try every one of the 529 positions described in the book. It was also all a bit too much for Burton's wife Isabelle. After his death she collected twenty-seven of his books, including the master copy of his thirteen-hundred-page translation of *The Perfumed Garden* and three decades' worth of notebooks and private journals, and made a bonfire.

/ 5 / WILLIAM GLADSTONE

The three-time British prime minister was famous for his high moral principles and his crusades to save fallen women. He spent his evenings during the 1850s roaming the slums of London picking up prostitutes, then he would take the fallen ladies back to his home and explain to them the error of their ways before flogging himself with a whip. The publication of his diaries in 1974 revealed that he also had a fondness for French erotic literature. An arch political enemy once asked Gladstone: "If you are saving fallen women, would you be so kind as to save one for me?"

/ 6 / FRANZ KAFKA

The venerated novelist had a huge secret stash of upmarket hardcore porn which he kept under lock and key in a safe on his bookshelf. His favorite top-shelf material was lesbian sex and bestiality, according to Kafka expert Dr. James Hawes. "Some of it is quite dark, with animals committing fellatio and girl-on-girl action. It's quite unpleasant."

/ 7 / PERCY GRAINGER

Australia's most popular composer, best known for his senti-mental ballads "An English Country Garden," "Molly On The Shore," and "Danny Boy," liked to wind down after a concert by whipping himself. He photographed it and wrote about it in great detail, scrupulously recording the number of lashes used and even the type of whip employed. In 1935 he founded the Grainger Museum at the University of Melbourne, built in a style described by the Australian press as "1930s lavatorial." This was where he intended to exhibit his unique collection of memorabilia, including his massive library of pornography. This would feature a set of photographs of the red and beaten bottom of Australia's greatest twentieth-century composer, plus various sex aids and life-size intimate papier-mâché models of his best friends. Grainger lost his testicles to cancer in 1957 and four years later spanked his last, at the age of seventy-nine. His dying wish was that his skeleton should also go on display, in the Grainger Museum—a request quietly ignored by the trustees.

〳 8 〵 KIM JONG-IL

North Korea's Dear Leader, not content with his status as Asia's biggest collector of pornography, also maintains a harem of around 2,000 imported blondes and young Asian women—the "Joy Brigade" comprising a "satisfaction team" for sexual favors, a "happiness team" for massages, and a "dancing team" for post-coital karaoke and dancing performances.

〳 9 〵 CHAIRMAN MAO ZEDONG

Although officially pornography was nonexistent under his rule, according to one of his doctors the Great Helmsman kept his own secret stash.

〳 1 0 〵 J. EDGAR HOOVER

The longest-serving director of the Federal Bureau of Investigation survived eight presidents, making himself untouchable by collecting dirt on the great and the powerful while keeping the wraps on his own deeply deviant lifestyle. Although Hoover amassed buildings full of documents on the intimate lives of millions of Americans, he left not one word about his own addiction to homoerotic pornography, or his fondness for mutual masturbation with leather-clad boys while reading aloud passages from the Bible, or for that matter his long relationship with his FBI right-hand henchman Clyde "Junior" Tolson.

Feet First

5 FAMOUS PODOPHILES

ʃ 1 ʃ FYODOR DOSTOEVSKY

Russia's most famous foot-lover was a thirty-four-year-old virgin when he married his first wife Maria in 1857. The event was not a great success: During the wedding reception he had an epileptic seizure and howled, foaming at the mouth, for two hours, then spent the rest of his honeymoon in a deep depression. He fared slightly better with his second wife, a twenty-two-year-old shorthand typist called Anna, twenty-five years his junior. Dostoevsky was crazy about Anna's feet and there were frequent references to toe-sucking in letters he wrote to her while he was away on business.

ʃ 2 ʃ VICTOR HUGO

The author of *The Hunchback of Notre-Dame* and *Les Misérables* was much given to toe-sucking. In an erotic footnote in *Hunchback*, Esmeralda is brought to the torture chamber and shown the tools, where her interrogator strips her "dainty" foot bare and places it helplessly into the apparatus. This is something you won't find in Walt Disney's version of *The Hunchback of Notre-Dame*, nor the farting prostitutes that appear in Hugo's novel.

ʃ 3 ʃ F. SCOTT FITZGERALD

Fitzgerald was aroused by women's feet, but unlike fellow literary foot fetishists Hugo and Dostoevsky, he was also morbidly obsessed with his own feet. No one, not even his wife or his lovers, were ever allowed to see them bare; shoes and socks stayed on even when he went paddling on the beach.

∫ 4 ∫ ELVIS PRESLEY

As a small boy, Elvis would wait for his mother to come home from her job at a laundry and then "rub her little sooties." As an adult it turned into a full-blown foot fetish, and he loved to fondle and suck women's toes. According to his biographer Pat Broeske, all of Elvis's women had to have pretty feet: "That was a requirement for a date with him."

∫ 5 ∫ TED BUNDY

The American serial killer and self-confessed foot fetishist escaped from jail twice before he was finally apprehended and admitted bludgeoning, strangling, and raping thirty victims. While on the run in Florida, Bundy took time out to use stolen credit cards to buy thirty pairs of socks.

History's 12 Randiest Royals

∫ 1 ∫ KING SOLOMON (c. 973–933 B.C.)

The wisest and yet the randiest of Jewish kings, Solomon reigned for forty years, during which time, according to the Old Testament, he "loved many strange women." He had seven hundred wives and anything up to three hundred mistresses, reputedly among the most beautiful women in all antiquity. He had a way with words, you see: According to the Song of Solomon, his chat-up technique included the lines, "thy hair is as a flock of goats" and "thy teeth are like a flock of sheep that are even shorn." Solomon's failure to produce more than a single heir, however, was said to be God's punishment for his promiscuity.

/ 2 / RAMSES II, "THE GREAT" (1279–1213 B.C.)

The Ancient Egyptians believed that their pharaohs were gods and were keen to keep the bloodline of their deities as pure as possible by encouraging sex with near relatives. Ramses II, the third king of the nineteenth dynasty of Egypt, had the second-longest reign in Egyptian history. He took two "principal" wives, then complicated matters by marrying his youngest sister Henutmire and the eldest three of his four daughters, Bintanath, Meritamen, and Nebettawi. In between fighting the Hittites and the Ancient Libyans and building statues of himself all over Egypt, Ramses also found time to pleasure two hundred concubines and father ninety-six sons and sixty daughters. Inappropriately, he gave his name to a leading brand of condom.

/ 3 / KING HENRY I (1068–1135)

The third Norman king of England succeeded his gay elder brother William. Blessed with allegedly phenomenal sexual stamina, he set an undefeated record for an English king by fathering at least twenty-one and possibly twenty-five illegitimate children.

/ 4 / KING CHARLES II (1630–85)

Nicknamed "Old Rowley" after a great old racehorse that had gone on to become a famous stud stallion, the king was allegedly the first royal personage ever to use a condom, although there are many dukes, earls, and barons today who can trace their lineage directly back to his failure to wear one. He fathered at least fourteen "official" bastards by seven different mothers, of whom Nell Gwynne, the Covent Garden orange seller and actress, was the best known. Another, Barbara Villiers, Duchess of Cleveland, survived him, having borne him six children. She was later alleged to have performed fellatio on a bishop and bitten off his penis.

/ 5 / AUGUSTUS II, "THE STRONG" (1670–1733)

The Saxon-born king of Poland, of whom it was said "left no stern unturned" over a half-century fathered three hundred and sixty-five bastards, give or take a dozen. It is only fair to record that there was also one legitimate heir. Augustus presided over an enormous warren of mistresses and found it so difficult to keep track of his bastards that he "accidentally" slept with at least one of his own daughters. Although his libido was one of the great marvels of the age, it didn't go down well with his Polish subjects, who were outraged by his private life, or with his wife Eberdine, who was so embarrassed by her husband's behavior that she refused to set foot in Poland throughout his reign.

/ 6 / KING JOHN V (1689–1750)

Portugal's inappropriately self-styled Most Faithful King cleverly combined his twin passions, Catholicism and sex, by sleeping with nuns. The king enjoyed open sexual relations with members of the Odivelas Convent which resulted in the birth of several illegitimate sons, known as "the children of Palhava," after the palace in Lisbon where they grew up.

/ 7 / KING LOUIS XV (1710–1774)

The Bourbon kings of France were known for their tireless sex lives, but that of Louis XV was the most astonishing of all. His personal brothel, the Parc-aux-Cerfs, was the grandest ever to service the needs of one man, stocked with a constant supply of healthy girls. It was widely rumored that he had to bathe daily in children's blood to renew his exhausted body. He also liked them young—as young as fourteen. It was thought that he was paranoid about catching syphilis and believed that very young girls statistically reduced his chances of something infectious lurking inside the royal codpiece.

/ 8 / KING FATAFEHI PAULAH (D. 1784)

Captain James Cook, on his third voyage in 1777, visited the Pacific island kingdom of Tonga, where he encountered King Fatafehi Paulah, thirty-sixth ruler of the Tu'i Tonga dynasty. The king, a hefty octogenarian, informed Cook that it was his royal duty to deflower every maiden on the island. Apparently his busy schedule required him to perform between eight and ten times a day, every day, and he had never slept with the same woman twice. It is estimated that, allowing for holidays and illness, King Fatafehi Paulah would have slept with approximately thirty-seven thousand and eight-hundred virgins during his reign.

∫ 9 ∫ EMPRESS CATHERINE II, "THE GREAT" (1762–1796)

The Russian Empress went through a string of lovers who were generally very large men, including Grigory Potemkin, a giant Russian known as "Cyclops." (He lost one eye in an argument over a game of billiards.) Potemkin's allegedly enormous penis was the subject of several persistent and apocryphal stories attached to Catherine, including one that she took a cast of her lover's member and consoled herself with it during his absences. The age gap between the Empress and her lovers grew less respectable as her reign progressed, and although obese and in chronic ill health she continued to drag young soldiers into her bed into late middle age. She was sixty when she took her last official lover, twenty-two-year-old Platon Zubov. Catherine's senile frolics were finally terminated in her sixty-seventh year. In her youth the Empress was an obsessive horse rider and refused to ride sidesaddle, which ladies of the day were instructed to do to avoid gynecological problems. It gave rise to a popular myth that she was crushed to death while having sex with a horse. In fact the old Empress fell off her toilet seat and died of a massive stroke while straining to poo.

∫ 1 0 ∫ KING WILLIAM IV (1765–1837)

Little wonder the Victorians decided to clean up their act after Britain's last Hanoverian monarch, or "Pineapple head," as he was known, thanks to his oddly shaped head. William fathered ten illegitimate children, five sons and five daughters, by his long-term lover, the Irish actress Dorothea Jordan, and one by a London prostitute, Polly Finch.

∫ 1 1 ∫ KING EDWARD VII (1841–1910)

Queen Elizabeth II's great-grandfather Edward "the Caresser" was said to have slept with about three different women a week for nearly half a century, which works out as a very conservative 7,800. Although considered a demon for "proper form," when it came to females, neither rank nor social status mattered to him, as he was equally happy in the arms of princesses or prostitutes. At his coronation in 1902 a special area set aside at Westminster Abbey for his various mistresses was nicknamed "the king's loose box."

∫ 1 2 ∫ KING IBN SAUD (1876–1953)

Their first ruling monarch of Saudi Arabia allegedly slept with three different women every night from the age of eleven until his death in 1953 aged seventy-two, although he had a night off during battles. He had an estimated forty-two sons and 125 daughters by twenty-two wives and married into more than thirty tribes, effectively uniting his new country in bed. Thanks to their founding father, today there are about 20,000 Saudi princes.

9 Famous Prudes

∫ 1 ∫ PRINCE ALBERT OF SAXE-COBURG-GOTHA

Although Queen Victoria lent her name to the golden age of prudery, by rights it should have been named after her upright, uptight husband, Albert. He surprised his wife by leaping out of bed very early on the morning after their wedding night to take a stroll. After that, Albert generally dealt with his wife's advances with German efficiency, always retiring to bed encased from head to toe in a woollen sleeping suit. Notoriously awkward in the company of women, his one and only known comment on the subject of sex was, "that particular species of vice disgusts me." Although the august testicles of the Prince Consort produced nine children, sex was strictly rationed out only as a means of increasing the size of the royal family.

∫ 2 ∫ ANTHONY COMSTOCK

Comstock served as a soldier in the Civil War, where he was shocked by the loose morals of his fellow soldiers and decided to become an anti-vice crusader. In 1873, after assiduously collecting all available pornographic material for his own noble purposes, he persuaded Congress to pass an act for the Suppression of Trade in and Circulation of Obscene Literature and Articles of Immoral Use, commonly known as the Comstock Act. The targets of Comstock's ire included the dissemination of information about birth control, which he believed was obscene, as well as other "impurities" including modern art and literature. Comstock was made a special agent of the Post Office, which gave him the right to open other people's mail. During his forty-year reign of terror he had thousands of people arrested, including a woman who called her husband a spitbub (rascal) on a postcard. In 1915 he brought several department store window dressers to court for dressing their naked mannequins in full view of the shopping public. During the trial the judge was moved to observe: "Mr. Comstock, I think you're nuts." Comstock liked to boast about the number of people that he had personally driven to suicide.

/ 3 / WILLIAM WITHERING

When the Swedish botanist Carl Linnaeus invented a brilliant new system for naming plants in the seventeenth century, it was largely based on the sexual behavior of plants. He divided them into classes by the number of "male genitals," the stamens (monandria, one stamen; diandria, two stamens), and then into orders by their pistils, the female "genitals." The plant-nookie references were all too much for the British physician William Withering, who dismissed the entire Linnaean botanical classification system as "too smutty for English ears" and "unspeakably vulgar." Withering took it upon himself to translate Linnaeus's sexually explicit terminology into harmless English equivalents. Thanks to his expurgated version, women could now discuss flower arrangements safely, without fear of embarrassment. A few Linnaean names, however, remained: The slipper limpet still answers to the name Crepidula fornicata.

/ 4 / NOAH WEBSTER

It took the dour Calvinist Webster twenty-two years to finish his *American Dictionary of the English Language,* contained definitions of 65,000 words, including the word "sodomy," defined simply as "a crime against nature." Even the Bible was too smutty for Webster, so he published a censored version in 1833, declaring it the greatest achievement of his life. In Webster's Bible, testicles become "peculiar members," leg became "limb," and female private parts, even wombs, are conspicuously absent.

/ 5 / LORD ROBERT BADEN-POWELL

Before he became a household name in England, Baden-Powell, heroic defender of Mafeking during the Boer War and founder of the worldwide Boy Scout movement, raised eyebrows with his outspoken views about the evils of prostitution, which made him a highly controversial figure within a British army that considered brothels essential for maintaining morale. In 1907, after returning to England from South Africa a national hero, Baden-Powell created the Scouts' Association. It was to be a "safe haven" for boys and young men away from the "depravities of women"; girls were "dirty" and young men who thought about them were "dirty minded little beasts." The movement was also a platform for his lifelong crusade against the evils of masturbation. B-P recommended that a young man beset by impure thoughts should run his "racial organ" under a cold water tap. He wrote in 1908: "Two men can be just as happy living together as any man and woman." It was wishful thinking. In 1912, aged fifty-five, and after taking fright and trying to make a last minute escape, he married a determined heiress called Olive, but soon after the honeymoon he began to complain of "agonizing headaches." They were cured when, after the birth of his third child, he permanently left the marital bed and slept on an open-air balcony.

∫ 6 ∫ T. S. ELIOT

In 1915 the Anglo-American poet and playwright, twenty-six years old and a virgin, married Vivienne Haigh-Wood, an English woman he had known for only a couple of months. He was such a prude that he couldn't bear the thought of shaving in front of his wife and spent the honeymoon sleeping on a deck chair. Eliot was apparently distressed by his wife's frequent and irregular menstrual leakages, which she tried to conceal by draping the bed with black silk sheets.

/ 7 / SIR WILLIAM ACTON

The nineteenth century was fertile territory for sex manuals on the perils of masturbation. In England the best-known author in this field was the physician Sir William Acton, who alerted his Victorian public to the dangers of "self-pollution" in his groundbreaking *Functions and Disorders of the Reproductive System*. Acton warned that masturbation could lead to ill-health and even premature death, and that the husband who overindulged in sex (three times a week was apparently more than enough) or became aroused too often was likely to develop "spermatorrhea," a tragic disorder that results in "general debility, inaptitude to work, disinclination for sexual intercourse" and, ultimately, impotence. Another British doctor, Isaac Baker Brown, meanwhile concluded that female masturbation led to hysteria, epilepsy, and insanity, and decided to protect women from these ills by preventative surgery in the form of the clitoridectomy—i.e., removal of the clitoris "either by scissors or knife—I always prefer the scissors." He was kicked out of the Obstetrical Society in 1867 when it turned out that he was promising to "cure" masturbation in women without letting them, or their husbands or families, know exactly what the cure entailed until the operation was over.

/ 8 / JOHN RUSKIN

The great British prude was twenty-eight when he married his cousin Effie Gray. Their wedding night did not go well. No one is quite sure exactly what happened when Effie removed her nightie, but Ruskin evidently found his bride's nakedness so shocking that he decided never to sleep with her again. A year later Ruskin was given the job of cataloging the entire collection of the great romantic landscape painter William Turner for the National Gallery. Ruskin, a great admirer of Turner, was aghast at his hero's hitherto secret fondness for sketching and painting girl-on-girl action and destroyed those works on the grounds that they were "grossly obscene." He explained later that Turner must have been mad when he drew them. Ruskin's fear of naked ladies never left him. In 1871 he founded the Ruskin School of Art, where, bizarrely, students were forbidden to draw or paint nude women.

/ 9 / LORD REITH

The puritanical founder of the British Broadcasting Corporation presided over a golden age of TV censorship, when radio announcers were expected to wear dinner jackets in front of the microphone and any employee suspected of adultery was fired immediately. The easily shocked Reith commissioned Eric Gill to make a nude sculpture of Prospero and Ariel above the door to Broadcasting House in London. Reith inspected Gill's finished work from street level and was perplexed by the enormity of Ariel's penis. He promptly sent one of his governors up the scaffolding with a notebook and tape measure, then informed Gill, "In my view this young man is uncommonly well hung." To Gill's horror, the organ was chiseled down to a size less likely to be "objectionable to public morals and decency."

10 Highlights of Casanova's Sex Life*

1. Kicked out of school for a homosexual offense, he went on to sleep with women, boys, nuns, and even a couple of his own daughters. He claimed a total of around ten thousand sexual conquests, although only 116 are actually named in his book.

2. His longest sex session was seven hours.

3. He got his biggest thrill eating oysters off women's breasts.

4. He had sex with one woman twelve times in a single day.

5. He specialized in seducing his friends' wives and daughters, often two at a time.

6. He was obsessed with trying to straighten his lovers' pubic hairs.

7. His greatest love, Henriette, was a cross-dresser who passed herself off as a castrato.

8. He seduced at least one ten-year-old girl and by today's standards would be locked up as a pedophile.

9. He tried out the very latest condoms made from pig's bladders, but found them unsatisfactory, placing his faith instead in a technique by which he inserted in his partner three gold balls, purchased from a Genoese goldsmith for about £50. He said this method had served him well, by and large, for fifteen years, with a couple of unfortunate exceptions.

10. After sleeping with a girl called Leonilda he was surprised to learn that he had impregnated her mother eighteen

* Casanova (1725–98) listed his dirty deeds in unflinching detail in an epic twelve-volume autobiography, *History of My Life*.

KARL SHAW

years earlier. The girl in turn also became pregnant by Casanova, which resulted in him fathering his own grandson.

10 Famous Wankers

∫ 1 ∫ ONAN

By reputation the biggest, and indeed only, Biblical wanker. In the Old Testament (Genesis 38:9), Onan, son of Judah, was obliged to marry his brother's widow, but he didn't want to impregnate her so he deliberately "spilled (his seed) on the ground." God was displeased with Onan's seminal wastefulness "wherefore he slew him also." With hindsight it is clear that Onan was sensibly practicing birth control rather than self-abuse, but the passage was misinterpreted and became the basis on which the Christian Church has condemned masturbation for centuries.

∫ 2 ∫ SAMUEL PEPYS

According to his diary, Pepys was a regular wanker and made an entry in his diary every time he knocked one out—often during church services. On one such solemn occasion, during a High Mass on Christmas Eve in 1666, the sight of the Queen and her ladies apparently led him to have a crafty wank while he was sitting next to his wife. His greatest triumph was when he managed to bring himself to orgasm while being ferried in a boat up the Thames, by just thinking about a girl he had seen earlier, without using his hands. He made his very last diary entry at the age of thirty-six, fearing that he was losing his eyesight.

∫ 3 ∫ JAMES BOSWELL

The diarist and author of *The Life of Samuel Johnson* was raised in Scotland as a strict Calvinist Presbyterian. As a youngster, Boswell was so plagued by guilt after being caught masturbating he considered castrating himself.

∫ 4 ∫ EDWARD LEAR

The Victorian polymath and "nonsense poet" suffered throughout his adult life from what he called "the Demon" epilepsy or "the Morbids," a state of mind that he attributed to excessive masturbation.

∫ 5 ∫ ANDRÉ GIDE

The French author and winner of the 1947 Nobel Prize for literature was kicked out of school for masturbating in class at the age of eleven. The family doctor threatened to castrate him if he didn't pack it in. He didn't: In his autobiography Gide fondly recalls knocking one out under the dining room table with a friend.

∫ 6 ∫ PAUL REUBENS

In 1991 the US comic actor most known for his Pee-wee Herman character was caught in a police "sting" operation, masturbating in a cinema while watching the X-rated film *Nancy Nurse*. Reubens's ordeal became the subject of several T-shirts, one of which read: I'M PULLING FOR PEE-WEE.

〔 7 〕 SALVADOR DALI

The Spanish Surrealist wanker was the first ever artist to make masturbation a significant theme of his work. One of his best-known paintings is called *The Great Masturbator*.

〔 8 〕 HAROLD ROBBINS

The American author said that wanking was the second most fun thing you could do on your own. The first was writing.

〔 9 〕 TRUMAN CAPOTE

The short story writer, novelist, and playwright said: "The good thing about masturbation is that you don't have to dress up for it."

〔 1 0 〕 ALLEN GINSBERG

In 1948 the American "beat poet," while quietly jerking off in his apartment in East Harlem, had a mystical vision in which he heard an angel reciting William Blake's "Songs of Experience." Ginsberg later spent eight months in a mental institution.

9 Prostitute Botherers

〔 1 〕 POPE ANACLETUS II

In theory, every Pope is handpicked by God, which means that even God occasionally gets it very wrong. Take Anacletus II, whose controversial succession to the papacy in the twelfth century was disputed by, among others, the French King Louis VI, "the Fat," leading to one of Christianity's great schisms. Anacletus went on to make himself even more unpopular by taking a prostitute mistress and having incestuous relations with several female relatives, including his sister, not to mention his disturbing habit of raping nuns.

∫ 2 ∫ THE DUKE OF WELLINGTON

Britain's great military hero and prime minister (1828–30) was also one of his nation's greatest skirt-chasers. His famous retort "Publish and be damned" was a response to the blackmailer Joseph Stockdale, who threatened to make public the memoirs of the Regency-era prostitute Harriette Wilson. Stockdale did publish, and so the whole of London was able to read about the Iron Duke's prowess between the sheets, which according to the high class tart was "most unentertaining . . . very uphill work." Wellington once shared a mistress, the French actress Mademoiselle George, with his greatest adversary, Napoleon. When asked to make comparisons, she replied diplomatically, "the Duke was the more vigorous."

∫ 3 ∫ CHARLES DICKENS

Even the Victorians found Dickens a bit priggish; in *The Pickwick Papers* he refers to trousers as "indescribables." His private life, however, was a remarkable contradiction of his public profile as a model of Victorian respectability. Like his contemporary William Gladstone he was involved in campaigns to "save" London prostitutes. Little wonder then that Dickens was keen to keep quiet about his own excursions to Paris brothels with his good friend Wilkie Collins, where he contracted venereal disease—probably gonorrhea—from a French prostitute. Dickens was embarrassed to write a note to his doctor explaining his predicament: "My bachelor state has engendered a small malady."

∫ 4 ∫ JAMES BOSWELL

Although Boswell was a famous man of letters, sadly, few of them were French. Between his first encounter with Dr. Samuel Johnson in 1763 and his death thirty-five years later, he was venereally infected nineteen times. Boswell's diaries, discovered more than a hundred years after his death, reveal him as a five-times-a-night addict with a predilection for dangerous sex with hookers in public places. Boswell treated his whores poorly; his tactic was to offer them half the going rate then rape them if they held out for more. Even as he lay dying of tuberculosis, he continued to chase prostitutes, ruefully reflecting in his diary that he couldn't help himself. Battling against clap and failing eyesight, he finally finished *The Life of Samuel Johnson* in 1791 and died four years later.

∫ 5 ∫ VINCENT VAN GOGH

Art's most famous suicide suspected that artistic creativity and a healthy sex life were mutually exclusive. Unfortunately, Vincent did not practice what he preached; he spent almost all of what little money he had in brothels. One of his favorite whorehouses in his southern French town of Arles was the subject of his painting *The Brothel*. A prostitute, Claudia Maria Hoornik, lived with him for over a year, modeled for several of his works, and gave birth to his son, Willem. He had a love-hate relationship with the sexually insatiable Paul Gauguin, with whom he briefly shared a house. Van Gogh was so deeply jealous of his friend's success with women that, in a fit of pique, he hacked off an earlobe and sent it to a local prostitute. No one is quite sure why he chose this particular gesture to demonstrate his ire, not even van Gogh. He was completely off his face on absinthe at the time and only had the haziest recollection of it the following morning.

/ 6 / F. SCOTT FITZGERALD

The author's wife Zelda made a disparaging remark about the size of his manhood on their wedding night, a taunt from which he never quite recovered. He spent the rest of his life fretting about the size of his penis, often visiting prostitutes to seek reassurance and find out how his willy compared with those of their other clients. After his mad wife was institutionalized, a hooker called Lottie satisfied his needs on a permanent basis and gave his fragile ego a much-needed boost by assuring him that size didn't really matter.

/ 7 / ISAAC MERRITT SINGER

According to Mahatma Gandhi, the Singer sewing machine was "one of the few useful things ever invented." Its inventor, one of the earliest heroes of American capitalism, also enjoyed a uniquely scandalous private life. The burly, bearded, six-foot-four-inch businessman spent a large portion of his vast fortune on New York prostitutes—only one of several twists in an unusually tangled private life. While legally married to Catherine

Singer for over thirty years, the woman he introduced to his friends, business associates, and employees as Mrs. Singer was in fact one Mary Ann Sponsler, mother of his ten illegitimate children. In 1861 Ms. Sponsler decided to blow the lid on his domestic situation when she saw him out with yet another "wife." Singer was arrested for bigamy and the American public was shocked to learn that he was in fact maintaining five separate households with a "wife" in each—four of them called Mary—and a combined total of at least twenty-four children, plus various other women besides who escaped motherhood. He was released on bail, but his reputation was ruined. In 1862 he sailed for Europe, never to return.

/ 8 / KING GEORGE V

Queen Elizabeth II's grandfather made regular trips to Bognor Regis and other seaside resorts on England's south coast, according to the historian A. N. Wilson, which were discreetly arranged so that he could entertain hookers as a refuge from his wife Queen Mary.

/ 9 / ERNEST HEMINGWAY

The US Nobel and Pulitzer Prize–winning author boasted that he was so highly sexed he needed a woman at least two or three times a day and had to take bromides to keep his sex drive under control. In Michigan and in Havana, Hemingway enjoyed the services of hookers and gave them nicknames like Xenophobia and Leopoldina. They became the basis for characters in his stories. Hemingway was the only mourner at Leopoldina's funeral and he paid the expenses. Like his friend F. Scott Fitzgerald, he fretted over the dimensions of a below average–size penis. The two great writers once compared organs—Hemingway concurred that they must both be normal.

10 Famous People Who Were Fond of Taking Their Clothes Off in Public

/ 1 / BENJAMIN FRANKLIN

America's founding father liked to sit stark naked in front of his open window thinking about bifocals, electricity, urinary catheters, and stoves. Some would call it indecent exposure, but he called it "taking an air bath."

/ 2 / WILLIAM BLAKE

The English poet-artist and his wife Catherine were sitting in their garden one day when his painter friend Thomas Butts dropped by. He found Mr. and Mrs. Blake stark naked, reciting passages from Milton's "Paradise Lost" to each other. Blake asked their friend to pull up a chair and join them. There is no report as to his response.

/ 3 / JOHN QUINCY ADAMS

Every morning in the White House the sixth US president rose at five, read the Bible, and took a nude swim in the Potomac. One morning the nude, pink president was bobbing up and down in the water when he was confronted by the lady journalist and war veteran's widow, Anne Royall, who had traveled to Washington to petition for a federal pension. According to some accounts

Royall sat on Adams's clothes until he agreed to answer her questions, earning her the first presidential interview ever granted to a woman, but the story is almost certainly apocryphal.

/ 4 / HENRY DAVID THOREAU

The US author was said to have had two great loves of his life: one was his brother John and the other was nature. John died tragically of lockjaw in 1842 and Thoreau was never quite the same again—he took to wandering naked through the local woods and streams. In 1844, while barbecuing fish at a local beauty spot, he accidentally sparked a major forest fire that for decades blighted one of the most beautiful places in America.

/ 5 / GEORGE MALLORY

The legendary mountaineer who climbed Everest "because it is there" liked to scale mountains in the buff. In 1912, wearing only sneakers, he and a friend attempted to climb a steep granite sea cliff near Land's End in Cornwall. Mallory's biographers Peter and Leni Gillman note that "their lack of clothing posed some interesting technical problems on the abrasive crystalline granite at the top of the route."

/ 6 / ROBERT BROOM

The famous Scottish doctor and paleontologist, conscious of his standing as a medical man regardless of whether he was delivering babies or collecting fossils, always dressed formally in a dark three-piece suit and turnup collars. Unless it got too hot, in which case he would strip completely naked.

/ 7 / CHARLES RICHTER

The co-inventor of the earthquake measuring system was described by his biographer as "a nerd among nerds" and an "at best marginally stable personality." Richter always dressed for work in a suit and tie, or sometimes two ties. In his spare time, however, the portly seismologist and his wife Lillian went on long nude hikes together and filmed their travels. Ironically, three thousand feet of film documenting the naked hikes of the Richters was destroyed when a fire swept through the house of Lillian's nephew after a 1994 earthquake.

/ 8 / MOHANDAS "MAHATMA" GANDHI

In his seventies, much to the surprise of Mrs. Gandhi, the skinny pacifist decided to "test" his celibacy by employing several young virgins to massage him, bathe him, and sleep with him in the nude. Gandhi's virgin sandwich attracted public attention in 1947 when it came out that the master was bunking nightly with his nineteen-year-old grandniece, Manu. Gandhi's entourage explained that the naked sleepovers were partly tests of purity for both participants, and partly an effort to stay warm in the winter chill.

/ 9 / SIR WINSTON CHURCHILL

The British wartime prime minister didn't care who saw him in the buff. He insisted on dictating letters to his secretary from his twice-daily bath, then would emerge stark naked and pace about the room. In 1941 Churchill stayed at the White House for twenty-four days and was often found lounging in the nude by servants who went to his room to serve him brandy. When

President Roosevelt arrived in his wheelchair at the door of Churchill's bedroom he was greeted by the naked prime minister with the words: "You see, Mr. President, I have nothing to hide."

∫ 1 0 ∫ LYNDON B. JOHNSON

An avid exhibitionist, LBJ liked to bully visitors to the White House into taking part in nude pool parties, including, on one occasion, the reluctant evangelist Billy Graham. During these skinny-dips LBJ always referred to his manhood as "Jumbo."

12 Famous Fetishists

1. Émile Zola—turned on by smells. There are so many olfactory references in the French writer's books that he is known as "the novelist with the quivering nostrils." Sadly he did not detect the whiff of poisonous gas emitting from a faulty stove in his Paris apartment, which caused his death by accidental asphyxiation in 1902.

2. René Descartes—turned on by cross-eyed women. The French philosopher probably had sex only once in his entire life, when he got a Dutch woman called Helena pregnant. He only did it as an experiment—he was writing an essay on fetal development. The man who said "I think, therefore I am," however, admitted he often thought long and hard about cross-eyed women, the result of a childhood crush on a cross-eyed schoolgirl.

3. Le Corbusier—chubby women. The great Swiss architect, famous for his love of large concrete edifices, also loved

large women. One of his less successful chat-up lines was "you are fat and I like my women fat."

4. James Joyce—dirty knickers. The Irish author was turned on by the sight of his wife Nora's dirty knickers and kept a tiny pair of doll's panties in his pocket: His party trick in public bars was to slip them over his fingers and "walk" them across the tabletop. He was also obsessed with Nora's farts. He wrote: "I think I would know Nora's fart anywhere. I think I could pick hers out in a roomful of farting women. It is a rather girlish noise not like the wet windy fart which I imagine fat wives have."

5. Elvis Presley—white panties. According to former girlfriend Barbara Leigh, Elvis was mostly turned on by "white lace panties with a bit of pubic hair coming out the sides."

6. Richard Wagner—silk underwear. Hitler's favorite composer took a fetishistic interest in his wife's knickers. He wrote several letters to dressmakers, ostensibly containing highly detailed instructions on how to make lingerie and various outfits for his wife, but was probably secretly ordering them for himself.

7. C. S. Lewis—fantasized about spanking. Called "God's storyteller," his fame rests on *The Chronicles of Narnia*, a series of seven children's classics about a fierce but benevolent lion who dies on a stone table to free his people from tyranny. Lewis wrote letters to friends revealing sadomasochistic fantasies and named a woman he hoped to spank, signing his letters Philomastix—"whip lover." Unsurprisingly, *Narnia* has inspired any number of Freudian theories: What, for example, are we to make of the fact that the children emerge into Narnia via what was

basically a closet-size vagina? As for talking beavers, best not to go there.

8. Algernon Charles Swinburne—flagellation. When the job of poet laureate fell vacant upon the death of Alfred Lord Tennyson in 1892, Queen Victoria remarked: "I understand Mr. Swinburne is the best of my poets." She was possibly unaware at the time of his reputation for cross-dressing and flagellation, not to mention the verses he had penned about Her Majesty's presumed sex life, especially the one about how she had been shagged by Wordsworth. Five feet tall, ginger-haired, and with an enormous head, Swinburne had an obsession with flogging that could be traced back to his schooling at Eton, where the headmaster of the day was so notorious for birchings that he was said to be more familiar with his pupils backsides than their faces. To be fair, there were clues to Swinburne's little problem in his works ("The Flogging Block," "Arthur's Flogging," "Reginald's Flogging," "A Boy's First Flogging," "Charlie Collingwood's Flogging," and *The Whippingham Papers*).

9. Dr. Samuel Johnson—bondage. Late in his career Dr. Johnson suffered a mental breakdown and was nursed back to health by Hester Thrale, wife of a well-to-do brewer, Henry Thrale. According to a mysterious diary entry, Johnson gave Mrs. Thrale a set of padlocks and had "insane thoughts about leg iron and handcuffs." According to another entry he shaved off all his body hair to see how long it would take to grow back. Dr. Johnson was once asked by the famous actor David Garrick to name his greatest pleasure in life, to which the great man of letters replied, "fucking."

10. Jean-Jacques Rousseau—flashing and bondage. The man who wrote "man is born free, yet everywhere he is in chains" enjoyed being tied up and beaten. Rousseau's autobiography, *The Confessions,* sold steadily for over two centuries thanks mostly to his admissions of sexual masochism and his fond recollection of the childhood spankings administered by a thirty-year-old governess— regular spankings that he grew overly fond of. As an adult he liked to loiter in dark alleys, exposing his backside to passing women.

11. H. G. Wells—turned on by hairy women. The first great English science fiction writer was in the habit of seducing the wives and daughters of his friends. One of his famous lovers was the novelist Dorothy M. Richardson, whom he later declared "most interestingly hairy."

12. Napoleon—liked smelly women. During one of his campaigns, he wrote a letter to his beloved wife. It read: "Dear Josephine, I will be arriving home in three days. Don't bathe."

7 British Monarchs Presumed to Be Homosexual

ʃ 1 ʃ KING WILLIAM II (C. 1056–1100)

The second of William the Conqueror's three surviving sons had red hair and lived in a near-permanent state of red-faced apoplexy, either of which could have accounted for his nick-name "Rufus." His reputation suffered at the hands of the dia-rists of the day—monks—who were so shocked by the king's "foul practices of Sodom" that the Pope threatened to excommunicate him. The Catholic Church doesn't go in for that sort of thing, apparently.

∫ 2 ∫ KING EDWARD II (1308–1327)

At the age of twenty-three Edward made an arranged marriage to twelve-year-old Isabella of France, an age gap thought not to be particularly disgusting by the standards of the day. The marriage was strained from the start by Edward's unusually close relationship with his courtier Piers Gaveston, who turned up for the wedding wearing a purple pearl-studded ball gown. It erupted into open warfare when the young king gave his favorite most of his wife's best jewelry. Edward later became infatuated with another courtier, Hugh Despenser, on whom he lavished land and riches. Edward's reign ended when infuriated opponents took revenge by capturing him and killing him by a method thought to be appropriate in the circumstances: the king was held down while a red hot poker was inserted into his rectum.

∫ 3 ∫ KING RICHARD I "THE LION-HEARTED" (1157–1199)

Although his exploits in the Third Crusade made him the hero of countless legends, Richard saw little of England and even less of his wife Queen Berengia. There are a number of apocryphal stories about his alleged male lovers, including his romantic attachment to his adversary, the Muslim leader Saladin (whom, in fact, he never actually met) and the gay minstrel Blondel (who almost certainly never existed). Richard fathered no heirs.

/ 4 / KING RICHARD II (1377–1399)

Richard's court was renowned for decadence and sartorial eccentricity. The king himself was known for his fantastic gemstone-covered ball gown, and (a dead giveaway for effeminacy in the fourteenth century) taking regular baths. Like Edward II, Richard fell under the influence of a disastrous favorite, Robert de Vere, Earl of Oxford. Meanwhile Richard's foreign adventures bankrupted the government, causing him to raise the hated poll tax, which led to the Peasants' Revolt of 1381. When de Vere died, Richard had a breakdown and fell into a deep depression, during which he was deposed and murdered.

/ 5 / KING JAMES I (1603–1625)

Rex fuit Elizabeth: nunc est regina Jacobus (Elizabeth was King, now James is Queen) was the witty Latin quip doing the rounds in 1603 when James I succeeded the Virgin Queen. The rumors started when he kissed one of his male favorites full on the lips during his own coronation. Although he fathered seven children, James's preference was for very young men, especially George Villiers, who found his way into James's bedroom as the king's cup bearer, then went on to become one of the richest nobles in England—arguably the most successful rent boy of all time.

/ 6 / KING WILLIAM III (1689–1702)

After the "Glorious Revolution," William's courtiers couldn't help noticing that their new king was immune to the charms of his young, attractive wife and co-ruler Queen Mary. It was whispered that "King Billy" was in fact sleeping with a Dutch page-boy, Arnold Joost van Keppel, who was mysteriously elevated to Earl of Albemarle. Queen Mary's indifference toward her husband has been interpreted as proof that she was also a lesbian, although it is more likely that she simply found the small, ugly, and hunchbacked William physically repulsive. The royal couple died heirless.

∫ 7 ∫ QUEEN ANNE (1665–1714)

The Queen was a gouty little woman who suffered from ill-health for most of her reign, her constitution weakened by seventeen childbirths. Her bed and her fondness for strong alcohol were usually shared by her Danish husband, Prince George. The question of who else occupied Anne's bed when George was gone was the subject of much speculation. Anne had a long, intimate attachment to a childhood friend Sarah Jennings (an ancestor of Diana, Princess of Wales). Sarah became Anne's lady of the bedchamber and her inseparable companion. By 1707, however, Anne had fallen out with her old friend, who was supplanted in the Queen's affections by another lady-in-waiting, the much younger Abigail Hill. It was whispered in court that the Queen and her new chum were more than just bridge partners. Ms. Jennings took her revenge in a devastating open letter, claiming that the Queen and Abigail Hill were lovers. Anne chose not to refute the allegation, and her continued silence was taken by many as a tacit acknowledgment that the rumors were true.

Love Hurts
10 SEXUAL TRAUMAS

1.   The punishment for male adulterers in ancient Athens was to thrust a radish up the offender's fundament.

2. Following the 1993 trial of Lorena Bobbitt, who cut off the penis of her husband John Wayne Bobbitt during a lovers' tiff, US newspapers reported a spate of copycat assaults on male genitalia. A Toronto woman snipped off her husband's penis with a pair of scissors during a domestic squabble, while in Los Angeles a woman was charged with cutting off her spouse's testicles, although the couple (the husband and wife, not the genitalia) were reunited a month later. In Jefferson, Missouri, a thirty-five-year-old woman was charged with tearing off her ex boyfriend's scrotum with her bare hands. In a domestic dispute in Hong Kong, the wife of forty-three-year-old Wong Cheong-do sliced his penis off, but doctors were able to sew it back because the quick-witted Wong dashed to the local hospital with it in his pocket. A thirty-five-year-old man in Saginaw, Michigan, required sixty-five stitches to his penis after his girlfriend bit him. Meanwhile, during a brawl in Davenport, Iowa, Jaime Johnson bit off a testicle belonging to one James Liske.

3. The Ibo tribe of Nigeria excels in a variety of punishments for adulterous couples. One involves tying the couple up and putting a stake through them, then carrying them off to a pool filled with crocodiles.

4. In 1992 Darryl Washington and Maria Ramos, a homeless couple, were injured when a train hit them while they were copulating on a mattress on the tracks at a New York City subway station. The couple subsequently filed a lawsuit against the Metropolitan Transit Authority for "carelessness, recklessness, and negligence." Their lawyer told the New York *Daily News*, "homeless people are allowed to have sex, too."

5. According to medical statistics, every year up to two hundred men break their penises during intercourse. The break is accompanied by a distinct cracking sound and the patient generally requires thirty to forty stitches, a splint, and complete bed rest for six weeks.

6. In 1993 the *Bangkok Post* reported that "quack" physicians had performed at least one hundred bogus penis-enlargement operations in Thailand. The operations involved injections of a "bulking agent," containing a mixture of olive oil, chalk, and various other substances. A Chiang Mai hospital official noted that he had seen victims' penises containing portions of the Bangkok telephone directory.

7. In 1993 the wife of Zhang Jingui cut off her spouse's penis with a pair of scissors, acting on the advice of a Beijing fortune-teller on how to improve their marital relations. The fortune-teller had concluded that the problem in the relationship was Zhang's tiny penis and that their only hope of saving the marriage was to remove it so that a new one could grow. In 2004 a fifty-five-year-old man in Wooster, Ohio, removed his own penis with a knife because he wasn't happy with it. For apparently similar reasons, a twenty-three-year-old from Arcadia, Florida, removed his genitalia with an electric saw. In the same year, thirty-four-year-old prisoner Clifford Roby sliced off his manhood with a Bic razor in Keene, New Hampshire, and flushed it down the toilet, explaining that it was "God's will."

8. "Love Stone" is a potion derived from toad venom and once commercially available in the United States as an aphrodisiac. The toad juices contain a hallucinogen known

as bufotenine that may stir the libido. It was banned after four men were reported to have died in New York in the mid-1990s after they ingested it. The manufacturers were swift to point out that the potion was only ever intended to be rubbed onto the genitalia.

9. In 2008 an Australian woman was accused of setting her husband's genitals on fire because she thought he was having an affair. Forty-four-year-old Rajini Narayan confessed to neighbors that she doused her sleeping husband's private parts with an alcohol-based solvent and then set him on fire after she saw him hug another woman. The charges were upgraded from arson to murder after her forty-seven-year-old husband Satish died from his injuries. Her husband jumped out of bed and knocked over the bottle of alcohol, causing the fire to spread and resulting in over $700,000 of damage to their town house and an adjacent property. Mrs. Narayan said: "I just wanted to burn his penis so it belongs to me and no one else. I didn't mean [for] this to happen."

10. In 1986 thirty-nine-year-old American Bruce Jensen of Bountiful, Utah, sought an annulment to his three-and-a-half-year marriage, citing "irreconcilable differences," upon the discovery that his wife was a man. The couple first met at the University of Utah Health Sciences Center, where the soon-to-be Mrs. Jensen, real name Felix Urioste, was masquerading as a female doctor. Jensen wed Urioste after the latter claimed to be pregnant with twins after their solitary sexual encounter. Urioste later said the twins were stillborn. He never let Jensen see him naked during their celibate marriage. The deception was

uncovered when Jensen filed a missing person report. Police subsequently learned that the absent Mrs. Jensen had a record for credit card fraud in Las Vegas, and had been arrested while traveling as "a bearded man." Jensen confessed, "I feel pretty stupid."

Adorable Ewe
10 ANIMAL PASSIONS

1857: Warren Drake, a soldier serving in the Utah militia in Echo Canyon, is found guilty of having sexual relations with a mare. A court-martial sentenced both Drake and the mare to death. The soldier's sentence was subsequently commuted to exile from the territory; the less fortunate mare was executed.

1952: A man from Nigeria is accused of committing an act of sexual indecency with a pigeon in Hyde Park, London. His resourceful defense counsel reminded the judge of a precedent in the 1930s, when a man was similarly accused of buggering a duck. On that occasion the accused had escaped scot-free after pointing out that a duck was a fowl, not a beast, and that he was therefore innocent of the charge of bestiality. The case against the Nigerian is dismissed, but he was fined £10 for taking the pigeon home and eating it.

1993: James Humfleet, age thirty-three, is charged with the murder of his uncle, Samuel Humfleet. According to the younger Humfleet, he was enraged after he stumbled across his uncle having sex with one of the two pit bulls belonging to the owner of the trailer in which they had been partying.

2004: The news agency Reuters reports that a fifty-year-old Zambian man hanged himself after his wife found him having sex with a hen. She caught him in the act when she rushed into their house to investigate a clucking noise. A police spokesman said: "He attempted to kill her but she managed to escape." The hen was put down after the incident.

2005: A man from Gig Harbor, Washington, died from injuries sustained while having sex with a horse on a farm in Enumclaw. Forty-two-year-old Kenneth Pinyan had had sex with horses several times before, and liked to film and distribute his encounters under the name "Mr. Hands." He died of acute peritonitis after being reluctant to explain the circumstances of his injury to doctors, thereby delaying his hospital treatment by several hours. Investigators said that the farm was well known in certain Internet chat rooms as a destination for people looking to have sex with livestock.

2007: A Dutchman accused of having sex with a sheep walked free because the animal was unable to testify. The man, from Haaksbergen, near Utrecht, was reported to police after a farmer caught him red-handed. Under Dutch law, bestiality is not a crime unless it can be proved the animal didn't want to have sex. The case was thrown out of court because the sheep couldn't take to the stand to testify that it didn't want to have sex and had suffered emotional stress.

2007: A twenty-year-old man is arrested for having sex with roadkill, in the form of a deer carcass he found on the side of the road while bicycling. The court hears that Bryan James Hathaway from Douglas County, Minnesota, had violated a

KARL SHAW

supervision order: He had been found guilty two years earlier of mistreatment of an animal after he killed a horse with the intention of having sex with it.

2008: A forty-four-year-old man from Michigan, Ronald Kuch, is found guilty of having sex with his girlfriend's dog. At the time of the incident the dog had been lying dead by the road-side for about a week after being hit by a car.

2010: A seventy-two-year-old man was arrested after having sex with a pig on a farm in Stepney, East London. A passerby phoned the police after spotting him abusing the animal while naked from the waist down. The manager of the farm said the seventy-two-year-old appeared to have deliberately singled out their most passive pig. "If he'd picked on one of the others, he would have been in serious trouble. They would have done him some damage."

2010: Paul Adlard, age sixty-four, from Bedworth, England, is arrested after filming himself having sex with his pet Old English Sheepdog. Police seized a camcorder from his home fol-lowing a tip-off from a neighbor who saw him stripped naked with the dog. Adlard told the court that he was drunk at the time of the incident and was having a spot of trouble in his marriage.

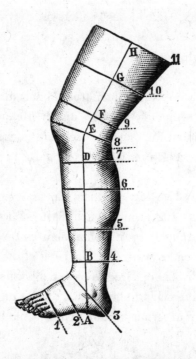

CHAPTER THREE
MEDICAL MISCELLANY

II Lost Body Parts

/ 1 / MICHAEL JACKSON'S NOSE

For some years before his death it was conjectured that the tip of Jacko's nose was missing, the result of either excessive plastic surgery or botched operations. Former close associates of Jackson admitted that the nose tip was in fact prosthetic and that the process of attachment was so painful and humiliating that he sometimes left it off and wore a surgical mask instead. According to rumors circulated on the Internet, the tip of the nose "fell off" as the dying singer was taken to the hospital.

/ 2 / MATA HARI'S HEAD

The Dutch-born erotic dancer, who was shot by the French as a spy in World War I, had her head removed. For many years it was kept in a Paris museum of anatomy, home to the mummified heads of about one hundred celebrity criminals, among 5,802 conserved body parts used by medical professors as teaching aids. In 2000 museum curators were baffled by the disappearance of Mata Hari's head from the collection. It has yet to be accounted for.

/ 3 / ISAAC NEWTON'S TOOTH

In 1816 a tooth said to have belonged to the great scientist changed hands in London for $3,633 (roughly $40,000 today). It was bought by an aristocrat who then had it set in a ring. The whereabouts of the tooth today are not known. In 1791 several

teeth formerly owned by the French writer Voltaire were also
made into fashion accessories.

/ 4 / CHE GUEVARA'S HANDS

After the guerrilla fighter's execution in Bolivia in 1967, his
hands were sawed off and put into a flask of formaldehyde, in
order to make a positive fingerprint comparison with records in
Argentina. Guevara's corpse, minus his hands, was later found
buried in a ditch at the end of the runway site of Vallegrande
Airport. It is not certain what became of the hands, although
according to some accounts they are somewhere in Cuba.

/ 5 / GERONIMO'S HEAD

The legendary Chiricahua Apache chief died in 1909, aged
eighty, and was still technically a prisoner of war. Nine years
later his grave was allegedly opened by six junior army officers
from Yale University, and his skull stolen. According to several
accounts the skull is currently one of several human artifacts
held at Yale. At the time of this writing the White House has
not yet responded to a request by Geronimo's great grandson
for help in recovering the skull.

/ 6 / JUAN PERON'S HANDS AND GENITALS

In 1987, thirteen years after the Argentinean dictator's death,
grave robbers stole his hands and genitals, with the help of an
electric saw, and demanded an eight million dollar ransom for
their return. The grave robbers have never been found, nor
have Peron's extremities.

| 7 | RENÉ DESCARTES'S HEAD

Upon his death from pneumonia at the age of fifty-four, the "father of modern philosophy" was buried in Stockholm but was later transferred home to France. During the exhumation, a captain of the Swedish guards allegedly removed his skull and substituted it with another. Descartes's skull then changed hands several times (it was sold for one hundred francs in 1829) and a number of "imposter skulls" cropped up. Apart from the "official" skull, currently residing in a container in the Musée de l'Homme in Paris, there are at least four other skulls, one in Stockholm and three in private collections—any one of which could have belonged to Descartes.

| 8 | A BOOKMARK MADE FROM WILLIAM BURKE'S SKIN

In the 1800s William Burke and his accomplice in crime William Hare were serial killers operating in Edinburgh, Scotland. They were responsible for at least sixteen murders, to obtain body parts to sell to surgeons for dissection and study. William Burke became a victim of the body-parts trade himself when he was hanged in 1829 and some of his skin was sold to collectors. According to legend, Charles Dickens bought a piece of Burke's skin, which he used as a bookmark.

| 9 | HOLY RELICS GONE MISSING DURING THE FRENCH REVOLUTION

These include a bottled sneeze of the Holy Ghost, a sigh uttered by Saint Joseph while he was sawing wood, the bones of the fish that Christ multiplied, and the tail of his ass.

⌠ 1 0 ⌡ SAINT ANTHONY'S JAWBONE

Known as the "quickest" saint in the history of the Catholic Church,* Saint Anthony was also known as a great speaker. Such a great speaker, in fact, that when his grave was opened thirty years after his death, his tongue was still going strong. In 1995 his jawbone was stolen from a church in Padua, allegedly by the Piovese Mafia family, in exchange for the head of the family not being sent to jail. Ironically, Saint Anthony is the patron saint of lost objects.

⌠ 1 1 ⌡ JESUS CHRIST'S FORESKIN

At one time there were fifteen foreskins of Jesus being worshipped in various places around Europe. In 1983 a relic of the Son of God's circumcision known in France as *Le Saint Prépuce*—the Holy Foreskin—went missing from a church in Calcata, thirty miles north of Rome. It had previously been in the news a couple of years earlier when it was damaged by a local priest who said he was "testing its elasticity."

10 Most Common Causes of Madness in the Eighteenth Century**

1. Moving into a new home
2. Squeezing a pimple
3. Old age

* Known not for a miraculous pace over 100 meters, but because he was canonized within twelve months of his death.
** As listed in the standard text on the subject of madness, written by the leading French physician Jean Esquirol.

4. Childbirth
5. The menstrual cycle
6. Shrinkage of hemorrhoids
7. Misuse of mercury
8. Disappointment in love
9. Masturbation
10. Bloodletting*

6 Notable Unipeds

∫ 1 ∫ SAMUEL FOOTE

The great English actor and dramatist was known for his Oscar Wildean wit and, like Wilde, his reputation was destroyed by homosexual scandal. In 1766 Foote was out riding when he fell off his horse, resulting in the amputation of one of his legs. It was replaced by a cork leg, giving rise to endless amusing foot and leg jokes amongst his colleagues. The Duke of York took pity and secured him a royal patent to build a brand-new Haymarket Theatre in Westminster. Foote used his gift for scathing wit to attack critics and friends alike. Most, like David Garrick, avoided Foote's public ridicule through flattery. Samuel Johnson, who considered Foote's wit "irresistible," was nevertheless obliged to threaten him with physical violence. In 1777 Foote was tried on a charge of homosexual rape when his former footman (no pun intended) John Sangster accused him of twice assaulting him. Foote was acquitted, but the scandal effectively ended his stage career.

---

* This would have been particularly confusing to a medical profession that also still believed bloodletting was a cure for madness.

/ 2 / ANTONIO LOPEZ DE SANTA ANNA

The hero of the Alamo survived several military defeats, sex scandals, opium addiction, and accusations of corruption to serve as president of his country eleven times and lived to die in bed at the age of eighty-two. Santa Anna had a leg torn off in a skirmish with the French in 1838. He recovered the severed limb and gave it a full state funeral. At public events he took to riding on horseback waving his new prosthetic cork leg over his head as a symbol of his sacrifices for his country. In 1847, again facing the United States at the Battle of Cerro Gordo in Mexico, Santa Anna was enjoying a quiet roast chicken lunch when his appetite was ruined by an uninvited regiment of Illinoisans, who stole his cork leg. Santa Anna hopped away to fight another day but the iconic limb remained in American hands, despite many requests from the Mexican government to return it. In the 1850s army veterans charged a nickel or a dime for curiosity-seekers to handle the leg in hotel bars. Santa Anna's prosthesis, a trophy of war, now resides in the Guard's Museum, Camp Lincoln in Springfield, Illinois.

/ 3 / HENRY PAGET, LORD UXBRIDGE

The British cavalry commander was famously renowned for his stoicism and "stiff upper lip." At the Battle of Waterloo in 1815 Uxbridge was sitting astride his horse next to the Duke of Wellington, when he was hit by French grapeshot. He informed Wellington, "by God, sir, I've lost my leg." The Duke casually observed the shattered limb and replied, "by God sir, so you have," then continued to survey the battlefield through his telescope. Several anecdotes testify to Uxbridge's composure during the horrific amputation and cauterizing procedure that followed. (His only comment was, "the knives appear somewhat blunt.") After the surgery the wounded noble called to a fellow officer, Sir Hussey Vivian: "I want you to do me a favor. Some of my friends here seem to think I might have kept that leg on. Just go and cast your eye upon it, and tell me what you think." Vivian picked up the severed limb and after examining it carefully informed Uxbridge that it was "in my opinion, better off than on." The limb went on open display and became a tourist attraction in the village of Waterloo in Belgium.

/ 4 / SARAH BERNHARDT

The "Divine Sarah" was the greatest actress of her day, a star of stage and screen and one of the first women to play Hamlet. Among her long list of lovers she claimed a unique royal treble by sleeping with King Edward VII, his bisexual son "Eddy" the Duke of Clarence, and the French Emperor Napoleon III. It was rumored that she and King Edward enjoyed copulating in a special silk-lined coffin which she kept in her bedroom for special "guests"; given "Bertie's" elephantine girth it was a fair bet that she was on top while he played dead. In 1905 she badly injured her knee onstage while performing the play *La Tosca*. The injury never healed and several years later the leg had to be amputated. But she bounced, or rather hopped, back with a Heather Mills–like determination to stay in the limelight. According to legend, while she was recovering from her operation the organizers of the Pan-American Exposition in San Francisco offered her $100,000 for the privilege of exhibiting her leg. Bernhardt cabled back: "Which leg?"

ʃ 5 ʃ DANIEL EDGAR SICKLES

The American Civil War general defied a number of public scandals, most notably the killing of his wife's lover, Philip Barton Key, for which he was acquitted with the first-ever use of temporary insanity as a legal defense in US history. His army career was ended at the Battle of Gettysburg when he was sitting on his horse and a cannonball hit his right leg, almost tearing it off. Sickles was apparently so unfazed by the event that he smoked a cigar on his way to the medical tent, where the leg had to be amputated. Sickles later donated his detached limb to the National Museum of Health and Medicine in Washington, D.C., in a little coffin-shaped box, along with a visiting card, marked "With the compliments of Major General D.E.S." The leg became Sickles's favorite chat-up line. Every year, on the anniversary of the amputation, he would visit the leg, bringing lady friends to the museum with him to impress them with tales of gallantry. The rest of Sickles was interred at Arlington National Cemetery after his demise in 1914.

ʃ 6 ʃ EDWARD TELLER

The Hungarian-born scientist known as "the father of the H-bomb" (although according to Wikipedia "he did not care for the title") was the inspiration for the eponymous mad scientist in Stanley Kubrick's 1964 film *Dr. Strangelove or: How I Learned to Stop Worrying and Love the Bomb*. In the film, Peter Sellers's Strangelove is a wheelchair-bound German scientist who has an uncontrollable mechanical hand that involuntarily makes Nazi salutes and threatens homicide. Teller lost his leg from the knee down after jumping from a station platform while trying to catch a train. A zealous advocate of all things nuclear, one of

Teller's ambitions was to detonate a bomb on the Moon, just to see what happened.

Xenophobe's Itch

10 POPULAR NAMES FOR SYPHILIS

1. French Pox (England, Italy, and Spain)
2. The Neopolitan Disease (France)
3. The Italian Disease (France)
4. The English Disease (France and Turkey)
5. The German Disease (Poland)
6. The Polish Disease (Germany and Russia)
7. Dutch Pox (Portugal)
8. The Portuguese Disease (Persia and Japan)
9. The Spanish Disease (Italy)
10. The Christian Disease (Turkey)

5 Famous People with Irregular Genitalia

/ 1 / ADOLF HITLER

The postmortem performed by Russian doctors on his partly burned body confirmed that, in the words of the old music hall song, *der Führer* did indeed have only one ball. Medical historians were divided as to whether the missing gonad had been removed surgically, possibly as a result of a bullet in the groin during World War I, or as was common practice when advanced syphilis reached its fatal stage. In 2008 an account left by the medic who treated Hitler during the Battle of the Somme in 1916 settled the matter by confirming that the famous testicle went missing on the Western Front. Dr. Johan Jambor told his priest that Hitler had been shot in the abdomen. Apparently Hitler screamed a lot, then asked him: "Will I still be able to have children?" There is, however, another version of events from the person who was best placed to know the truth. According to Eva Braun, Hitler's testicular damage was the result of a boyhood mishap with a wild alpine goat.*

/ 2 / NAPOLEON BONAPARTE

In spite of his remark, made on St. Helena: "Women! When you don't think of them you don't need them!," Boney did need women and lots of them, although he was not quite the romantic French lover of popular imagination. For most of his life he was plagued by impotence, and his marriage with Josephine was a childless, frustrating affair. She blamed his performance in bed for the marital breakdown. His semen, she said, was "no use at all . . . just like so much water." The Little General's penis continues to be a bone of contention. Removed surreptitiously during his autopsy, it ended up in the hands of a priest called Vignali, who then smuggled it home to Corsica. It was passed down by Vignali's family until 1916, when they sold it to a British collector—who, in turn, sold it to a Philadelphia collector, A.S.W. Rosenbach. The penis changed hands a few more times until it turned up for auction in 1972 at Christie's in London. Mounted in a velvet Cartier box, it was approximately one inch long, resembled a fossilized pork scratching, and was

---

* The Allies had a clear testicular advantage in World War II. According to WWII records detailing the health of conscripted men, the British army had nine soldiers with three testicles apiece.

listed as "a small dried-up object." It was a major disappointment, failing to reach even the reserve price. Five years later
the penis was put up for sale again at a Paris auction house and
this time it was bought by an American urologist for $3,000.

/ 3 / GENERAL FRANCISCO FRANCO

Like Hitler, the Spanish dictator lost some of his manhood
through an injury sustained in battle. He was shot in the lower
abdomen at El Biutz, near Ceuta, Morocco, in June 1916, when
he was a captain in the Spanish army. He went on to father a
daughter, Carmen Franco y Polo, in 1926, then ten years later
joined the military uprising that led to the Spanish Civil War,
assumed leadership of the Fascist Party, and ruled Spain for
thirty-six years with an iron fist—but only one ball. Although
he was one of the twentieth century's most durable dictators,
unlike his fascist contemporaries Hitler and Mussolini, Franco
was not the most charismatic of leaders. Hitler once described
meeting him as "less pleasurable than having four or five teeth
pulled." Severe illness forced Franco to resign in 1973, but he
lingered on much longer than even his doctors or his supporters anticipated. At last on his deathbed two years later, Franco
was told that General Garcia wished to say good-bye. "Why?"
Franco enquired. "Is Garcia going somewhere?"

/ 4 / GRIGORI RASPUTIN

Russia's greatest love machine and hairy antihero of the last
days of the Russian czars belonged to a religious sect called
Khlysty, whose believers thought they could get closer to God via
group sex. He was able to persuade women that by submitting

their bodies to him in a spare bedroom he called his "Holy of Holies" they could purge themselves of sin. It sounded so much more exciting than Russian Orthodoxy, and even though his body stench was overpowering, his conquests literally bathed themselves in perfume to mask the smell. By the time of the putrid prophet's death he had deflowered almost every female aristocrat in Saint Petersburg. After being variously poisoned, shot, and drowned by a group of vengeful Russian aristocrats in 1916, Rasputin's penis was hacked off and discarded, but it was retrieved by a servant who turned it over to a woman who took it with her to Paris, where she preserved it in a small velvet-lined oak box. The box held the key to the biggest mystery all—Rasputin's great success with women. When it was opened in 1984 the organ was said to have resembled "a blackened over-ripe banana, about a foot long."

⌠ 5 ⌡ CHAIRMAN MAO ZEDONG

Most of the time the Great Helmsman had only one thing on his mind, and it wasn't the struggle for proletarian leadership of the democratic revolution. His underlings discovered that the quickest way up the Communist Party ladder was to keep their aged leader happy with a permanent supply of young women. Mao suffered from temporary bouts of impotency and was treated with injections of ground deer antlers and a secret formula called H3, but his sexual appetite, if not his performance, seemed to increase with age. Well into his seventies, he was still shedding his drab military uniform to bed several young women at a time. He regularly suffered from venereal disease but refused any treatment or to abstain from sex. The young girls whom he continued to bed considered an infection caught from their Chairman a badge of honor and testimony to their close personal relationship with Mao. According to his physician Dr. Li, Mao had an undescended testicle, but because of his general ignorance of human physiology did not realize that it wasn't normal, and no one ever dared tell him otherwise.

10 Contemporary Cures for the Black Death

1. Wash the victim in goat urine.
2. Apply the entrails of a newborn puppy to the victim's forehead.
3. Drink menstrual blood.
4. Pierce your testicles.
5. Inhale fumes from a latrine.
6. Commit incest on an altar.
7. Smoke tobacco.
8. Apply dried toad to the bubo.
9. Eat the pus-filled boil of plague victims.
10. Eat a little treacle after rainfall.

12 Radical Remedies for Hair Loss

1500 B.C.: Egyptian men treat their hair loss by reciting a magic spell to the sun god Ra and then swallowing a mixture of onions, iron, red lead, honey, and alabaster.

420 B.C.: The ancient Greek physician Hippocrates applies sheep's urine to his bald patch, sadly to no avail.

47 B.C.: Julius Caesar* is incredibly sensitive about thinning hair and tries all of the popular remedies of the day, including rubbing his head with myrrh. His lover Queen Cleopatra suggests a cure made from ground up, burnt domestic mice, horse teeth, bear grease, and deer marrow.

A.D. 210: Chinese people in the Han Dynasty prevent hair loss by eating rat flesh or by applying a mixture of dried and ground-up animal testes.

1610: The incredibly vain King Louis XIV of France loses most of his hair after a severe illness and takes to wearing a voluminous, powdered, curly wig, thus setting a fashion trend for men for the next two hundred years.

1654: A medical handbook published in London advises men to put chicken shit on their scalps as a cure for baldness. It is also said to work for infertility, bad breath, head lice, and aching breasts.

1800: Napoleon Bonaparte tries the very latest cure for baldness; dog's paws and asses' hooves are the main ingredients.

1901: Dr. Delos Parker announces that male pattern baldness is the result of abdominal breathing and advises men to wear corsets. Parker explains that women who wear tight corsets don't use their diaphragms as much and therefore retain their hair.

---

* Ironically his name Caesar is from the Latin *caesaries* meaning "abundant hair."

1950: Scandinavian farmers still favor a traditional cure for baldness, available since the nineteenth century. It involves coating the head with cow dung for twenty minutes twice weekly. Another traditional treatment involves being licked by a cow.

1990: A popular Japanese treatment for baldness recommended washing hair with a bottle of special shampoo while listening to a Mozart CD.

1995: University researchers conclude that there is no guaranteed cure for male pattern baldness which will leave you with your testes intact, but note that "while castration may be a cure, it is not commercially acceptable." The side effects of castration include loss of body hair, a falsetto voice, a tendency to obesity, insomnia, a weak bladder, and poor eyesight.

2010: Mexicans rub wax extracted from killer bees to cure baldness and hemorrhoids: one simply rubs it into the problem area.

50 Workplace Health Problems

    Bakers' Eczema
    Billingsgate Hump (a problem for fish porters)
    Boilermakers' Deafness
    Bricklayers' Itch
    Biscuit Makers' Dermatitis
    Budgerigar Fanciers' Lung

Bullmans' Hand
Cable Makers' Rash
Chain Makers' Cataracts
Cigar Makers' Cramps
Cigarette Cutters' Asthma
Cobblers' Mouth
Combers' Fever
Confectioners' Dermatitis
Cornpickers' Pupil
Cotton Mill Fever
Cotton Twisters' Cramp
Covent Garden Hummy (curvature of the spine)
Dairyman's Itch (caused by a form of VD found
    in cows)
Diamond Cutters' Cramps
Dockers' Itch
Dustmans' Shoulder
Feather Pluckers' Disease
Fireman's Eye (afflicts potters who fire kilns,
    not firemen)
Fish Handlers' Disease
French Polishers' Dermatitis
Gold Smelters' Cataracts
Glassworkers' Cataract
Grocers' Itch
Harpists' Cramps
Hatters' Tremor
Miners' Elbow
Mushroom Workers' Lung
Nailmakers' Cramps
Nuns' Bursitis

Paddy-field Foot

Paprika-splitters' Lung

Printers' Asthma

Pork Finger (afflicts abattoir workers)

Potters' Rot (lead poisoning)

Poultry Pluckers' Finger

Seal Finger (unique to sealers and whalers)

Shipyard Conjunctivitis

Tailors' Ankle

Tea Tasters' Cough

Tripe Scrapers' Disease

Tulip Finger (afflicts market gardeners)

Upholsterers' Mouth

Wool Sorters' Disease (anthrax, also known
   in France as "Bradford Disease")

Weavers' Bottom

10 Self-Harmers

1667: Isaac Newton sticks a bodkin—a large, blunt needle—
into the back of his eye socket between his eyeball and the
bone and jiggles it about to see if it would induce optical effects,
nearly blinding himself in the process. Then he stares directly
into the sun with one eye for as long as he possibly can, just to
see what happens. Although he escapes any permanent damage, he has to lie down in a darkened room for days before his
eyesight recovers.

1982: Police are baffled by a flash fire that sweeps through the
London flat of Norik Hakpisan, burning the twenty-four-year-

old student alive. It later transpired that Hakpisan had perished during an unsuccessful attempt to cure his severe case of hemorrhoids with a can of petrol—a traditional cure, according to his family.

1993: French postman Jean Cellise bleeds to death in Toulouse after cutting himself open to check that his doctors had removed his appendix properly.

1993: Thirty-two-year-old Italian Armando Botalezzi is rushed to the hospital after attempting a nose job with a pair of pliers and a kitchen knife. Botalezzi explains later that he couldn't afford plastic surgery and had decided to "whittle it down a bit" himself. He claimed he would have been successful if only he hadn't kept fainting at the sight of his own blood.

1994: A twenty-eight-year-old British man who couldn't wait to have his left leg amputated by the National Health Service decides to do something about it himself by laying his limb on a railway line in front of a train. Ian Hudson of Winnall, Winchester, had damaged his leg in a motorcycle accident six years earlier. In spite of twenty operations he still had to hobble around on a special boot, caliper, and crutches. After watching a slow-moving railway maintenance vehicle slice his leg off cleanly above the knee, Mr. Hudson said that he had no regrets and was looking forward to having his brand-new artificial leg fitted.

1994: Workmates of a fifty-two-year-old Brazilian lumberjack Luciano Bastos are hugely impressed when their colleague loses his right hand in a logging accident. Bastos refuses to make a fuss and simply fits himself out with a hook. Not another word was spoken about the ordeal, until he tries to take his hat off and accidentally removes his eye.

1995: Twenty-six-year-old Terry Grice from Grand Ridge, Florida, carefully constructs a wooden clamp with which to hold his penis and testicles in place, then slices them off with a circular saw. Grice says later that he did it because he was depressed. Fortunately he recovered from his state of depression long enough to throw the severed organs into the back of his pickup truck, then drive fifty miles to the nearest hospital to have them sewn back on.

2000: A British woman, Heather Perry, age twenty-nine, from Gloucester, drilled a two-centimeter hole in her head in an attempt to cure her chronic fatigue syndrome. The twenty-minute procedure, an ancient surgical technique known as trepanning, went wrong and she required urgent medical assistance. She said later: "I'm the first to admit it sounds totally ridiculous, but I felt something radical needed to be done."

2004: A sixty-seven-year-old Romanian man was rushed to the hospital after he accidentally cut off his own penis and fed it to his dog. Constantin Mocanu, from Galati, told doctors he couldn't sleep because of a noisy chicken. He decided to kill the bird but claimed he mistook his penis for the chicken's neck and chopped it off. When he realized what he had done, he threw the severed organ to the dog, which ate it. Surgeon Nicolae Bacalbasa said he was unconvinced by the man's story.

"It's like the Bible says. If your right hand gives you trouble then cut it off. The man is sixty-seven and he may have had reasons to punish his organ."

2007: Howard Shelley, a forty-two-year-old construction site manager from Bletchley, England, performs a DIY sex change using a kitchen knife and rubber bands. His wife Janet, happily married to Howard for fifteen years, did not have a clue about her husband's gender confusion until after the procedure, performed sober and without painkillers, when her husband drove five miles in agony to his GP and demanded an appointment.

9 Reasons Why Laughter Isn't Always the Best Medicine

400 B.C.: Greek artist Zeuxis laughs himself to death after painting a portrait of an old woman. According to legend, the woman had commissioned a painting of Aphrodite but insisted on sitting as the model.

206 B.C.: The Greek stoic philosopher Chrysippus of Soli keels over and dies laughing after giving his donkey some wine, then watching it try to eat some figs.

1410: Martin I of Aragon, last legitimate descendant of Wilfred the Hairy, dies at a banquet from a lethal combination of dyspepsia and uncontrollable laughter.

1566: Pietro Aretino, Italian writer of erotic prose, falls backwards off his chair and dies after laughing too hard at a rude joke told to him by his sister.

1599: Nanda Bayin, King of Burma, dies laughing after being informed by a traveling Venetian merchant that Venice was a free state without a monarch.

1660: Thomas Urquhart, Scottish Royalist, writer, and eccentric, laughs himself to death upon hearing the news that King Charles II had been restored to the throne.

1975: Alex Mitchell, a fifty-year-old bricklayer from King's Lynn, England, collapses and dies after laughing nonstop for twenty-five minutes during an episode of the TV series *The Goodies* featuring a Scotsman in a kilt kung fu–fighting with some bagpipes. His wife Nessie writes and thanks the creators of the comedy program "for making Alex's last minutes so happy."

1989: An easily amused Danish audiologist, Ole Bentzen, kicks the bucket while watching the allegedly humorous *A Fish Called Wanda*. Bentzen's heart rate was later calculated at between 250–500 beats per minute, causing cardiac arrest. The official verdict on his death is that he "died from mirth."

2003: Damnoen Saen-um, a fifty-two-year-old Thai ice cream salesman, dies laughing in his sleep. His wife is unable to wake him during his two minutes of fatal hilarity and he expires, presumably of heart failure or asphyxiation.

7 Categories of Human Feces*

1. Separate hard lumps, like nuts—passed with difficulty
2. Sausage-shaped but lumpy
3. Like a sausage but with cracks on the surface
4. Like a sausage or snake, i.e., smooth and soft
5. Soft blobs with clear-cut edges—easily passed
6. Fluffy pieces with ragged edges—a mushy stool
7. Watery, no solid pieces—entirely liquid

Gone with the Wind
10 SUFFERERS OF FLATULENCE

ʃ 1 ʃ GOD

According to Isaiah 16:11 the Lord said, "Wherefore my bowels shall sound like an harp for Moab." Sadly there is no guidance in the Bible as to how this Mighty Wind may have smelt.

ʃ 2 ʃ EDWARD DE VERE, EARL OF OXFORD

He accidentally broke wind while bowing to Queen Elizabeth I and was so embarrassed by the incident he decided to keep a low

---

* The Bristol Stool Scale was developed by gastroenterologists Kenneth W. Heaton, M.D., and Stephen J. Lewis, M.D., of the University of Bristol, UK, in 1997. The Scale is a diagnostic tool used to evaluate a patient's bowel habits and helps to improve communication between doctor and patients too embarrassed to discuss their bodily functions, known to some in the trade as "shameful shitters."

profile and threw himself into extensive traveling abroad. When he finally returned to the court after a seven-year absence, the Queen greeted him with "My Lord, I had forgot the fart."

∫ 3 ∫ SAMUEL PEPYS, DIARIST

"Wind doth now and then torment me about the fundament extremely . . . I had a couple of stools forced after it and did break a fart or two, but whether I shall grow better upon it I cannot tell."

∫ 4 ∫ JOSEPH PUJOL, PETOMANE

The nineteenth-century Frenchman Joseph Pujol was so adept at controlling the flow of his flatulence that he could sound musical notes. Performing as Le Petomane (the fartiste) he made a career out of it and in his prime was one of the highest paid performers in France.

∫ 5 ∫ SIR HENRY LUDLOW, BRITISH PARLIAMENTARIAN

In 1607 the MP for Ludgershall, Wiltshire let rip a fart in the House of Commons that was so enormous the poet Ben Jonson wrote an epigram about it.

∫ 6 ∫ ROBERT HOOKE, "THE FATHER OF MODERN SCIENCE"

His diaries chronicled his flatulence in conjunction with barometric pressure; he believed that there was a link.

∫ 7 ∫ WOLFGANG AMADEUS MOZART

According to his letters, he was very proud of his flatulence and wrote about it in detail to his mother and cousin. His wooing of his wife Constanze consisted mostly of fart jokes, which she apparently found irresistible.

∫ 8 ∫ QUEEN VICTORIA

She ate very quickly, mixed whiskey with her claret, and consequently was a martyr to her wind. In 1897 John Norton, the proprietor of the Australian journal *Truth* was tried for libel after describing Queen Victoria as "fat, flabby, and flatulent."

∫ 9 ∫ CHARLES DARWIN

Darwin suffered lifelong bouts of trapped wind and excessive flatulence, which he attempted to cure by going for months without sugar, salt, bacon, or alcohol, also by lemon sucking, sipping acid, applying vinegar to his neck, ice cold baths, and cold water douches. There was also more technical quackery, involving tying heavy batteries to his stomach and electric chains around his neck. He discovered the theory of evolution but unfortunately for his wife Emma he never found the antidote to his nocturnal trumps.

∫ 10 ∫ MARILYN MONROE

According to Hollywood legend, when Clark Gable and Marilyn appeared together in the 1961 movie *The Misfits,* the two costars had a torrid affair. This claim is rubbished by Gable's biographer David Bret, who reports that Monroe's interest in Gable was not returned, mostly because he was put off by her constant farting.

10 People Who Were Killed by Their Doctors

/ 1 / QIN SHI HUANG

The first emperor of unified China died at the age of fifty after ingesting some highly toxic mercury pills given to him by his physicians. They told him the pills would give him eternal life.

/ 2 / KING RICHARD I

King Richard "the Lionheart" was laying siege to a castle in France when he was hit by a crossbow bolt in the shoulder. Richard hung on for eleven days, expiring from blood poisoning on the evening of Tuesday, April 6, 1199. Before he died he absolved the young archer who had shot him, saying: "Youth, I forgive thee. Take off his chains, give him one hundred shillings and let him go." Royal magnanimity was not extended to Marchadeus, the Jewish physician who hastened Richard's death while attempting to remove the arrowhead. He was later executed. Richard's premature death was not all bad news. It brought his brother John to the throne, which in turn led to the signing of the Magna Carta, the fundamental statement of English liberties and a precursor to the American Declaration of Independence and the French Rights of Man.

∫ 3 ∫ KING CHARLES II

On Monday, February 2, 1685, as King Charles II was being prepared for his morning shave, he suffered a stroke. His physicians bled him, purged him, shaved his head, and applied blister-raising cantharides plasters to his scalp, pressed red-hot irons against his skin, administered twice-hourly enemas of rock salt and syrup of buckthorn, and made him drink metals dissolved in white wine (thought to be an emetic). He was then required to swallow therapeutic potions of oriental bezoar stone from the stomach of a goat and boiled spirits from a human skull. On February 7, after five days of being tortured, as one historian recounted, "like a red Indian at the stake," his body raw with burns and blisters, the king succumbed and lapsed into a merciful coma, dying the following day. The king's final words were, "I am sorry, gentlemen, for being such a time a-dying."

∫ 4 ∫ ROBBIE BURNS

Scotland's most famous son contracted a severe case of rheumatic fever in 1795 when he lost his appetite, suffered trembling fits, and spent sleepless nights wracked with pain. Taking his doctor's advice he walked out into the bitterly cold muddy waters of the Solway and stood in it up to his waist for as long as he could stand it, then downed several glasses of port wine. Emaciated beyond recognition and weakened by the "cure" to the point where he couldn't stand unaided, Burns collapsed at home where he died four days later.

∫ 5 ∫ GEORGE WASHINGTON

On December 13, 1799, the sixty-seven-year-old former president came down with a throat infection and was visited by Dr.

James Craik, who tried "two copious bleedings," a cantharides blister, two doses of calomel, and an unspecified "injection" which "operated on the lower intestines." Two more physicians arrived that afternoon to bleed Washington yet again, then made him inhale vinegar in a vapor mixed with steam, followed by more calomel and "repeated doses of emetic tartar" which produced "a copious discharge from the bowels." Between them they drained about 35 percent of the blood in his body within twelve hours. At this point Washington told his doctors he preferred to die without further intervention. Meanwhile the architect and inventor William Thornton rushed to Mount Vernon and proposed to revive Washington by rubbing his skin and blowing air into his lungs followed by a transfusion of lamb's blood, but friends of the deceased president wouldn't allow it.

∫ 6 ∫ JAMES A. GARFIELD

In 1881, just three months after he was sworn in, Garfield was felled by two bullets fired by the assassin Charles Guiteau: one grazed Garfield's arm but the other lodged itself somewhere inside his body. Over a period of eighty days, sixteen doctors were consulted on the president's condition. The first on the scene jabbed a finger into Garfield's open wound then inserted a non-sterile probe to find the bullet, doing so much damage that it misled several other doctors who arrived later into believing that this was the path made by the bullet and that the missile had hit Garfield's liver. An army surgeon general then helpfully stuck an unwashed digit into the wound as deep as he could, soon followed by the navy surgeon general who probed with his finger so deeply that he actually punctured the president's undamaged liver. Garfield's fever rose and he was put on a diet of milk and brandy. Meanwhile the surgeons continued to poke and prod about inside the president's body for the bullet with their fingers. The government called in their expert, Alexander Graham Bell, with his latest invention, a crude metal detector, to help locate the offending missile. After several passes with his device Bell announced that he had found the bullet. When the physicians set about cutting Garfield open to remove it they realized with horror that Bell's equipment had actually located the metal springs under the mattress—the bullet however continued to elude them. For some period after the shooting, Garfield was fed rectally. By the time he died of a massive, fatal heart attack, his doctors had turned a three-inch-deep, harmless wound into a twenty-inch-long contaminated gash stretching from his ribs to his groin. The president's autopsy determined that the bullet had in fact lodged itself some way from the spine and that Garfield would have survived if everyone had just left him alone. Garfield's medical bill was $18,500. At his trial, Charles Guiteau argued that it was the incompetence of Bell and the doctors, not he, that had killed the president. Worth a try, but he was hanged anyway on June 30, 1882.

∫ 7 ∫ JOHANN SEBASTIAN BACH

Bach was a victim of John Taylor, the most famous eye surgeon of his day, self-styled "Opthalmister" to the Pope and "every crowned head in Europe." Taylor relied on a crude technique for the removal of cataracts known as couching, an invasive procedure using unsterilized instruments by which the opaque lens was displaced from the eye. The immediate results were usually good, but the operation was inevitably followed by serious infection. Bach suffered agonies from repeated incisions into this eyes followed by treatment with mercury ointment, and his death was hastened after the operation by septicemia from Taylor's dreaded couching needle. Modern historians speculate the cause of death may have also been complicated by stroke.

/ 8 / THOMAS JEFFERSON

In 1825 Jefferson complained that he was having "difficulty in making water" and called in his physician Robley Dunglison who prescribed "bougies"—an incredibly painful procedure, without anesthetic, in which flexible cylinders were introduced through Jefferson's urethra. Jefferson found relief for his immediate problem, but the unsterilized technique introduced bacteria, leading to damage to Jefferson's kidneys. He gradually grew worse with occasional periods of good health. The exact cause of his subsequent death has been conclusively determined but it was undoubtedly hastened by toxemia from a kidney infection and uremia from kidney damage.

/ 9 / KING GEORGE V

On January 20, 1936, the king fell into a coma following a series of bronchitis attacks, and the royal doctor Lord Dawson of Penn was summoned to Sandringham. Shortly before midnight Dawson slipped a hypodermic syringe containing a lethal mixture of cocaine and morphine—now commonly known as a "whizzball"—into the king's jugular vein. Dawson's medical notes confirmed that he had not terminated the king's life to end his suffering—the king was unconscious and therefore was not in any pain—but simply for the sake of the morning papers.

The moment of death was deliberately timed to ensure that the news, in Dawson's words, "received its first announcement in the respectable morning papers, such as the *Times*, rather than the less appropriate field of the evening journals." Dawson even phoned the *Times* to warn them to hold the front page and to expect an important announcement shortly. The early death also suited Dawson because it allowed him to get back to his busy private practice in London.

∫ 1 0 ∫ JOSEPH STALIN

In December 1953 the seventy-four-year-old Soviet leader was felled by a stroke and lay helpless on the floor in a pool of his own urine, unable to call for help. As no one dared to go into his rooms uninvited, it was hours before his bodyguards finally summoned the courage to open his door—plenty of time for Stalin to reflect upon the fact that he had recently ordered the arrest and torture of most of his best doctors. By the time help finally arrived the terrified medics were reluctant even to touch Stalin to take his pulse. However, leeches were applied to his ears and he was administered enemas of magnesium sulphate and spoonfuls of weak tea. He died five days later.

12 Revealing Facts about the Human Condition

1. An average person produces 25,000 quarts of spit in a lifetime, enough to fill one Olympic-size swimming pool.
2. On average, your underwear contains about ten grams of fecal matter. Washing your underwear in a machine along

with other clothes simply spreads the fecal contamination around.

3. You have close cousins of the gonorrhea bacteria living in your mouth and throat.

4. The average American adult stool is smaller, harder, darker, about half the size, and much less likely to float than its third-world equivalent.

5. According to the most recent UN estimates (2010), 638 million people in India—5 percent of the population—defecate out of doors, in public. Modesty permits, however, that Indian women can only defecate in public after dark and in the woods, a practice that frequently exposes them to snake bites.

6. The average person burps about fifteen times a day, mostly because of swallowed air, the rest from fermentation of undigested food.

7. One of the most common causes of asthma is inhaled cockroach shit.

8. Farts are created mostly by E. coli and other bacteria inside your gut. Flatulence runs in families, because they have a tendency to harbor similar intestinal parasites, along with an inclination to eat the same types of foods.

9. Your sweat is made up of the same components as urine: water, salts, and urea. It also contains traces of chemicals found in wasp poison and skunk spray. Some people stink more than others because their bodies lack a particular enzyme that absorbs a smelly protein made by bacteria in the stomach.

10. Adult men usually pee in a narrower stream than women do because sex and children can affect the women's tissues there. This unusual fact was used to test virginity

centuries ago: if a woman peed like a man, she was thought to be a virgin.

11. Nine-tenths of ordinary household dust is dead human skin. Every seven years you can literally claim to be a new you because your outer covering will have completely replaced itself: the old you is in the vacuum cleaner bag.

12. Vomit tastes bitter because it contains hydrochloric acid, which in a concentrated form can eat through stainless steel.

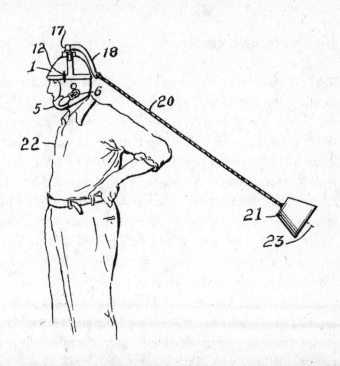

CHAPTER FOUR

WIZARDS OF ODD

9 Clueless Explorers

1687: French explorer Robert Cavelier de La Salle travels the length of the Mississippi, almost entirely by foot, all the way to the Gulf of Mexico, then returns to France claiming the entire valley for King Louis XIV. Unfortunately La Salle's discovery was a fluke he was unable to repeat. When he returned to the New World to find the Mississippi again he landed by mistake on the Texas coast, some four hundred miles west of his intended destination. He and his crew wandered thousands of miles on foot looking for the Mississippi, completely lost. His men died of thirst and attacks by marauding Indians. He eventually found his way back to his ship and sailed for Canada, only to get lost again, finding himself back in the Gulf of Mexico. La Salle tried again, but by this time his crew had had enough; on his third unsuccessful attempt they mutinied against the prospect of more hardship, and murdered him.

1793: John Thomas Evans, the son of a Methodist preacher from Caernafon, Wales, sets off for North America to find a lost tribe of Welsh Indians, taking with him a Welsh Bible so that he could pray with his long lost kinsmen in their ancestral language. Despite having little knowledge of the local geography and believing that America is populated with woolly mammoths and has mountains made of salt, Evans braves freezing weather conditions and attacks by Sioux natives. After two years of searching he hears not a single word of Welsh. He returns to civilization and writes in his journal, "there is no such people as the Welsh Indians." His spirit crushed, Evans drinks himself to death in a Saint Louis bar two years later, aged twenty-eight.

1811: The English botanist Thomas Nuttall spent the biggest part of his adult life walking across North America collecting hundreds of plant specimens, but his survival skills left something to be desired. His fellow travelers christen him "le fou" (the fool), after checking his gun before an Indian raid and finding it filled with dirt: he had been using it to dig up plants. Nuttall spent most of his time completely lost. He frequently wandered away from his group, engrossed in his work and could never find his way back. One night a search party was sent out to look for him and when he saw them approach him in the dark, he mistook them for Indians and ran off. His rescuers chased him for three days without success, until he accidentally wandered back into the camp unassisted. On another occasion Nuttall somehow strayed one hundred miles away from his group and was so exhausted that he collapsed and lost consciousness. A passing Indian took pity on him and carried him three miles to the river and paddled him home in a canoe. Against all odds, he eventually found his way back to England, where he was acclaimed as a world-leading authority on the flora and fauna of the American Northwest.

1825: Gordon Laing, a young Scottish army officer serving in the Royal African Colonial Corps sets off to find the fabled lost city of Timbuktu, although his health and mental state are described as "delicate" and his grasp of African geography "hazy." Laing records very little in his scientific journal over the coming months, apart from random observations such as "I must not meddle with the females of the country." After being attacked and left for dead by Taureg tribesmen, and having traveled 2,650 miles of unmapped, hostile desert with horrific multiple injuries, Laing reaches his goal and enters the fabled city of

Timbuktu on August 13, 1826. He looks everywhere for the glittering palaces and nubile lovelies he had heard of, but found only a poor, run-down frontier town full of mud huts and bandits. Weirdly, Laing wrote home that Timbuktu "has completely met my expectations." He spends the next five weeks going mad, strutting through the streets in full dress uniform announcing himself as the King of England's emissary. On his way home, on September 22, 1826, three days after leaving Timbuktu, he was killed by Tauregs, throttled by two men with his own turban, then decapitated and left for the vultures.

1834: The Scottish botanist David Douglas braved whirlpools, grizzly bears, robbery, frostbite, snow blindness, and near starvation in the Rocky Mountains. Despite rapidly deteriorating eyesight, he covered over ten thousand miles of the Northwest like a roving, frostbitten Mr. Magoo, literally bumping into trees. His sight impairment led to an epic blunder. He returned home from one of his trips to the Rockies and announced the discovery of two giant peaks, which he named Mount Hooker and Mount Brown after distinguished British botanists. For almost seventy years they were the subject of great excitement and speculation and were listed on every map as the two highest peaks in the Canadian Rocky Mountains, but thwarted the best efforts of experienced mountaineers to find either of them. The search for Douglas's giant peaks was finally brought to a close when someone carefully reread his original journals and noticed that he had claimed to have climbed both peaks in a single afternoon. In 1834, while looking for plants in Hawaii, the optically challenged Douglas stumbles into a pit that had been excavated to trap wild cattle and is gored to death by a bull.

1846: The career of British explorer John Ainsworth Horrocks is tragically cut short when he sets out to conquer the hitherto impenetrable hinterland of South Australia with several goats, a bull called Harry, and an unnamed camel imported from Tenerife. The addition of the camel to the party is seen as a logistical masterstroke because previous expeditions, equipped with horses and bull, had all perished in the fierce heat. The decision turned out to be less of a coup than anticipated when not long into the journey the camel attacked their cook, biting a large chunk out of his head. A couple of days later the recalcitrant camel strikes again, lurching into Horrocks just as he was loading his gun, causing him to accidentally shoot himself in the lower jaw, knocking out half of his teeth. Horrocks dies in agony from his injuries several days later, the first explorer to be shot dead by his own camel.

1865: Realizing that preparation is the key to any successful expedition, the pioneer missionary Dr. David Livingstone sets off across Africa with seventy-three books, weighing a total of 180 pounds. He eventually agrees to discard some of his portable library, but only after his exhausted porters had carried them for three hundred miles. As the journey continues his library grows progressively smaller until only his Bible remains. (Not very sensible, but still not quite in the same league as the French explorer-priest Alexandre Debaize who in 1878 reached the African town Ujiji packing twenty-four umbrellas, two suits of armor, and a portable organ). Livingstone died in Africa in 1873, after braving illness and years of paddling up and down snake-infested rivers, none of them, alas, leading to source of the Nile. Along the way, he converted only one African, who later lapsed.

1897: The Swede Salomon August Andrée and companions Knut Fraenkel and Nils Strindberg set off on an ill-fated attempt to reach the North Pole by hydrogen balloon, despite little experience in large balloons and none in Arctic conditions. All three men die a couple of weeks after landfall from severe food poisoning after dining on undercooked polar bear.

1933: Maurice Wilson, the manager of a women's clothes shop in Yorkshire, England, attempts the first-ever solo ascent of Mount Everest by crash-landing a plane on the slopes of the world's highest peak, then walking to the summit. There are a couple of flaws in Wilson's bold plan. He doesn't own a plane and has never flown one before or done any mountain climbing, but Wilson is resolute. After buying a three-year-old Gipsy Moth plane and naming it Ever Wrest, he books himself some flying lessons. After a few sessions he decides he is ready for his great adventure. The British and Nepalese authorities hear about Wilson's plan and do their best to stop him, but he slips out of the country and flies five thousand miles to India, where he is forced to abandon his plane and complete the rest of his ascent on foot. Hiking overland through Tibet, he arrives at the foot of Mount Everest on May 17. Wilson is convinced he can surmount any obstacle, including the world's highest peak, via a combination of fasting and prayer. His Sherpas begged to differ and abandoned him at 21,000 feet, but Wilson climbs on, braving increasingly desperate weather and dying of exposure. A year later, a British party found his frozen corpse and beside it his diary. Wilson's final entry, for May 31, was: "Off again, gorgeous day." When Wilson was found there was women's clothing in his rucksack, and he was wearing women's underwear.

10 Martyrs to Science

433 B.C.: The Greek philosopher and physician Empedocles was the first person to realize that the Moon shines by reflected light and is also known as the world's first chemist because of his important insight into the nature of matter. In another insight, Empedocles comes to believe that he is a God. In order to demonstrate his immortality to his supporters, he jumps into the crater of Mount Etna. The volcano spews out one of his bronze sandals but there has been no sign of the owner since.

1500: The first manned rocket flight is attempted by a Ming Dynasty Chinese official called Wan Hu. He builds a wheelchair and attaches to the base forty-seven rockets filled with a combustible mixture of charcoal, saltpetre, and sulfur. Seated in his wicker chair and grasping a large kite in each hand to keep him airborne, he braces himself and signals to his assistants to light the rockets beneath him. The fuses blaze and the gunpowder ignites in a mighty explosion. Wan Hu's assistants look skyward for signs of their master, but in vain. When the billowing clouds of smoke clear there was nothing left: no chair, no kites, no Wan Hu. The experiment is presumed a great success but, tellingly, there are no attempts to repeat it.

1767: The thirst for medical knowledge inspires the great Scottish surgeon and anatomist John Hunter to inject pus from the weeping sores of a gonorrhea-infected prostitute into the glans of his own penis to find out how the disease was transmitted. Unfortunately for Hunter the prostitute he chooses to take his sample from also suffers from syphilis; a mistake that will delay Hunter's marriage for three years and from which he never completely recovers. It was also bad news for venereology, because Hunter mistakenly concluded that syphilis and gonorrhea were stages of the same infection, setting back the study of both diseases for many years.

1785: The accident-prone French chemist Jean-François Pilâtre de Rozier and his companion Pierre Romain become the world's first air disaster victims when their hot air balloon crashes near Wimereux in the Pas-de-Calais during an attempt to fly across the English Channel. By way of preparation, de Rozier tested the properties of hydrogen by filling his mouth with the gas, then expelling it over an open flame, thus proving that hydrogen is highly flammable and that there are less painful ways of losing all of your facial hair.

1786: Despite having no formal scientific education the Swede Karl Wilhelm Scheele made formidable contributions to chemistry. He discovered oxygen more than a year before Joseph Priestley identified the gas, but didn't publish his results. Scheele went on to discover an astonishing eight elements, including, chlorine, fluorine, manganese, barium, molybdenum, tungsten, and nitrogen, but in every case someone else got the credit. Scheele might have gone on making great discoveries if it hadn't been for his curious habit of tasting every chemical he worked with, including such lethal substances as mercury and hydrocyanic acid—a chemical so deadly that even inhalation or contact with the skin could lead to a horrific, painful death. Any one of these could have accounted for his sudden and premature death at his laboratory workbench at the age of forty-three.

1799: The chemist Thomas Beddoes speculates that certain "factitious airs" have great therapeutic qualities and has the alarming insight that inhalation of hydrogen or methane might cure tuberculosis. Beddoes tests his theory by piping methane gas into the sick rooms of tuberculosis patients—the other end of the pipe connected to some flatulent cows on a nearby lawn. Fortunately he was unable to repeat the trick with hydrogen. At the cutting-edge of most of Beddoes's more questionable research was his nineteen-year-old assistant, Humphry Davy, inventor of the miner's lamp. Beddoes persuaded Davy to inhale carbon monoxide, which he did, with near-fatal consequences. Davy only avoided slipping into a deep and lethal sleep because he dropped the inhaler mouthpiece before collapsing. Beddoes then persuaded his young assistant to inhale about eighteen liters of laughing gas from a used sick bag.

1804: Stubbins Ffirth, a doctor from Philadelphia, drinks fresh vomit from yellow fever patients to prove it is not a contagious disease. Ffirth does not fall seriously ill and claims he was vindicated, but his efforts were in vain. Yellow fever is extremely contagious, but only if transmitted directly into the bloodstream, for example, from a mosquito bite.

1806: The Prussian polymath Alexander von Humboldt is fascinated by the discovery that electrical currents can produce muscle contractions. Humboldt undertakes a series of horrific self-experiments by which he attaches electrodes to various parts of his body. He once spent an afternoon in convulsive agony after idly sticking an electrode into the cavity left by a freshly extracted tooth to see what would happen. Some of his experiments with electricity on animals were more unsettling.

In order to collect electric eels for experimentation, Humboldt and his assistants herded about thirty horses into an eel-infested lake, where they were trapped and shocked repeatedly until the agitated eels were too exhausted to pose any danger to the humans. Several horses drowned in agony in the first few minutes.

1889: The medical talents of the French physician Charles-Édouard Brown-Séquard found a curious outlet as a young man when he took to swallowing whole sponges attached to a string, and pulling them back up again so he could study his gastric juices. In 1854 he went to Mauritius, just in time for a local cholera epidemic that took the lives of eight thousand people. He helped to organize a hospital and drank victims' vomit to test the efficacy of opium as a cure. After a fortunate recovery in 1889 at the age of seventy-two, Brown-Séquard surprised a packed meeting of Europe's leading physicians with an intimate revelation. Having chopped and ground up the testicles of puppies and guinea pigs and injecting himself with the resulting compound, Brown-Séquard claimed he was now physically thirty years younger and was able to "visit" his young third wife, Elizabeth, every day without fail. His *liquide testiculaire* caused a stir in the international medical establishment and generated a wave of similar experiments hoping to re-create his elixir of youth, albeit briefly. His wife left him for a younger man and shortly after that Brown-Séquard dropped dead from a cerebral hemorrhage.

1989: E. Frenkel, one of a growing number of psychic healers in Russia, claims to have successfully used his psychic powers to stop moving vehicles, including bicycles and cars. Frenkel decides he is ready for something bigger and steps in front of a freight train in the southern city of Astrakhan. The train driver later reported that the psychic walked onto the tracks with "his arms raised, his head lowered, and his body tensed." Frenkel died from his injuries.

10 People Who Were Too Smart for Their Own Good

1. The single most influential medical scholar in antiquity was the first-century Roman Pliny the Elder, whose forty-seven-volume book *Historia Naturalis* was the most authoritative text on scientific matters right up to the Middle Ages. *Historia Naturalis* was so influential that by the time anyone got around to seriously challenging his teachings, Pliny the Elder had been dead for over a thousand years, after discovering during the eruption of Vesuvius in A.D. 79 that there was no cure for standing next to a volcano to get a better look.

2. The Greek poet and critic Philitas of Cos was a stickler for grammar. He is said to have studied erroneous word usage so intensely that he lost track of mealtimes and accidentally starved himself to death.

3. The sixteenth-century Italian polymath Girolamo Cardano wrote on a wide variety of subjects, including medicine, astronomy, philosophy, and mathematics. As a physician he gave the first clinical description of typhus fever. His passion for gambling led him to discover one of the most fundamental laws of the theory of probability. His reputation as a mathematician was so great that he was

consulted by Leonardo da Vinci on questions of geometry. As a sideline Cardano also earned international fame as the most successful astrologer of his day, and was hired to cast horoscopes for the crowned heads of Europe. He predicted his own death, down to the very hour, at the age of seventy-five. When the time arrived and Cardano found himself in robust good health, he committed suicide rather than be proven wrong.

4. The great Hungarian mathematician Paul Erdös was a prodigy who, at the age of three, could multiply three-digit numbers in his head. Outside the world of mathematics he was totally dysfunctional; he was eleven years old before he learned to tie his shoelaces and twenty-one before he realized that he had never learned how to butter bread—a revelation that came to him when he went abroad for the first time without his mother. "I can make excellent cold cereal," he said once, "and I could probably boil an egg, but I've never tried." Erdös lived only for mathematical problems. He had no family, no job or hobbies, nor even a fixed address. He carried all his worldly belongings with him in a small battered suitcase, and spent his life as a perpetual houseguest of various colleagues all over the world. He would turn up unannounced and say: "My brain is open." Erdös was not the easiest of houseguests: According to his hosts, he had no idea how to wash his own underwear. He had an amazing facility for remembering telephone numbers and would phone friends and colleagues all over the world with no consideration of the local time. He was hopeless at remembering names and faces, even those of his closest friends. One of the few people Erdös called by his Christian name was his friend

Tom Trotter; Erdös always called him Bill. Erdös once bumped into a fellow a mathematician and asked him where he was from. "Vancouver," came the reply. "Oh, then you must know my good friend Elliot Mendelson," said Erdös. The man replied, "I *am* your good friend Elliot Mendelson." He died in 1996 at the age of eighty-three of a fatal heart attack at a mathematics conference in Warsaw while in the middle of working on another equation. By that time Erdös had more than fifteen hundred published papers to his credit, but had never learned how to boil water to make himself a cup of tea.

5. The physicist Paul Dirac, one of the founders of quantum mechanics and widely regarded as one of the greatest physicists of all time, once said he got his ideas by lying on his back with his legs in the air so that the blood ran to his head. The most remarkable thing about that statement is that Dirac said it at all. For most of his adult life his spoken vocabulary was said to have been limited to three replies: "Yes," "No," and "I don't know." Dirac spent several years as head of the physics department at Florida State University where his students found his answers so monosyllabic that they named a unit of measure after him: the Dirac unit of volubility, equal to one word per year. He was so taciturn that some of his short-term acquaintances believed that he was actually dumb. He married the sister of the famous Hungarian theoretical physicist Eugene Wigner. Shortly after their wedding the couple bumped into an old friend of Dirac's who had not yet heard about the marriage. Dirac's friend wondered who the attractive woman with the professor might be. "Sorry," replied Dirac. "I forgot to introduce you, this is Wigner's sister."

6.   The British scientist Sir Nevill Mott, winner of the Nobel Prize for Physics in 1977, was notoriously absentminded. Before working at Cambridge University, Mott spent some time as professor of physics at Bristol University. One day after visiting London, Mott took the train back from Paddington to Bristol. Just as he was about to arrive, he remembered he was no longer a professor of physics in Bristol, so he took the next train back to London and from there he took a train to Cambridge. Just before he arrived, Mott remembered he had traveled up to London by car. So he took the next train back to London, found his car, and drove to Cambridge. Just before he arrived, Mott finally remembered that he had been accompanied that morning by his wife.

7.   The US congressman Clement Vallandigham was a famous opponent of Abraham Lincoln. He also enjoyed a career as a prosperous and successful lawyer until a famous court case in 1871. Vallandigham was defending a man accused of shooting another man dead in a barroom brawl. While cleverly demonstrating how the murder victim could have inadvertently shot himself, Vallandigham grabbed a pistol he thought was unloaded, reenacted the event for the benefit of the jury, and shot himself in the process. Having proved his point, the defendant was acquitted.

8.   In 1993 Garry Hoy, a thirty-eight-year-old lawyer in Toronto fell to his death after he threw himself against a window on the twenty-fourth floor of the Toronto-Dominion Centre in an attempt to prove to a group of visiting law students that the glass was "unbreakable." His first attempt failed to break the glass, as did his second. Unfortunately the impact popped the glass out of the

window frame, and he fell more than three hundred feet to his death.

9. During World War II the Allies were preoccupied with the possibility that Germany might be able to build a nuclear bomb if they gained access to Norway's stocks of heavy water (deuterium oxide). A committee was set up to investigate the possible threat with the code name MAUD. It got this name after a telegram arrived from the top Danish physicist Niels Bohr, ending with the words, AND TELL MAUD RAY KENT. Allied scientists were convinced that this could only be a coded message, possibly an anagram. Churchill's top cryptologists were set to work on decoding the message. They came up with RADIUM TAKEN (presumably by the Nazis?)—U AND D MAY REACT—indicating an atomic reaction using uranium and deuteronium abbreviated D—and MAKE UR DAY NT. The mystery was finally unraveled when it turned out that Bohr was sending a message to his housekeeper called Maud Ray who lived in Kent.

10. According to his biographer, John McNeill, the inventor Thomas Midgley Jr., inadvertently had more impact on the atmosphere than any other organism in Earth's history. In 1916 Midgley discovered that leaded petrol was the solution to an annoying problem called engine "knock," a destructive phenomenon that occurred in internal combustion engines, characterized by overheating, jerky motion, and sluggish response. Today, thanks to Midgley, children all over the world have lower IQs because their brains have been poisoned by lead. A decade later, the well-meaning Midgley had another bright idea. Refrigeration at that time was a risky business because fridges used dangerous, unstable

gases; in 1929 a leaky refrigerator at a hospital in Ohio killed more than a hundred people. Midgley discovered that chlorofluorocarbons (CFCs) were an almost perfect substance for fridges, air-conditioners, and aerosol cans. In 1931 he demonstrated just how safe CFCs were by filling his lungs with the vapor and exhaling it to extinguish a candle. He was lauded as a genius. It was only much later that CFCs were found to destroy the ozone layer. The chlorofluorocarbons that had cooled the world and chilled its food were also destroying its protection against the sun's rays. Midgley never knew how much havoc he had wreaked with leaded petrol and CFCs because he died long before anyone else realized their impact. In 1940 he contracted polio, which left him wheelchair bound. Finally and fatally he devised a contraption comprising ropes and pulleys that allowed him to hoist himself out of bed without assistance. On the morning of November 2, 1944, his wife found him dead, having strangled himself in his final invention.

9 Discredited Scientific Theories

/ 1 / HOLLOW EARTH THEORY

In 1691 the great British astronomer Edmond Halley (of Halley's Comet fame) read a paper to the Royal Society setting out to prove that the Earth was a giant hollow shell, comprising three concentric shells, nesting inside one another like giant Russian dolls. The two larger shells were roughly the same size as Mars and Venus, while the solid inner sphere was about the size of the planet Mercury. The interior of the Earth, he explained to his audience, was also inhabited. He never got around to specifying what sort of creatures these underground species might be, but he went on to explain that they had a special light source that would occasionally burst out through fissures in the North Pole, spreading through the atmosphere as the aurora borealis display. We don't know what Halley's fellow scientists made of all this elaborate subterranean speculation because, perhaps wisely, he never mentioned it again in public. Halley was not the only scientist to seriously consider hollow earth theory. Fifty years earlier the German Athanasius Kircher suggested that giants made of fire lived beneath the Earth's crust, although relatively speaking, Kircher's theory wasn't all that odd, given that he also believed that the plague was caused by rotting mermaids.

∫ 2 ∫ HOLLOW SUN THEORY

Sir William Herschel was one of the most distinguished astronomers of the eighteenth century. He completed detailed surveys of the northern sky, cataloguing thousands of stars, and still found time to discover the first new planet in recorded history: Georgium Sidus, which he named in honor of his patron, King George III. (He was not amused when they had decided call it Uranus instead, and refused to call it anything other than Georgium Sidius for the rest of his life.) Herschel also had some odder theories concerning the Sun. He knew that the surface of the Sun was too hot to support life, but he also believed that beneath the Sun's surface lay a more temperate zone where intelligent beings lived. These beings, Herschel revealed, lived in a society very much like our own. He found at least a couple of scientists who agreed with him, including the famous French physicist Dominique Arago. As recently as 1952 the German Godfried Buren reprised Herschel's argument, hypothesizing that inside our hollow Sun lurked a cool region with lush vegetation. Buren was so pleased with himself that he offered the considerable sum of 25,000 DM to anyone who could disprove his theory. When the German astronomical society did precisely that, Buren refused to pay up, until they took him to court and won.

/ 3 / WE ARE NOT ALONE IN THE SOLAR SYSTEM THEORY

As the features of the planet Venus are permanently obscured by dense clouds, it was assumed for many years that it rained a lot—a bit like Seattle but nearer the Sun. Another puzzling feature of Venus is that, like the Moon, it is sometimes observed as a crescent, but with the dark area slightly illuminated. A German professor, Franz von Paula Gruithuisen, found the cause of this phenomenon. It was not, as most people now believe, the result of refraction in the planet's atmosphere, it was due to the Venusian custom of setting the forests ablaze to celebrate the succession of their new emperor. Gruithuisen went on to write various papers on the subject of extraterrestrial life forms, including "Discovery of Many Distinct Traces of Lunar Inhabitants, Especially of One of Their Colossal Buildings," in which he claimed that he had seen roads, cities, and a star-shaped temple on the Moon. Still, he got to have a small lunar crater named after him. Gruithuisen was not alone in thinking that we are not alone. The Dutch mathematician, astronomer, and physicist Christiaan Huygens speculated that the planet Jupiter was blessed with large supplies of hemp. How did he know this? The clues lay in Jupiter's moons. According to a fashionable theory of the day, the Earth's moon was provided by God as a navigational guide for seafarers. As Jupiter had four moons, it followed that the planet had four times as many sailors. And where there were lots of sailors, Huygens reasoned, there were lots of boats. Lots of boats implied lots of sails and ropes to work the sails. And rope required loads of hemp . . . QED. More recently, the twentieth century American astronomer Percival Lowell, who endowed the famous observatory that bears his name, studied Mars for fifteen years, mapping the "canals" he could see on the surface. For many years his books *Mars and Its Canals* and *Mars as the Abode of Life* were hugely influential to astronomers and scientists alike, including Nikola Tesla and Guglielmo Marconi, who both claimed they had received radio signals from Martians.

⁄ 4 ⁄ GOLD FROM URINE THEORY

Nothing quite demonstrated the craze for strange scientific experimentation in the seventeenth century quite like the curious case of Hennig Brand. For some reason, and no one is quite sure why, Brand, a merchant from Hamburg, came to believe that he could turn human urine into gold. In 1669 he collected a small lake of human urine—between fifty and sixty buckets full in all. Each bucket took at least a fortnight to fill. He then allowed the urine to stand and putrefy until, in his own words, it "bred worms." Ignoring the protests of his wife, he then boiled it down into a waxy residue, then left it in his cellar for several months until it had fermented and turned black. Brand then heated the black, fermented urine and distilled it into a large beaker. What remained, Brand was disappointed to discover, was not gold. It did, however, have some unexpected and peculiar properties. It glowed in the dark and was highly combustible; he had accidentally invented phosphorous. Notwithstanding the fact that half the neighborhood must by now have been aware of Brand and his malodorous lake of ancient piss, he proudly demonstrated his new discovery to his friends, heralding it as one of the best-kept secrets of science. But what to do with this stinking byproduct of sixty buckets of old piss? In the 1750s Swedish chemist Karl Scheele worked out how to make phosphorus in bulk without the smell of urine. Unfortunately one of the first uses of the new substance was in the manufacture of matches, resulting in "phossy jaw," one of the most horrific occupational diseases known to mankind, in which the victims' jawbones would literally rot and glow in the dark. It was only treatable by surgical removal of the jawbone.

/ 5 / USSHER CHRONOLOGY

In 1650 an Irish priest from Armagh named James Ussher published a huge book called *The Annals of the Old Testament*. The project, which occupied two thousand pages in Latin, was a formidable piece of academic research that took up twenty years of Ussher's life and caused him to go half blind in the process, but the most important piece of information in the whole book appeared in the very first paragraph of the very first page. By adding together the life spans of all the descendants of Adam, Ussher worked out that God created Earth on Saturday, October 22, 4004 B.C. At 6:00 p.m., to be precise. What happened before that, at half past five for example, Ussher didn't say, or rather couldn't. According to Christian doctrine, before 6:00 p.m. on October 22, 4004 B.C., time itself did not exist. Ussher was congratulated by almost everyone for his stunning piece of historical scholarship because it confirmed something Christians had assumed to be correct for centuries: that the world and mankind were as old as each other, that is, not very old at all.* In 1675 a London bookseller, Thomas Guy, started publishing Bibles with Ussher's date printed in the margin of the work. Guy's Bible became immensely popular, although this may have had more to do with his engravings of bare-breasted biblical women than the inclusion of Ussher's chronology. A few years later the Church of England also began printing Ussher's date in its official Bible, and before long the date was appearing in Bibles so often that it was practically accepted as the word of God. Ussher's date for the age of the Earth continued to hold sway, largely unchallenged, for the next two hundred years or so, and was still being printed in the margin of Bibles right into the twentieth century.

/ 6 / OMPHALES HYPOTHESIS

The Victorian naturalist Philip Gosse was the author of a number of successful books on zoology and marine biology, but is mostly remembered for his strangest, *Omphales*, published in 1884. Gosse was preoccupied with the knotty problem of whether or not the Biblical Adam possessed a belly button. It

* The Catholic establishment was not known for being reasonable with people who entertained doubts about the literal accuracy of the Bible—the Inquisition cut out the tongue, strangled, then burned Giulio Vanini when he suggested that there might be a logical explanation for the Biblical miracles—there were still one or two skeptics who pointed out that, for example, according to Ussher, the Earth was not as old as recorded Chinese history.

goes without saying that, strictly speaking, Adam didn't need an umbilical cord having never spent time in a womb, but as the prototype for all men, was he equipped with all the working parts? Gosse's conclusion in his book *Omphales* (Greek for navel) was that Adam did indeed have a belly button. God had created Adam's navel—and the fossil record—to create the impression that the world was very old. It was an almighty hoax to tempt humankind and test their faith. Gosse thought his explanation was a work of genius and sat back to enjoy the plaudits, but to his astonishment they didn't come. Scientists simply sniggered, while fellow Christians disliked the implication that God was a practical joker. When thousands of copies of *Omphales* remained unsold, Gosse was mystified. Convinced that the title of the book was the problem, he reissued it with the more accessible title of *Creation* but it didn't help. Crushed by overwhelming indifference he gave up science and took up watercolor painting.

∫ 7 ∫ PHRENOLOGY

First hypothesized in the nineteenth century by the German doctor Franz Joseph Gall who believed that a person's personality is dictated by the shape of his or her head. Gall had many followers, including the British Prime Minister David Lloyd George, who was known to have a keen interest in the subject, and once asked for a meeting with the author C. P. Snow after noticing that he had "an interestingly shaped head." Another phrenologist, Cesare Lombroso, the founder of modern criminology, believed that murderers were born, and claimed to have found certain common physical characteristics of "the criminal type" in the failed regicides Guiseppe Fieschi and Karl Eduard Nobiling, notorious for their respective attempts on the lives of the king of France and the emperor of Germany, including "facial asymmetry, enormous jaws, developed frontal sinus and protruding ears." In the 1890s, Italian phrenologists examined two men who tried to kill the king of Italy and concluded that because their heads were oval-shaped, they were predisposed to regicide. Although his discredited theories died with him, Cesare Lombroso's own pickled head is still preserved for all to see in the Museum of Criminal Anthropology in Turin.

∫ 8 ∫ AIDS FROM SPACE THEORY

The cosmologist Fred Hoyle coined the expression "big bang" to describe the theory that the universe was created by a huge explosion. Hoyle actually believed that "big bang" cosmology was nonsense and was ready to argue with anyone who said otherwise. When he came up with the term during a radio talk show, it was intended as a joke. Annoyingly for Hoyle, "big bang" stuck, and he was often attributed with creating the original theory. His reputation went into eclipse when he claimed that life on Earth evolved from microbes falling from cometary tails about four billion years ago. According to Hoyle, the AIDS virus arrived from space in the mid-1970s, and was originally passed to humans from rainwater via cuts on their feet. Hoyle went on to postulate that humans had evolved protruding noses with downward pointing nostrils to keep alien pandemic from falling into them from above. Hoyle's obituary in the journal *Nature* pointed out, "he put his name to much rubbish."

/9/ DINOSAUR FARTS THE CAUSE OF GLOBAL WARMING

In 1991, three US scientists, Simon Brassell, Karen Chin, and Robert Harman, published a paper on their study of dinosaur farts and proposed that millions of years' worth of flatulence passed by dinosaurs during the Cretaceous period "may have been a contributor to global warming." They came to their conclusion after studying fossilized dinosaur dung and detecting signs of bacteria and algae, indicating that they digested their food by fermenting it, a process that releases methane. A number of fellow scientists, however, detected a whiff of bullshit. Eric J. Barron, a Pennsylvania State University climatologist, noted with delicate understatement: "I wonder whether or not there were enough dinosaurs to make that substantial a contribution to atmospheric chemistry."

15 Military Eccentrics

1. Queen Victoria's father, Edward, Duke of Kent (1767–1820) was a brutal and tyrannical disciplinarian, known as the "Flogging Duke" for his fondness for thrashing his soldiers at the drop of a hat. His predilection was first noticed during his command in Gibraltar as colonel of the Royal Fusiliers, where he flogged his men to the point of mutiny, then shot two of the ringleaders and had a third flogged to death. The added bonus for the Duke was that he was sexually aroused by the sight of men being whipped, which also caused him to wet his trousers. When news of the mutiny filtered back to England, the Duke was quietly removed and sent to Canada. He simply

viewed his new posting as a fresh opportunity for more outrageous punishments, and the number of floggings in the Duke's new regiment went up roughly in line with his laundry bill.

2. During heavy fighting in Beirut in 1983 the Syrian Defense Minister, General Mustafa Tlass, instructed his men to stop attacking Italian peacekeeping soldiers because of his lifelong crush on the Italian actress Gina Lollabrigida. General Tlass told his men: "Do whatever you want with the US, British, and other forces, but I do not want a single tear falling from the eyes of Gina Lollabrigida." Tlass divulged that he had also had a "thing" for Madonna and Marilyn Monroe.

3. The British naval commander, Admiral Sir Algernon Charles Fiesché Heneage, or "Pompo" as he was known to the men under his command, was obsessive about his personal appearance. He wore his hair set in curls and took 240 shirts to sea with him; the dirty ones were sent home for laundering on any available ship bound for England. He was more fastidious than his fellow Brit, submarine commander Sir Herbert Shove, who generally carried two white rats in the pockets of his uniform.

4. The Confederate General Thomas J. Jackson had several nicknames before he earned the moniker "Stonewall" at the first battle of Bull Run by sitting astride his horse "like a stone wall" while bullets flew around him. He was also known as "Tom Fool" Jackson for his eccentric mannerisms. The general believed that one side of his body weighed more than the other, so whenever he walked one arm was raised to restore his balance. He also always stood while eating and would often fall asleep

with food in his mouth. When he was a junior officer he wore his thick army greatcoat throughout a long and very hot summer because he had not received an order to do otherwise. He was also a strict Presbyterian, hence the nickname "Deacon Jackson." His deep religious convictions also meant that he refused to fight on Sundays. During the thick of the battle of Mechanicsville in 1862, Jackson spent the Lord's day praying alone on a nearby hill, refusing to speak to anyone, while his troops took heavy casualties. He was accidentally shot in the arm by his own men during the battle of Chancellorsville, and his arm had to be amputated. He died of pneumonia a week later.

5. The Greek commander General Hajianestis, who led his country's army in the war with Turkey in 1921, was thought by many to have been certifiably insane, but in fact he showed a keen sense of self-preservation. Rather than rouse himself to command his troops he stayed in bed pretending to be dead. Another ploy he used was to claim that he couldn't get up because his legs were made of glass and that they might break if he moved.

6. One of the Duke of Wellington's senior commanders during the Peninsular War, Sir William Erskine, was certifiably mad and twice had been confined to a lunatic asylum. Wellington heard of his appointment with stunned disbelief, and immediately wrote to the Military Secretary in London for an explanation. The Secretary replied, "No doubt he is a little mad at intervals, but in his lucid intervals he is an uncommonly clever fellow, and I trust he will have no fit during the campaign, although I must say he looked a little mad as he embarked." During one of Erskine's less lucid intervals he was found at dinner when

he should have been defending a strategically important bridge. He eventually sent five men to defend it. When a fellow officer queried his decision Erskine thought better of it and sent a whole regiment, but pocketed the instruction and forgot all about it. His mental health wasn't the only problem. Erskine's eyesight was so poor that before a battle he had to ask someone to point him in the general direction of the battlefield. He eventually committed suicide by jumping out of a window in Lisbon. Found dying on the pavement, he asked bystanders "Why on earth did I do that?"

7. The Prussian king and military genius Frederick "The Great" had a complete disregard for casualties or human life, including his own. He drank up to forty cups of coffee a day for several weeks in an experiment to see if it was possible to exist without sleep. It took his stomach three years to recover. Frederick would always open a vein before a battle to calm his nerves, and when the tide turned against him he fought on with a vial of poison ready for suicide. His wounded men were expected to find their own way off the battlefield and back to hospitals as best they could and were denied rations. As only one in five who entered a Prussian military hospital came out alive, men deserted by the thousands rather than risk being buried alive in one, and hundreds more committed suicide. When his campaign funds ran short, Frederick saved money by skimping on his soldiers' uniforms: there was so little material in them they couldn't even be fastened, so many of his men froze to death. One day, he was surprised to find one of his best soldiers shackled in irons. When he asked why, he was told that the man had

been caught having sex with his horse. Frederick ordered: "Fool—don't put him in irons, put him in the infantry," then apologized to the soldier for taking his horse away from him.

8. The Civil War General Richard S. Ewell—Old Bald Head as he was known to his Confederate troops—was a brave but flawed military leader. He served under General Jackson, and in 1862 he was seriously wounded at the second battle of Bull Run. Ewell returned to the army with a new wooden leg and newly married to a rich widow he always referred to as "Mrs. Brown." He escaped further injury, except for an incident when his wooden leg received a direct hit from a Yankee sharpshooter's bullet. Ewell was small, highly strung, and hypochondriacal. He claimed he couldn't sleep in a normal position and spent his nights curled around a camp stool. He was convinced that he was suffering from a mysterious internal disorder and lived almost entirely on a diet of frumenty—a dish of hulled wheat boiled in milk and sweetened with sugar. Ewell also harbored the delusion that he was a bird. This problem became frequently apparent whenever he cocked his head to one side, pecked at his food, and made chirping noises. To complete the picture, Ewell was also known for his beaky nose.

9. Orde Charles Wingate was a brilliant but unorthodox military leader in the Second World War. His three campaigns in Palestine, Ethiopia, and as commander of the Chindits led Winston Churchill to call him "a man of genius"; others found him simply "barking mad." Wingate's personal habits included several novel theories about achieving good health. He believed that the best

way to stay fit in the tropics was to eat half a dozen raw onions a day, drink tea strained through his socks, and to completely avoid bathing. Even more baffling was his habit of strolling around in front of his fellow soldiers stark naked. He dictated letters in the buff and held interviews while lying naked on a bed and combing his body hair with a toothbrush. Wingate made a lasting impression on the future Israeli ambassador by giving him an hour-long lecture on Zionism while completely naked. He terminated the interview in his usual manner, by drawing attention to the miniature alarm clock strapped to his finger. His brief career was tragically ended, at the age of forty-one, by an airplane crash in Burma. No identifiable remains of Wingate were found, save for his trademark outsize pith helmet.

10. The French military hero Marshal MacMahon crushed a Paris left-wing uprising in 1871 and went on to become president of France from 1873 to 1879. One day he was visiting a field hospital when he came across a soldier who lay ill with a tropical fever. "That's a nasty disease you have there," sympathized the great man. "You either die of it or go crazy. I've been through it myself."

11. The Duke of Wellington had more to occupy his mind at Waterloo than the small matter of defeating Napoleon. Wellington's ally, the famous Prussian field marshal, Leberecht von Blücher, suffered from fits of senile melancholia, which led him to experience bizarre hallucinations. Blücher once confided to Wellington that he was pregnant and about to give birth to an elephant; worse still, the man who had raped him was a French soldier.

12. The Russian Czar Paul I suffered from paradomania—an unnatural obsession with militaria. The entire Russian army, of which Paul was commander in chief, was forced to adopt the antiquated Prussian uniform of his hero Frederick the Great, right down to the last detail of old fashioned gaiters and powdered pigtails. Paul became fanatical about his soldiers' uniforms right down to the last epaulette, always at the expense of military efficiency. He made them wear costumes that were so tight fitting that they made breathing difficult and fighting practically impossible. Underneath they wore straightjackets to make them stand erect, and on their heads they wore thick, heavy wigs with iron rods inserted in them to make the hairpiece sit straight. To make his soldiers goose-step perfectly without bending their legs, he strapped steel plates to their knees. The night before a parade his men would labor until dawn to cover their wigs with grease and chalk. They all knew that even a hair out of place could mean arrest, a thrashing, or deportation.

13. Brigadier-General John Nicholson (1821–1857) was one of the British Empire's bravest military heroes, known as the "Hero of Delhi" after losing his life while putting down the Indian Mutiny of 1857. Nicholson, described by one biographer as a violent, repressed homosexual with an unusual attachment to his mother, was equally famous for his breathtaking sadism. He kept the heads of executed Indian mutineers on his desk as paper weights and invented the tactic of blowing away mutineers from the mouths of cannons. Nicholson was once tipped off that someone had poisoned the regimental soup; he tested it by forcing it down the throat of a monkey and when

it expired on the spot, he strung up the cooks from the nearest tree. Later that evening Nicholson strolled into the British mess tent at Jullunder and informed the gathered officers, "I am sorry, gentlemen, to have kept you waiting for your dinner. I have been hanging your cooks."

14. General Earl Horatio Herbert Kitchener, immortalized as the poster art icon of the British army recruitment drive for World War I, enjoyed his reputation as the hard man of the British Empire: he once claimed that in the heat of battle he caught a bullet in his teeth. While fighting the Boers in South Africa in 1900, Kitchener complained that the enemy didn't fight fairly. They were always on the move or taking advantage of surrounding cover, he said, instead standing quite still in the open while they were shot down by British rifles and machine guns. When he wasn't catching bullets in his teeth, Kitchener took time during military campaigns to correspond with his cousin Florence about interior decoration and fabric design. Kitchener's favorite aide-de-camp, Oswald Fitzgerald, was the talk of the mess. They lived together for the last nine years of their lives and died together, lost at sea in June 1916 when their warship, HMS *Hampshire,* struck a mine and sank in the North Sea en route to Russia.

15. The British Allied commander Field Marshal Bernard Law Montgomery "Of Alemain" was known to be both arrogant and highly ambitious. His chief of staff Sir Alan Brooke commented to King George VI at a social function in 1944 that the problem with "Monty" was that "every time I meet him I think he's after my job." The King replied, "You should worry. When I meet him I always think he's after mine." Monty's odd behavior at the front often left

his long-suffering chiefs of staff scratching their heads. One day in France in 1944 a young officer returned from the hospital after being wounded. Monty summoned the young man to his caravan and ordered him to strip. The puzzled officer did as he was told. Monty peered at him for a while, then ordered him to dress, saying, "I wanted to assure myself that you are fit for duty. You can go now." In 1967 Montgomery urged the House of Lords to throw out a bill to legalize gay sex, warning that it would be a "charter for buggery . . . this sort of thing may be tolerated by the French, but we're British—thank God." In 1985 the book *Monty at Close Quarters* was published, a collection of anecdotes by men who served under Monty during World War II. It was known in the trade as "Monty at Hind Quarters."

10 Secret Weapons

1. In the 1920s the Soviet leader Joseph Stalin tried to rebuild his depleted Red Army by creating a regiment of hybrid half-men, half-apes. He turned to Russia's top animal breeding scientist, Ilya Ivanov, to apply his skills to the quest for a new super-warrior. Uncle Joe told him: "I want a new invincible human being, insensitive to pain, resistant and indifferent about the quality of food they eat." In 1926 Ivanov was sent to Africa with £100,000 to conduct experiments in impregnating chimpanzees, meanwhile a center for the experiments was set up in Georgia—Stalin's birthplace—for the apes to be raised. Ivanov's experiments in Africa were a failure, and he

returned to the Soviet Union. Meanwhile in Georgia, experiments using monkey sperm in human volunteers were similarly fruitless. The disgraced scientist was sentenced to five years' jail, which was later commuted to five years' exile in the Central Asian republic of Kazakhstan in 1931. A year later he died, reportedly after falling sick while standing on a freezing railway platform.

2. During World War II the Allies called upon their finest scientific minds to give them a competitive edge. America turned to the Harvard chemist Dr. Louis Fieser, inventor of napalm. Fieser unveiled a brand-new secret weapon he was confident would bring to an early conclusion to the war with Japan—the incendiary bat. His plan was to collect millions of bats and keep them cold, thereby inducing a state of hibernation. The slumbering bats would then be released over Japan, each carrying a tiny incendiary device containing one ounce of napalm. As the bats fell they would warm up, settle under the eaves of buildings and set fire to them. Fieser imagined a "surprise attack" with fires breaking out all over Tokyo at 4:00 in the morning. The plan was abandoned after trials at the Carlsbad Army Air Field in New Mexico, when a number of bats, blown out of the target area by high winds, set fire to and destroyed a US army hangar and a general's car.

3. In the 1930s Adolf Hitler tried to persuade the Allies that Germany had a death ray. Leading British scientists dismissed the claim as the ramblings of a madman, but Britain's Air Ministry was uncertain. Just to be on the safe side, it offered a £1,000 prize to anyone who could invent a death ray capable of killing a sheep at one hundred yards.

4.   Geoffrey Nathaniel Pyke was civilian adviser to Combined Operations, a British military unit briefed to think up novel ideas for defeating the enemy in the late 1930s. Pyke hatched a series of eccentric plans that were to earn him the name "Professor Brainstorm." His first plan was to avert World War II by presenting the results of an opinion poll to Hitler showing that the majority of Germans wanted peace; Hitler would see the results, become discouraged, and call the whole thing off. Pyke assumed that the fascist dictator was probably dead against opinion polls per se, so he planned to flood Germany with students, disguised as golfers, carrying clipboards in one hand and golf clubs in the other. Although Germany was not at that time known to be a nation of golf enthusiasts, he did manage to persuade a few students to dress up as golfers and travel to the home of the Third Reich. Unfortunately Hitler had other ideas, and invaded Poland anyway. Pyke's next project was a motorized "torpedo sleigh" to aid travel in occupied Norway. The sleigh was to be driven slowly up a slope to tempt the Germans into giving chase. Halfway up the slope the torpedo was to be released to roll down onto the Germans and blow them up. Just in case the equipment fell into enemy hands it was to be marked with a sign in German warning people to keep clear: DANGER—SECRET GESTAPO DEATH RAY. Alternately, Pyke suggested, the sleighs were to be marked OFFICERS' LATRINE FOR COLONELS ONLY. The Germans, Pyke explained to his employees, were a very obedient race.

5.   The British scientist Bertie Blount, known to his friends as "The Colonel," was briefed to investigate ingenious methods of assassinating Adolf Hitler by using chemical

or bacteriological agents. Blount came up with a plan to kill Hitler using anthrax, and pondered ways of hiding the lethal agent. He suggested the assassin could wear glasses or false teeth, or perhaps should have a "physical peculiarity such as wearing a truss or a false limb." He also advised, "Guns and hypodermic syringes disguised as fountain pens are usually not a bit convincing and are likely to lead to the death of the operator before he has had any opportunity of making his attack." After much discussion the project was quietly shelved.

6. Lieutenant-Colonel Dudley Clarke was an expert at devising epic strategic bluffs to confuse the enemy about British plans during the Second World War. His most important contribution to the war effort was the creation of a phantom army in Southeast England, designed to convince Hitler that the Allied invasion was heading for Calais. The deception was maintained by phony traffic signals, bogus supply dumps, cardboard tanks, plywood airplanes, and canvas landing craft. To complete the illusion, there were even genuine royal visits. Some of Clarke's ideas to baffle the enemy were less effective. The removal of road signs caused such chaos on the home front that they had to be put back. Clarke's scheme to fool Mussolini into believing that General Wavell intended to retake British Somaliland in 1940 backfired completely. Far from reinforcing their position, the Italian army retreated into Eritrea, which was the real British target. The Luftwaffe once paid tribute to a Clarke design—a dummy railhead in Egypt—by dropping a wooden bomb on it. The most notable hiccup in Clarke's career came in 1941 when he was arrested in Madrid by Spanish police, who found him wearing women's clothes and full makeup, flirting with some German spies. The British intelligence services asked Lord Gort, governor of Gibraltar, to interview Clarke to establish that he was sane. The cross-dressing colonel claimed he was trying out the costume for a secret mission.

7. During the Cold War, Britain hatched a secret plan to build a nuclear landmine operated by live chickens. The device, weighing seven tons, was the size of a small truck and designed to be buried or submerged by a British army retreating from Soviet forces. The landmine had a plutonium core surrounded by high explosives and was to have been detonated by remote control or timer, causing mass destruction and radiation contamination over a wide area to prevent enemy occupation. Scientists working on the project realized that there was one technical hitch. The bomb could fail in winter if vital components froze, so they explored ways of keeping the inner workings warm. One proposal put forward was to fill the casing of the nuke with live chickens, who would give off sufficient heat, prior to suffocating or starving to death, to keep the delicate explosive mechanism from freezing. Despite the potential importance of chickens to the project, the mine was mysteriously codenamed "Blue Peacock." The idea of a chicken-powered nuke was so outlandish that, when operation Blue Peacock was finally declassified on April 1, 2004, the press took it as an April Fools' Day joke. A government official replied to the media that it was not: "The Civil Service does not do jokes."

8. In 1944 America developed its own bird-powered secret weapon, the pigeon-guided missile. It was the brainchild of the famous behavioral psychologist Burrhus Frederic

Skinner, who realized that missile guidance technology at the time was unreliable, subject to frequent jamming, and also expensive and difficult to package inside a bomb casing. He had a brilliant idea; he had already trained pigeons to dance, to do figure eights, or play tennis—why not train pigeons to guide bombs? Pigeons were ideal for this purpose: they were immune to jamming, inexpensive to maintain, and were small and light. Skinner set about making a bomb divided into three compartments, and into each he strapped a pigeon. As a bomb headed toward earth, each pigeon would see the target on its screen. By pecking at the image, the birds would activate a guidance system that would keep the bomb on the right path until impact. Successful pecking was rewarded with grains of seed; at one point he tried marijuana seed, but it turned out the pigeons would become less focused on their task. Unbelievably, Skinner's idea received initial support and the US Navy ran with it for five years until the project was eventually dropped, largely because pigeons were easily distracted by clouds. The two dozen pigeons that Skinner had trained went home with him to live at the bottom of Skinner's garden.

9. The CIA once considered making a fake video of Saddam Hussein having gay sex with a young man in order to destabilize the tyrant ahead of the Iraq war. The tape, which was to have shown the Iraqi leader apparently romping with a teenage youth, was supposed to shock the Iraqi people into rising up against their leader and thus make the invasion a lot easier. Intelligence chiefs also produced a fake video of Osama bin Laden and his henchman sitting around a campfire sipping alcohol

and talking about having sex with men, but it was never shown.

10. According to the people who had the job of keeping him alive, the FBI tried to assassinate the Cuban president Fidel Castro on more than six hundred occasions. The bungled bids to kill Castro began immediately after the 1959 revolution that brought him to power, when a CIA agent sent from Paris failed to snuff him out with a cunningly disguised pen-syringe. Some of the attempts to kill him were more fanciful. The CIA recruited one of Castro's former lovers to track him down and finish him off. She was given poison pills, which she hid in a jar of cold cream, but the pills dissolved. She toyed with the idea of slipping cold cream into Castro's mouth while he was snoozing, but lost her nerve. On another occasion a poisoned chocolate milkshake was placed in a freezer; by the time it was offered to Castro, it was frozen solid and had lost its potency. There were other attempts to prepare bacterial poisons to be placed in Castro's handkerchief or in his tea and coffee, but none got off the drawing board. In 1960 the CIA tried to dose some of Castro's cigars with a virulent toxin, slipped into his private stash during a trip to the United Nations. They later aborted similar plans to load his cigars with explosives, or with a hallucinogenic drug to give him a wild acid trip to embarrass him during a public appearance. In arguably the most bizarre plot of all, the CIA planned to steal Castro's "charisma" by planting thallium salts—a powerful hair remover—in his shoes during a trip overseas so that his famous beard would fall out. When the CIA found out that Castro enjoyed scuba diving they bought a diving suit and

contaminated the regulator with fungus spores, hoping to give him a rare skin disease: the diplomat assigned to hand over the "dirty" suit accidentally gave him a clean one instead. The CIA explored the possibility of placing an exploding conch at Castro's favorite diving spot. The plan was to find a shell big enough to contain a lethal quantity of explosives, which would then be painted in bright colors to attract Castro's attention when he was underwater. In his autobiography *Shadow Warrior,* retired CIA operative Felix Rodriguez confessed to three trips to Cuba to assassinate Castro. In 1987 the Iran-Contra committee asked Rodriguez if he ever took part in the CIA's infamous attempt to poison Castro's cigars. "No sir, I did not," he replied. "But I did volunteer to kill that son of a bitch in 1961 with a telescopic rifle."

CHAPTER FIVE
COURTING THE MUSE

10 Ironic Stage Exits

1934: The US magician Benjamin "Black Herman" Rucker performs his popular "buried alive" act, which begins with his internment in a coffin, then resumes when he is exhumed several days later, for the last time. He collapses and dies onstage from a heart attack but the audience thinks it is part of the act and refuses to leave. Huge crowds gathered outside the funeral home to see the end of the "trick," so his assistant decided to charge admission, explaining: "It's what he would have wanted."

1958: The British actor Gareth Jones, while playing a character who dies of a heart attack on the live TV show *Armchair Theatre*, dies of an actual heart attack between scenes. The director instructs the rest of the cast to improvise to make up for his absence.

1958: The US comedian Harry Parke dies while performing as his well-known character "Parkyakarkus" (a pun on "park your carcass") onstage with Milton Berle. As Parke slumps into his costar's lap, Berle asks, "Is there a doctor in the house?" and the audience laughs, unaware of Parke's predicament. The show director asks crooner Tony Martin to cover with a song to keep the audience diverted. Martin obliges with "There's No Tomorrow."

1960: Baritone Leonard Warren succumbs to a fatal cerebral hemorrhage while performing the opera *La forza del destino* at the New York Metropolitan Opera. He had just finished Don Carlo's Act III aria, which begins, "Morir, tremenda cosa" ("to die, a momentous thing").

1971: The US fitness guru Jerome Irving Rodale appears on the *Dick Cavett Show* and boasts "I'm in such good health that I fell down a long flight of stairs yesterday and I laughed all the way . . . I've decided to live to be a hundred," then dies of a heart attack onstage. According to some witnesses, Cavett asks his guest, "Are we boring you, Mr. Rodale?" The episode was never broadcast.

1974: The fifty-nine-year-old conductor Carl Barnett dies of a heart attack onstage while conducting Bach's "Come, Sweet Death." His death occurred on April 23, 1974. It was his first and last performance of the piece.

1985: Yoshiyuki Takada, one of five performers of Sankai Juku, an avant-garde Japanese dance troupe, plunges six stories to his death from the side of Seattle's Mutual Life building. His rope broke while he was performing a piece called "The Dance of Birth and Death."

1986: Actress Edith Webster, during a performance of *The Drunkard* in Baltimore, has a fatal heart attack after singing several robust choruses of "Please Don't Talk About Me When I'm Gone."

1994: A French clown, Yves Abouchar, chokes to death while receiving a custard pie in his face from a colleague.

1996: Richard Versalle, a tenor performing at the New York Metropolitan Opera, suffers a heart attack and falls ten feet from a ladder to the stage after singing the line "You can only live so long," from the opening scene of *The Makropulos Case*. It is a Czech opera about an elixir that confers eternal youth.

Blame It on the Booger
10 CURIOUS REFERENCES IN POPULAR CULTURE LEAST LIKELY TO BE USEFUL TO YOU ON A QUIZ SHOW

1. The 1968 Mothers of Invention song "Let's Make the Water Turn Black" tells a true story of two teenage friends of the composer Frank Zappa, Ronnie Williams and Dwight Dement, who saved their own mucous on the pane of Ronnie's bedroom window. The experiment, which involved the pair smearing the content of their nasal passages on a single window over a period of seven months to see if dried mucous could block light, was subsequently destroyed with the aid of a putty knife under orders from Ronnie's mother. After having no contact with Zappa for many years, Ronnie showed up in the front row of a 1975 concert in California, shouting, "Do the song about the boogers," and was invited onstage as a special guest.

2. For hundreds of years until the end of the nineteenth century, priests in Britain were affectionately known as: "bollocks" or "bollacks." This little known fact formed the basis of a successful legal defense in 1978 when the British punk band the Sex Pistols used it to save their debut album, *Never Mind the Bollocks, Here's The Sex Pistols* from a nationwide ban.

3. The Paraguayan president Alfredo Stroessner (1954–89) is the world's only dictator to have had a popular dance named after him, "the General Stroessner Polka." Stroessner's security chief liked to play a polka during torture sessions to drown out the screams of his victims. He once had the secretary of the Paraguayan Communist Party torn apart with a chainsaw, to the accompaniment of Stroessner's polka. The entire proceedings were relayed to Stroessner by telephone to ensure that he didn't miss anything.

4. In 2001 the US rock band Tenacious D, featuring lead vocalist Jack Black, released the song "Rock Your Socks," in which they reference a Cleveland Steamer: "All we're askin' you to do/Is drop trou/And squeeze out/A Cleveland Steamer on my chest." The Cleveland Steamer is a colloquial term for defecating on another person's chest, then rocking back and forth imitating the motion of a steamroller. The origin of the term, possibly a reference to the first location of this act in the early 1920s, is disputed. In 2003 a Detroit, Michigan, talk radio show was fined $27,500 after discussing the Cleveland Steamer on air during a "half-hour educational discussion."

5. Armin Meiwes, the German cannibal who had a friend for dinner in 2001, has provided the inspiration for several works by metal bands, including the 2007 Marilyn Manson album *Eat Me, Drink Me* and Rammstein's 2004 single "Mein Teil," featuring the lyric, "you are what you eat." In 1965 the calypso singer Mighty Sparrow had a hit with "Congo Man," a song about a cannibal who dines exclusively on white people "until his belly upset."

6. The Anglo-American poet and playwright T. S. Eliot is regarded as one of the giants of twentieth-century poetry, thanks to such works as "The Waste Land." He also wrote a number of verses about cats, the basis for the longest-running show in Broadway history, plus several obscene poems: the "Columbo and Bolo verses," largely about defecation and violent sex, as yet undiscovered by Sir Tim Rice or Lord Andrew Lloyd Webber.

7. The 1999 single "When I Grow Up," by Garbage featuring lead singer Shirley Manson, contained the lyrics "Happy hours/Golden showers," a reference to urophilia—sexual excitement derived from urinating. The band's followup single was the James Bond title theme "The World Is Not Enough."

8. When Chuck Berry dealt with the often neglected issue of masturbation in "My Ding-A-Ling" in 1972, it gave him the only No. 1 of his career, despite attempts to have the song banned. The Who experienced no such difficulties when they released their 1967 single "Pictures of Lily," described by its writer Pete Townshend as "a ditty about masturbation and the importance of it to a young man."

9. "I Love You," by Barney the Purple Dinosaur was the most played torture music in the Guantanamo Bay detention camp.*

10. Casual acquaintances of the work of US rock band Steely Dan may be forgiven for supposing that they acquired their name from their founding members. The name however derives from the William Burroughs novel *Naked*

* Used to keep prisoners awake during sleep deprivation sessions.

Lunch, in which "Steely Dan" is a large metal strap-on dildo that is crushed in an entertaining manner by a formidable German bulldyke prostitute.

Hope I Die Before I Get Old
10 CLASSICAL COMPOSERS WHO DIDN'T MAKE THEIR FORTIETH BIRTHDAY

Vincenzo Bellini (died from gastroenteritis, 33)

Georges Bizet (heart failure, 36)

Frédéric Chopin (tuberculosis, or possibly cystic fibrosis, 39)

George Gershwin (brain cancer, 38)

Felix Mendelssohn (a stroke, 38)

Wolfgang Amadeus Mozart (rheumatic fever, 35)

Giovanni Battista Pergolesi (tuberculosis, 26)

Henry Purcell (tuberculosis, 26)

Franz Schubert (typhus fever, or possibly syphilis, 31)

Carl Maria von Weber (tuberculosis 39)

10 Ways to Overcome Writer's Block

1. The prolific French author Honoré de Balzac swigged up to fifty cups of strong black coffee a day. He died aged fifty-one from heart failure aggravated by caffeine poisoning.
2. Agatha Christie got her inspiration by eating apples in the bath.

3. The Pulitzer Prize–winner John McPhee used to tie himself to the chair in front of his typewriter with the belt of his bathrobe until he had written something.

4. Victor Hugo gave all of his clothes to his servant with strict instructions not to return them until he had done some writing.

5. The Irish author James Joyce overcame writer's block by jerking off. One day a fan walked up to him and said, "Let me shake the hand that wrote *Ulysses.*" Joyce thought for a while and replied, "No, best not, it's done lots of other things too."

6. Charles Dickens got his inspiration by checking out the local morgue, just hanging out for days watching new bodies arrive.

7. The US poet Vachel Lindsay believed that germs were the cause of his writer's block. On December 5, 1931, he swallowed a whole bottle of household disinfectant. His last words were, "I got them before they got me."

8. Robin Moore, author of *The Green Berets,* always did his best writing standing up, stark naked.

9. Ernest Hemingway wrote nude, standing up, with his typewriter at about waist level. While suffering from severe and seemingly endless writer's block, he blew his head off with his favorite shotgun at his home in Ketchum, Idaho.

10. Robert Louis Stevenson wrote the whole of *Dr. Jekyll and Mr. Hyde* under the influence of cocaine. It helped him write and twice revise the sixty-thousand-word book in six days flat.

Premature Death as the Subject of a Pop Record

THE TOP 10

/ 1 / "TEEN ANGEL," BY MARK DINNING, 1960

Concerning the avoidable death of the narrator's sixteen-year-old girlfriend, who is pulled clear of their car as it stalls on a railway track in front of oncoming train, but returns to look for a missing ring.

/ 2 / "TELL LAURA I LOVE HER," BY RAY PETERSON, US 1960/RICKY VALANCE, UK 1960

Tommy's impractical plan to raise money to buy a wedding ring for Laura by winning a car race ends in tragedy when his vehicle inexplicably overturns and bursts into flames on a curve.

/ 3 / "EBONY EYES," BY THE EVERLY BROTHERS, 1961

A young soldier on leave arranges to have his fiancée join him so they can be married, but she is lost in a tragic aviation disaster, possibly due to inclement weather. *"The plane was way overdue so I went inside to the airlines desk and I said 'Sir, I wonder why 1203 is so late?' He said 'Aww, they probably took off late or they may have run into some turbulent weather and had to alter their course.' "*

/ 4 / "TERRY," BY TWINKLE, 1964

Two lovers fight, and the biker boyfriend speeds off on a motorcycle to his death. Accusations of bad taste led to a ban by the

BBC and British TV's top pop show, *Ready Steady Go!* Future Led Zeppelin guitarist Jimmy Page was a session musician on this track.

/ 5 / "LAST KISS," BY J. FRANK WILSON AND THE CAVALIERS, 1964/PEARL JAM, 1999

Tastefully based on an actual news story of 16-year-old lovers Jeanette Clark and J. L. Hancock, who perished when their car hit a tractor-trailer on a road in rural Barnesville, Georgia. The local gas station attendant, helping with the recovery of the bodies, failed to recognize his own dead daughter. It was a stroke of luck, however, for songwriter Wayne Cochran, who lived nearby and just happened at the time to be working on a song about a road accident.

/ 6 / "LEADER OF THE PACK," BY THE SHANGRI-LAS, 1964

Betty's love for Jimmy, the leader of a local motorcycle gang, turns to despair when her parents put pressure on her to get rid of him. Upset, Jimmy roars off on his bike leading to inevitable death on a rain-slicked surface.

/ 7 / "LAURIE (STRANGE THINGS HAPPEN)," BY DICKIE LEE, 1965

The song's narrator meets a quiet girl with very cold hands at a dance, only to find out later she was dead all along. Luckily, the sweater he lent her turns up neatly folded on her grave.

∫ 8 ∫ "ODE TO BILLIE JOE," BY BOBBIE GENTRY, 1967

The narrator's mother informs the family over dinner of the apparent suicide of one Billie Joe McAllister, who jumped off the Tallahatchie Bridge. The narrator, possibly the suicide's girl-friend, loses her appetite upon hearing this, but not her father, who observes, *"Well, Billie Joe never had a lick o' sense; pass the biscuits, please."*

∫ 9 ∫ "HONEY," BY BOBBY GOLDSBORO, 1968

Husband mourns his deceased wife, who dies a few years after planting a tree, and is consequently reminded of his wife every time he sees the tree. In the 1970s it received more British air-play than was strictly necessary when the BBC radio deejay Tony Blackburn had an on-air mental breakdown while going through a divorce with his wife Tessa and played the song on a loop. Voted by the users of CNN.com as the worst single ever; the Beach Boys once considered releasing a version but thought better of it.

∫ 1 0 ∫ "SEASONS IN THE SUN," BY TERRY JACKS, 1974

A man with an unspecified terminal illness says good-bye to family and friends. Originally recorded as "Le Moribund" (The Dying Man) by Belgian singer-songwriter Jacques Brel. The b-side of the single was the little-known "Put the Bone In," in which a woman in a butcher shop begs the butcher to "put the bone in" for her because "her doggy had been hit by a car."

9 Guilty Pleasures

1. Adolf Hitler was delighted with his Christmas present from Joseph Goebbels in 1937—fifteen Mickey Mouse cartoon films. Four years later, however, he declared Mickey an enemy of the Third Reich and banned him in Germany.

2. The only Western films allowed to be shown in Albania during Enver Hoxha's dictatorship were those starring the English comedian Norman Wisdom—or "Pitkin," as he was known to his legions of Albanian fans. No one is quite sure why Wisdom's films alone escaped censorship. It could be that Hoxha considered them ideologically sound: The downtrodden Pitkin, struggling against the decadent Mr. Grimsdale in such films as *Pitkini Ne Dyqan* (Pitkin at the Store) and *Pitkini Ne Spital* (Pitkin in the Hospital), was seen as enacting a Communist parable on the class war—a member of the oppressed proletariat triumphing against capitalism. Or it could have been that the plot lines were just so silly that even Hoxha's legendary paranoia was not alerted. In any event, as the country's only permitted Western film star, Norman Wisdom became Albania's second biggest national folk hero after Mother Teresa.

3. The genocidal Yugoslav President Slobodan Milosevic, who died while on trial for sixty-six counts of genocide and crimes against humanity, liked to listen to Frank Sinatra's classic "My Way" in his prison cell. Milosevic became a Sinatra fan while working as a New York banker in the 1970s.

4. The Libyan leader Colonel Muammar Gaddafi is the No. 1 fan of singer Lionel Richie. He was invited to perform at Gaddafi's "concert for peace," held to mark the twentieth anniversary of a US raid on Tripoli in which his adopted daughter, Hanna, was killed. Richie announced onstage: "Hanna will be honored tonight because of the fact that you've attached peace to her name."

5. Robert Mugabe, president of Zimbabwe, is a big fan of Elvis Presley; his thirty-bedroom mansion in the capital Harare is called Gracelands, in honor of his hero. His favorite living artist is Britain's own 1950s Elvis clone Sir Cliff Richard. When informed that Bob Marley would be performing at Zimbabwe's 1980 Independence Day celebrations, Mugabe complained that the Marley was "too scruffy" and suggested Sir Cliff perform instead. Sadly, the wholesome singing knight of the garter was otherwise engaged, so Marley's performance went ahead as planned, performing to a crowd of one hundred thousand that included Prince Charles.

6. Mahmoud Ahmadinejad, the president of Iran, is a fan of the Irish crooner Chris de Burgh, especially his hit single "Lady in Red." In 2009 de Burgh became the first Western artist given permission to perform a gig in Iran since the Islamic revolution thirty years earlier, but his shows were canceled following Ahmadinejad's crackdown on post-election protests.

7. Saddam Hussein's favorite film was *The Godfather*. It was also a big influence on his management style: Saddam had at least fifty-three of his relatives killed, including two sons-in-law, the Kamel brothers. In August 1995, following a falling-out with Saddam's son Uday, the

brothers defected to Jordan, taking their wives with them. After telling the CIA everything they knew about Iraq's weapons program, the brothers became homesick and wanted to go back. Their father-in-law promised that no harm would come to them if they returned. Taking a line almost directly from the mouth of Michael Corleone, Saddam asked Hussein Kamel, "Would I kill the father of my grandchildren?" He had them shot immediately upon their return.

8. Coincidentally, *The Godfather* is also the favorite film of North Korea's Dear Leader Kim Jong-il. Kim owns more than twenty thousand videos, although his taste in films is less than revolutionary, judging by his extensive library of classic westerns, especially John Wayne films, or his comprehensive collection of Daffy Duck cartoons. Kim also has a full set of James Bond films. He is not too crazy, however, about *Die Another Day*, in which he was parodied as the insane, power-mad son of a North Korean dictator. He was allegedly so annoyed that he stabbed his minister of culture with a ballpoint pen and spat at the screen. Kim is also allegedly a big fan of Brit bluesman Eric Clapton.

9. Osama bin Laden was crazy about Whitney Houston, according to his former mistress, Kola Boof. She claims that the al-Qaeda fugitive kept her as a "sex slave" for four months in 1996 and that bin Laden thought Whitney was "the most beautiful woman he'd ever seen." He was so smitten by the infidel singer that he wanted to marry her, buy her a big house in Khartoum, and have her husband Bobby Brown killed. He also had a soft spot for Van Halen and the B-52s.

When the Shit Hits the Fan
10 GREAT MOMENTS IN CREATIVE DEFECATION

1929: While fellow surrealists Max Ernst and René Magritte are painting allusive images of the psyche, the Spanish artist Salvador Dali depicts people taking a shit. Dali's ardor for ordure began when he was very young; he liked to introduce an element of surprise into his mother's daily chores by hiding his turds in unexpected places around the house.

1961: Italian artist Piero Manzoni, the Godfather of poop-based art, exhibits a series of ninety one-ounce cans containing his own excrement, titled *Artist's Shit*, allegedly in response to a remark by his father, who told him, "Piero, your work is shit." In June 2002, the Tate Gallery in London announced it had purchased tin No. 4 of Manzoni Jr.'s feces for about $38,000. In October 2008 tin No. 83 was offered for sale at Sotheby's, with a not-to-be-sniffed-at estimate of $80,000–$110,000.

1972: The novelty song "How Much Is that Doggy in the Window?" was a No. 1 hit in the United States for Patti Page in 1952. More controversially, the song is also considered by many to be the crowning glory of the career of film director John Waters, connoisseur of, in his own words, "bad bad taste." In the final scene of *Pink Flamingos*, to the tune of "How Much Is that Doggy in the Window?," the actor Divine scoops up and eats a poodle's turd from the sidewalk.

1990: G. G. Allin, (born Jesus Christ Allin because his dad wanted him to have the best possible start in life) troubled front man of several US "scum punk" bands, including the Scumfucs, the Disappointments, and the Murder Junkies, rewrites the rule book on audience participation. During a performance Allin, who according to one critic was "so vile that he makes Marilyn Manson look like a Sunday school teacher," defecated onstage, smeared some of it on his body, ate some of it, then flung the rest of it at the crowd. Most of his shows ended prematurely, often in his arrest. Having maintained that he would eventually commit suicide onstage, Allin dies of an overdose shortly after his final performance three years later.

1995: An abstract picture by the artist Anton Henning, painted with the artist's own feces, gets "a mixed reception," according to the German newspaper *Bild* when it goes on display at Frankfurt's Museum of Modern Art. Henning says he had eaten a large meal to give himself sufficient material for the painting. "I enjoyed a meal of Koenigsberg dumplings, mustard gherkins, beetroot, potatoes, watermelon and lemon juice, Rheingau Riesling wine, and a big brownie," he tells *Bild*.

1998: The United Kingdom's most prestigious award in art, the Turner Prize, is won by Chris Ofili, best known for his paintings using elephant dung. He is reported to have used this ingredient in all his works (a guarantee of authenticity), with the original materials smuggled in from Africa. Subsequent provisions were excreta from the London Zoo, dried in an airing cupboard. Ofili remarks during the award ceremony that the important thing was to know whether art was "good art or bad art," and not whether it contained elephant dung. His works include *7 Bitches Tossing Their Pussies Before the Divine Dung* and *The Adoration of Captain Shit*.

2002: Metal band Dillinger Escape Plan open at England's prestigious Reading Festival. They decide to warm things up as DEP vocalist Greg Puciato defecates on stage, puts the mess in a bag, and throws it at the audience, then announces: "This is an example of shit on stage, which is all you're gonna get here today."

2005: An untitled work by the American artist Tom Friedman fails to attract a minimum bid of $45,000 at an auction held at Christie's. The work is described as "a two-foot white cube with a barely visible black speck set right in the middle of the top surface." The black speck was not paint or charcoal or chalk, or any other material usually associated with art. According to the description in the auction catalog it is ".5mm of the artist's feces."

2008: The American photographer Andres Serrano exhibits sixty-six photos of poo produced by dogs, jaguars, bulls, and the artist himself. "I wanted to take a close-up look at shit," Serrano explains. He admitted doubts about his latest project, but said he asked God for direction. The first photograph he took was a self-portrait of his own shit and when the film came back from the processing lab, "I realized I saw a face in it. It was a sign!" Serrano's *Piss Christ*—a photograph of a crucifix submerged in a glass of the artist's urine—caused a scandal when it was exhibited in 1989, not least because he got a $15,000 grant from the US government for the work.

2008: The American artist Paul McCarthy, best known for his "inflatable sculptures," creates a pile of giant inflatable dog turds, titled *Complex Shit*. McCarthy's sculpture causes havoc when it breaks free from its mooring outside a gallery in Switzerland and takes down a power line in Bern.

12 Depressed Artists

537 B.C.: Greek sculptor brothers Bupalos and Athenis hang themselves after a series of bitchy attacks by the poet Hipponax, who apparently didn't approve of their sculpture of him.

1640: Abraham van der Doort, Dutch painter and official keeper of King Charles I's art collection, opts for suicide rather than own up to losing one of the king's favorite miniatures.

1816: English painter Robert Fagan, after falling behind on a commission for a series of murals and under mounting financial pressure, throws himself out of an upstairs window in Rome.

1846: English artist Benjamin Robert Haydon, stung by criticism that he is not very good at painting, puts a pistol to his head and fires, but somehow manages not to kill himself. He then takes a razor, braces himself at the door, and cuts his own throat from right to left, but so badly that he has to do it again. After a second attempt, this time cutting from left to right but still missing the carotid artery, he collapses. His wife and daughter downstairs hear a thump as his body hits the floor, but assume he is manhandling his final gigantic, unfinished painting. His daughter finds him later, when she comes into the room and slips on a puddle of her father's blood. Despite all of Haydon's avowed interest in anatomy he hadn't even known how to cut his own throat properly.

1866: Léon Bonvin, French watercolorist, hangs himself from a tree in the forest of Meudon after a Parisian art dealer rejects his paintings.

1890: Dutch expressionist Vincent van Gogh, clinically depressed after hacking off an earlobe in a fit of pique and sending it to a local prostitute, becomes a voluntary inmate in an asylum at Saint Rémy. He absconds and shoots himself at the scene of his last painting, *Cornfields with Flight of Birds*, dying two days later, aged thirty-seven.

1894: American painter Henry Alexander, depressed by lack of funds, drinks carbolic acid on his second day as a guest at the Oriental Hotel in New York.

1908: Austrian painter Richard Gerstl, distraught after a brief romantic fling with Mathilde, wife of the composer Arnold Schoenberg, sets fire to his studio, then hangs himself in front of his studio mirror, then disembowels himself with a butcher knife for good measure.

1948: American abstract expressionist painter Arshile Gorky, after a run of bad luck, during which his studio burns down, he undergoes a colostomy for cancer, his neck is broken, his painting arm temporarily paralyzed in a car accident, and his wife of seven years leaves him, taking their children with her. He hangs himself from various trees before finding one he likes, at age forty-four.

1956: After several attempts to drown himself, Jackson Pollock, American abstract expressionist painter, drives his car into a tree a mile from his home at age forty-four.

1965: Performance artist Alberto Greco gives his final performance, overdosing on barbiturates and leaving notes on how the experience feels. The word *fin* is found written on his bottle of barbiturates.

1970: Mark Rothko, the Russian-American abstract expressionist painter, overdoses on barbiturates then slashes his wrists in his studio after years of complaining that he hates being called an abstract painter.

10 Banned Authors

∫ 1 ∫ WILLIAM SHAKESPEARE

King Lear, about an old king who gives up his throne and goes mad, was banned in Britain from 1788 to 1820 because it was "inappropriate" in light of King George III's mental illness.

∫ 2 ∫ CASANOVA

His autobiography, *Memoires,* in which he fondly reflects upon losing his virginity in bed between two sisters and persuading a nun to give him a hand job during a game of cards, was banned by the Pope (1834) and by Mussolini (1935).

∫ 3 ∫ JONATHAN SWIFT

Gulliver's Travels, for its politically sensitive themes of corruption, antiwar sentiments, and the injustices of colonization, was banned in several countries—Swift had to publish it anonymously. It was also banned in Ireland for "wicked and obscene" descriptions of public urination.

∫ 4 ∫ CHARLES DARWIN

From 1926–1937 *On the Origin of Species* was variously banned in the Soviet Union, Nazi Germany, Yugoslavia, Greece, and by the US state of Tennessee. In the United Kingdom, the book was banned from the library of Trinity College, Cambridge, where Darwin had been a student.

∫ 5 ∫ ARTHUR CONAN DOYLE

In 1929 the Soviet Union banned *The Adventures of Sherlock Holmes* for "occultism."

∫ 6 ∫ JAMES JOYCE

His novel *Ulysses* upset the Catholic Church with graphic accounts of sex and defecation. The full version of the book was banned in Britain and the United States for nearly twenty years. When the "obscene" *Dubliners* was published in 1922, it was burned on the streets of Dublin.

∫ 7 ∫ GEORGE ORWELL

Initially turned down by the New York publisher Dial Press because there was "no market for animal stories in the United States," Orwell's satirical allegory *Animal Farm* was banned in the Soviet Union because of its anti-Stalinism and by several US states, fearful that American children would be exposed to communism. Animal Farm is still banned in China and North Korea because of its anticommunist analogy, and in most Islamic countries because of its pork content.

∫ 8 ∫ D. H. LAWRENCE

The "obscene" *Lady Chatterley's Lover* was banned in Britain and subject to a famous obscenity trial in 1960. During the trial, prosecution council Mervyn Griffith-Jones asked the jury: "Is it a book that you would even wish your wife or your servants to read?" He also took the trouble to keep a detailed tally of the novel's profanities, informing the jury that the word "cunt" occurred fourteen times. Not only was the book banned in Australia, but the book describing the British trial, *The Trial of Lady Chatterley,* was also banned.

∫ 9 ∫ DAN BROWN

The Da Vinci Code, although a work of fiction, was banned in Lebanon and in Iran after Catholic clergy complained about its portrayal of Christ marrying Mary Magdalene and fathering a child.

∫ 1 0 ∫ J. K. ROWLING

The Harry Potter series was subject to more than five thousand attempts to remove books from US schools and public libraries between 2000 and 2010 by vigilant parents protecting their children from Potter and his twisted tales of the occult. Harry Potter is also banned in Australia by a Queensland primary school library for "dangerous stories teaching children about murder and casting spells."

10 Bitchy Authors

1. "To me, [Edgar Allan] Poe's prose is unreadable, like Jane Austen's. No, there is a difference. I could read his prose on a salary, but not Jane's."
—Mark Twain on Jane Austen

2. "Horrible, shameful, blasphemous, filthy in word, filthy in thought"
—William Makepeace Thackeray on Jonathan Swift

3. "There are two ways of disliking poetry. One way is to dislike it, the other is to read Pope."
—Oscar Wilde on Alexander Pope

4. "I don't think Browning was very good in bed. His wife probably didn't care for him very much. He snored and had fantasies about twelve-year-old girls."
—W. H. Auden on Robert Browning

5. "The work of a queasy undergraduate scratching his pimples"
—Virginia Woolf on James Joyce's *Ulysses*

6. "The Hitler of the book racket"
—Percy Wyndham Lewis on Arnold Bennett

7. "He was dull in company, dull in his closet, dull everywhere. . . . He was a mechanical poet."
—Samuel Johnson on Thomas Gray

8. "A poor creature who has said or done nothing worth a serious man taking the trouble of remembering"
   —Thomas Carlyle on Percy Bysshe Shelley
9. "An outstandingly unpleasant man, one who cheated and stole from his friends and peed on their carpets"
   —Kingsley Amis on Dylan Thomas
10. "When his cock wouldn't stand up he blew his head off. He sold himself a line of bullshit and he bought it."
    —Germaine Greer on Ernest Hemingway

12 People Who Didn't Get the Beatles

/ 1 / DICK ROWE, HEAD OF DECCA RECORDS IN 1962

"Guitar groups are on the way out . . . the Beatles have no future in show business."

/ 2 / JAMES BOND, SECRET AGENT

In *Goldfinger* (1964), Bond tells Jill Masterson that "drinking Dom Perignon '53 above the temperature of 38 degrees" is "as bad as listening to the Beatles without earmuffs."

/ 3 / NOEL COWARD, BRITISH COMPOSER AND PLAYWRIGHT, SUMMARIZING A BEATLES CONCERT IN 1964

"Bad mannered little shits . . . the noise was deafening throughout and I couldn't hear a word they sang or a note they played, just one long ear-splitting din."

∫ 4 ∫ WILLIAM F. BUCKLEY, US AUTHOR AND COMMENTATOR, 1964

"The Beatles are not merely awful, I would consider it sacrilegious to say anything less than that they are godawful. They are so unbelievably horrible, so appallingly unmusical, so dogmatically insensitive to the magic of the art, that they qualify as crowned heads of anti-music."

∫ 5 ∫ *NEWSWEEK* REVIEWER, FEBRUARY 24, 1964

"Musically, they are a near disaster; guitars slamming out a merciless beat that does away with secondary rhythms, harmony and melody. Their lyrics (punctuated by nutty shouts of "yeah, yeah, yeah!") are a catastrophe, a preposterous farrago of Valentine-card romantic sentiments."

∫ 6 ∫ AMERICAN TV HOST DAVID SUSSKIND IN 1965

"The most repulsive group of men I've ever seen."

∫ 7 ∫ ROBERT ELMS, AUTHOR AND BROADCASTER

"A sanitized and anemic version of American blues-inspired rock and roll . . . they turned something that was once sexy and raw and had roots into something that was totally soulless, playground sing-along music".

∫ 8 ∫ DAVID KEENAN, AUTHOR AND MUSIC CRITIC

"The Beatles are the absolute curse of modern indie music . . . my favorite Beatle is Yoko Ono; without Yoko's influence I don't think there would be any Beatles music I could listen to."

∫ 9 ∫ RICHARD SMITH, JOURNALIST, REVIEWS
SGT. PEPPER'S LONELY HEARTS CLUB BAND

" . . . why making records on drugs isn't always a good idea and why you shouldn't let Ringo sing . . . if not the worst, then certainly the most overrated album of all time."

∫ 1 0 ∫ ELVIS PRESLEY AND RICHARD NIXON

In 1970 Presley met with President Richard Nixon at the White House and was granted a private tour of FBI headquarters. An FBI memo records that during Presley's visit he told them that, "The Beatles laid the groundwork for many of the problems we are having with young people by their filthy unkempt appearances and suggestive music while entertaining in this country during the early and middle 1960s."

∫ 1 1 ∫ MICHAEL DEACON, DAILY TELEGRAPH
MUSIC CRITIC

" 'Love Me Do' . . . a melody so weepingly banal it sounds like a fingering exercise for primary-school recorder practice."

∫ 1 2 ∫ AMAZON.COM CUSTOMER REVIEW OF
SGT. PEPPER'S LONELY HEARTS CLUB BAND

"I just bought this CD and I don't see what all the hype is about. My teacher always talks about the Beatles but they have no lyrical skills, my cousin Rodney is a better songwriter than these clowns. I think they should remix these songs with 50 Cent or Snoop, then they'd really get some fans behind them."

7 Oversexed Writers

⌡ 1 ⌡ LORD BYRON

Byron's sex life got off to a flying start when he was seduced by his nanny, an alcoholic Calvinist Bible teacher named Mrs. Gray, when he was nine years old. Although short, fat, and clubfooted, Byron's verse made him the heartthrob of his generation; while women swooned over his dark, smoldering looks, men imitated his moody, brooding silences and even his limp. Females everywhere were anxious to throw themselves at this most famous of writers, and he was keen to oblige. The eccentric Lady Caroline Lamb was one of his easier conquests. Their torrid affair led her to conclude that Byron was "mad, bad and dangerous to know"; he was unimpressed when she sent him a lock of her pubic hair as a keepsake. In addition to Byron's estimated five hundred female conquests (he spent so much on female prostitutes that the owner of a brothel once advised him to slow down) there were various homosexual flings, including one with a fifteen-year-old choirboy and another with the English boxing champion, "Gentleman" John Jackson, not to mention sundry Greek youths. Byron's sex life scandalized London but he completely overstepped the mark with his more than brotherly love for his half sister Augusta Leigh. Byron's incest was so shocking that there were doubts about his sanity. He briefly considered suicide. "I should, many a good day, have blown my brains out," he reflected, "but for the recollection that it would have given pleasure to my mother-in-law." In 1816 he left England, never to return, leaving in his wake a trail of broken hearts, illegitimate children, and greatly boosted sales. In Venice Byron kept up his reputation for exotic sexual experimentation and his expensive taste in whores. The greatest romantic poet of them all even had a romantic name for the venereal disease he contracted there—"the curse of Venus."

∫ 2 ∫ HONORÉ DE BALZAC

When Balzac wrote about rich, bored aristocrats with little better to do but sleep with one another he was drawing on rich personal experience. Although short, fat, and very scruffy, he received thousands of fan letters from female admirers, some of which contained indecent propositions he was only too happy to exploit on his huge, circular divan bed. Balzac was far from fussy; according to his biographer: "He slept with aristocrats, courtesans, and trollops indiscriminately, displaying in his love life the same dazzling diversification that appeared in his writing." Balzac's amatory adventures were relaxation from phenomenal bouts of work. He spent between fourteen and sixteen hours a day writing at his table and thought that sex was a drain on his creativity. After several months of abstinence he was once tempted into a Paris brothel, but complained afterward "I lost a novel this morning."

∫ 3 ∫ ALEXANDRE DUMAS

The author of *The Count of Monte Cristo* and *The Three Musketeers* wrote more than six hundred and fifty books. (Not as prolific as the romantic novelist Dame Barbara Cartland, who could knock out six thousand words between lunch and dinner, but then Ms. Cartland never found time to share her duvet with three, four, or even five lovers simultaneously.) Making the best of his lifelong insomnia, the randy French author boasted that he needed several mistresses at a time because, "if I had only one she would be dead at the end of the week." Dumas fathered dozens of bastards but acknowledged only three, including a daughter by a nineteen-year-old, Emilie Cordier, when he was fifty-seven. He died of syphilis, aged sixty-eight.

∫ 4 ∫ GUSTAVE FLAUBERT

The French novelist's non-literary life was marked by his life-long addiction to brothels, which regularly brought him into contact with various exotic venereal infections. In 1849 the twenty-seven-year-old author left France with his friend, the writer Maxime Du Camp, to undertake the infamous "whore-house tour" of the Middle East. During his trip he kept copi-ous notes about his experiences. In Egypt Flaubert marveled at the performance of a dancer named Kuchuk Hanem, who per-formed "The Bee"—a striptease reputedly so erotic that the mu-sicians had to be blindfolded. He wrote up his activities with various other Egyptian performers, including one "on top of whom I enjoyed myself immensely and who smelled of rancid butter" and another with "ample breasts" and a verse from the Koran tattooed along her right arm.

∫ 5 ∫ GUY DE MAUPASSANT

France's greatest short story writer was a sexual athlete of reputedly superhuman prowess. In his relatively short life he claimed to have slept with several thousand women and boasted he could achieve orgasm six times an hour. He put his legendary stamina down to a fanatical fitness regime, which included rowing up to forty miles day on the Seine. He once boasted that he was "no more tired after making love three or four times as I am after twenty." A group of fellow young writers heard about Maupassant's alleged sex drive and challenged the author to prove himself. Maupassant bet them he could satisfy six prostitutes in an evening. A restaurateur accompanied the author to a brothel to act as referee. They stopped counting at twenty and the friends paid up. He died of tertiary syphilis in a lunatic asylum.

/ 6 / GEORGES SIMENON

Behind every great French writer there is a prostitute. Or two. Step forward Georges Simenon, the Belgian-French pulp fiction novelist who created the pipe-smoking Inspector Maigret, one of the best-known characters in detective fiction. Simenon claimed that in order to keep his creative juices flowing he needed sex three times a day. In his seventies, he confided to the film director Federico Fellini that he had slept with about ten thousand women, of whom about eight hundred were prostitutes. His second wife begged to differ. This was a gross exaggeration, she said—a total of twelve hundred was nearer the mark.

/ 7 / GRAHAM GREENE

Although married for sixty-four years, Greene had an extraordinary appetite for adultery, which he wasn't shy about writing about in his books. His *The End of the Affair* was based on the ménage à trois involving Greene, the politician Harry Walston, and his wife Catherine Walston. When his long-standing mistress Catherine challenged him about rumors that he paid women for sex, Greene scribbled down a list of his forty-seven favorite prostitutes and handed it back to her. The women in the list had nicknames such as Russian Boots, Channel Islands Girl, Blackmail, Bishop Hooper, Black Pants, Bond Street French, and Caesarian. Greene also confessed that he often fantasized about having sex with the Queen.

10 Succinct Pop Critiques

∫ 1 ∫ POET, FOOL OR BUM, BY LEE HAZLEWOOD (1973)

"Bum." —Charles Shaar Murray, *New Musical Express*

∫ 2 ∫ YEAH!, BY DEF LEPPARD (1996)

"Nah." —author unknown, *New Musical Express*

∫ 2 ∫ LET'S GROOVE, BY EARTH, WIND & FIRE (1981)

"Let's not." —Johnny Black, *Smash Hits*

∫ 3 ∫ RUN TO THE HILLS, BY IRON MAIDEN (1982)

"Don't think I wasn't tempted." —Red Starr, *Smash Hits*

∫ 4 ∫ GTR, BY GTR (SUPERGROUP FOUNDED BY GENESIS GUITARIST STEVE HACKETT AND YES GUITARIST, STEVE HOWE, IN 1986)

"SHT." —J. D. Considine, *Creem*

∫ 5 ∫ ROBOTS, BY KRAFTWERK (1978)

"Zzzzzzzzzz." —Dean Porsche, *ZigZag*

∫ 6 ∫ "I'M ALIVE," BY ELO (1980)

"A blatant lie. Product." —Deanne Pearson, *Smash Hits*

∫ 7 ∫ AWAY FROM THIS TOWN, BY STILL LIFE (1982)

"And the further the better." —Robin Smith, *Record Mirror*

∫ 8 ∫ LIKE A ROCK, BY BOB SEGER (1986)

"Exactly, Bob. Prehistoric." —Kevin Murphy, *Sounds*

∫ 9 ∫ "WASTING TIME," BY STRANGEWAYS (1979)

"Yes, mine." —Robin Banks, *Sounds*

∫ 1 0 ∫ FOREVER YOUNG, BY ALPHAVILLE (1984)

"Should have been strangled at birth." —Morrissey, *Smash Hits*

Terrible Typos
12 EMBARRASSING LITERARY BLUNDERS

1631: The first of several typos in various editions of the Bible, the most notorious error is found in a King James edition, published in London. With the omission of the word "not" in the

Seventh Commandment, it reads "Thou Shalt Commit Adultery." The publisher is fined £300 and the book became known as The Wicked Bible. Later, a 1653 printing declares: "Know ye not that the unrighteous shall inherit the kingdom of God?" and was henceforth known as The Unrighteous Bible. Other editions of the Bible not recommended for Christian fundamentalists include: the Printers Bible—in the 1702 edition of the King James Bible, he is quoted as saying, "Printers [not "princes"] have persecuted me without cause"; the Sin On Bible—a 1716 edition encourages readers to "sin on more" [instead of "sin no more"]; the Wife-Hater Bible—an 1810 version reads, "If any man come to me, and hate not his own wife [not "life"], he cannot be my disciple": the Camels Bible—an 1832 edition has Rebekah leaving her tent to meet Isaac with a group of camels [not "damsels"]; the Murderer's Bible—a mid-nineteenth-century Bible had Mark 7:27 read: "Let the children be killed" [not "filled"].

1817: On June 18, the *Times* of London covers the opening of the Waterloo Bridge by the Prince Regent, reporting that "The Royal party then pissed over the bridge." The entire composing-room staff was reportedly fired the following day.

1840: The poet Robert Browning has critics scratching their heads over a verse in his new poem "Pippa Passes," which contains the lines: *"Owls and bats, cowls and twats, monks and nuns in a cloister's moods/adjourn to the oak-stump pantry."* Browning genuinely thought "twat" was another word for a nun's headdress. It is, however, then, as it is now, slang for a female vagina.

1914: President Woodrow Wilson is dating a widow named Edith Galt, a tidbit covered by the *Washington Post* in its gossip column.

The item should have read: "Rather than paying attention to the play, the President spent the evening entertaining Mrs. Galt." What was actually printed in the first edition, however, was: " . . . the President spent the evening entering Mrs. Galt."

1940: The *Washington Post* prints the headline on the front page of its first edition: FDR IN BED WITH COED. In fact, as the story eventually made clear, President Roosevelt was in bed with a cold.

1944: *Harvey,* the story about Elwood P. Dowd and his imaginary friend Harvey, a six-foot-three-and-one-half-inch-tall rabbit, opens on Broadway. In a theater review a critic informed readers that the main character "was followed around by a six-foot-tall white rabbi."

1961: The international edition of the *New York Times,* published in London, refers to the Archbishop of Canterbury as the "red-nosed Archbishop." It should have read "red-robed."

1996: The Coca-Cola Company is alerted to a typographical error in the word "disk" in the copyright information on two million twelve-packs of its soft drink. The notice reads: "The red dick icon and contour bottle are trademarks of the Coca-Cola Co."

2002: The MSNBC cable channel apologizes for a typographical error in an onscreen caption identifying the name of an interview subject. The network screened an interview with the black Republican politician Niger Innis. The caption spelt his first name with an extra *g*.

2009: The BBC News website runs a story about two male penguins caring for a small chick with the headline, "Gay penguins rear adopted chick." It was later altered to read "Male penguins raise adopted chick."

2009: The president of a college in Iowa apologizes for a mistake in a handbook distributed to about ten thousand students before the error was discovered. A calendar entry for February 16 was supposed to read "Black History, Lunch and Learn." Instead, it read "Black History, Linch and Learn."

2010: The publisher Penguin Australia is forced to pulp seven thousand copies of its cookbook *The Pasta Bible* when a recipe in the book for tagliatelle with sardines and prosciutto, which should have called for "freshly ground black pepper," called for "freshly ground black people." "Why anyone would be offended, we don't know," commented Bob Sessions, head of publishing.

12 Musical Bans

Fourth Century B.C.: Plato calls on the Greek republic to ban pop music because it leads to low morals.

1936: Adolf Hitler bans the playing of Mendelssohn because the composer is Jewish.

1956: ABC radio is successful in getting Cole Porter to change the words of "I Get a Kick out of You." Porter's original lyric was, "Some get a kick from cocaine." The cleaned up version is "Some like the perfume in Spain."

1957: Capitol Records receive hundreds of complaints about a picture on the front cover of the Five Keys album *On Stage!* To some, the finger of lead singer Rudy West looks like a penis. Subsequent issues of the album cover are airbrushed.

1958: Jerry Lee Lewis steps off a plane in London arm in arm with his wife Myra, who he reveals is also his cousin and "about thirteen." A tabloid newspaper furor ensues when it turns out that the rocker was also a serial bigamist who first married at the age of fourteen. His tour is canceled, and he is banned from playing in Britain.

1959: Although it has no lyrics at all, Link Wray's guitar instrumental "Rumble," is banned by US radio stations who fear the title will promote teen violence. Despite the boycott the song sells more than a million copies. Link follows up with a single called "Jack the Ripper."

1967: The Beatles' "A Day in the Life" was widely banned because of perceived drug references, the first of many. "I Am the Walrus" is also banned by the BBC for use of the word "knickers." Meanwhile the Fab Four accidentally snub Imelda Marcos by failing to take up her invitation to tea in Manila; all Beatles recordings are banned in the Philippines.

1966: The singer P. J. Proby is banned from appearing on ABC TV's dance show *Shindig* after he accidentally split his pants during a concert in London. It is feared that Proby is splitting his pants deliberately.

1969: Jim Morrison of the Doors is arrested in Miami after he asks the audience, "Do you wanna see my cock?" They did.

1969: "Je T'Aime . . . Moi Non Plus" by Jane Birkin and Serge Gainsbourg is banned by US and European radio stations for content of an explicit sexual nature. The record's chance of getting playlisted are not helped by Gainsbourg's line about the joys of going "entre tes reins" ("between your kidneys" or up your bum, allegedly).

1970: The Rolling Stones release their new single "Cocksucker Blues," a ploy to get them out of a contractual obligation. It works.

1971: The Malawian dictator Dr. Hastings Banda bans the song "Delilah," made famous by the Welsh singer Tom Jones, in deference to a favorite mistress of the same name.

9 Dead Drummers

1975: Al Jackson, best known as a founding member of Booker T. & the MG's, was known as "the Human Timekeeper" for his drumming ability. Jackson is shot dead in his home; reports conflict on whether the culprit was a burglar or his estranged wife, who had already shot him in the chest a few months earlier. He decided not to press charges, but was in the process of a divorce.

1978: Keith Moon, reckless but seemingly indestructible drummer of the Who, dies at the age of thirty-two—having survived his repeated practice of blowing up hotel toilets with explosives—from an accidental overdose of sedatives he had been prescribed to alleviate his alcohol withdrawal symptoms.

1980: John Bonham, hard drinking drummer in Led Zeppelin, dies of pulmonary edema—waterlogging of the lungs caused by the inhalation of vomit. At the coroner's inquest it emerged that in the twenty-four hours before he died, Bonham had drunk forty measures of vodka.

1983: Dennis Wilson, founding member and the drummer of the Beach Boys—and allegedly the only one who could actually swim—dies of drowning after attempting to rescue four kilos of cocaine from under his boat in the Pacific Ocean.

1984: Nicholas "Razzle" Dingley, drummer with Hanoi Rocks, is a passenger in a car driven by Mötley Crüe lead singer Vince Neil. While speeding and under the influence of alcohol, Neil loses control of the vehicle, crashing it into an oncoming car. Razzle is pronounced dead on arrival at hospital, aged twenty-four. Mötley Crüe would go on to title their box sets *Music to Crash Your Car To, Vol. 1* and *2.*

1992: Jeff Porcaro, founding member of Toto, dies in a bizarre gardening accident. The thirty-eight-year-old drummer was using a garden pesticide that he was allergic to, triggering a heart attack. An autopsy showed he was afflicted with heart disease.

1998: Cozy Powell, drummer with Jeff Beck and Rainbow among others, dies while driving his car at 104 mph in bad weather on the M4 motorway near Bristol, England. At the time of the crash, Powell's blood alcohol reading was over the legal limit, he wasn't wearing a seatbelt, and he was talking to his girlfriend on his mobile phone.

2008: Ola Brunkert, former session drummer for the Swedish band ABBA, is found with his throat cut in his garden on the Spanish island of Majorca. His death was ruled "accidental." Apparently Brunkert put his head through a glass door in the dining room of his house then put a towel around his neck and staggered into the garden, where he collapsed and bled to death.

2008: Buddy Miles, best known as a member of Jimi Hendrix's Band of Gypsies, dies of congestive heart failure at age sixty. According to friends, "he turned off his defibrillator and was ready for heaven."

5 Artists and Writers Who Were More Wasted Than Keith Richards

∫ 1 ∫ THOMAS DE QUINCEY

The first and still the finest literary dope fiend, the author of *Confessions of an Opium Eater* first took opium as a treatment for toothache and immediately discovered it was the drug for him. As he put it, "Here was the secret of happiness, about which philosophers had disputed for so many ages, at once discovered: happiness might now be bought for a penny, and carried in the waistcoat pocket." He started off by taking an "opium holiday" every three weeks, then every Saturday night, then, inevitably, his intake became daily, and then virtually hourly, by which time his habit comprised a daily intake of up to eight thousand drops of opium and five or six glasses of laudanum. It caused him to lose all his teeth and his skin to take on the appearance of cracked parchment. Although his gift for writing never quite deserted him, the drugs slowly destroyed his memory and he was incapable of dressing unaided. He also frequently set fire to his hair while poring over his manuscripts by candlelight. His lodgings were crammed with books and old newspapers until there was no room for him to work or sleep; he would simply leave them and move elsewhere. He was hopeless with money and usually in debt but refused to sell any of his books to pay it off. He once approached a friend for a loan of seven shillings and sixpence. By way of security, he offered a screwed-up ball of paper, which he said was a "document." It turned out to be a £50 note. *Confessions* set the template for many writers who attempted to follow in de Quincey's junkie footsteps.

/ 2 / ARTHUR RIMBAUD

The French poet is regarded as the greatest artistic bad-lad of the nineteenth century. Just in case anyone was in any doubt about this, he wrote a piece called "Arsehole Sonnet" and used a rival poet's work as toilet paper. Rimbaud began one of the most notorious collaborations in literary history when he attracted the attention of the much older, not to mention recently married, poet Paul Verlaine by sending him five of his lewdest poems. Rimbaud and Verlaine ran away together and spent the next three years traveling Europe, spending Verlaine's money, taking drugs, and drinking implausible amounts of absinthe. Rimbaud's friendship with Verlaine was volatile and often violent; their idea of a quiet night in was to stab each other with kitchen knives wrapped in towels followed by energetic bouts of anal sex. One evening things got out of hand and Verlaine shot Rimbaud in the wrist; the latter wound up in the hospital, the former in a Brussels prison. The arresting officer described Rimbaud as "incomprehensible and repulsive," also mysteriously reporting that the poet's penis was "short and not very voluminous," while his anus was "dilated quite markedly." Verlaine was sentenced to two years in prison, where he was visited by a priest, who, after listening to Verlaine's lengthy confession, asked, " . . . but you've never slept with animals?" The recuperating Rimbaud meanwhile announced that he was working on a "series of masturbating poems." Verlaine left prison in January 1875 and entered a Trappist retreat, but soon left and hurried to Stuttgart to meet Rimbaud. Absinthe did not, however, make the heart grow fonder, and his former lover repulsed him with violence. Later, Rimbaud, finding himself short of cash, blackmailed Verlaine by threatening to spill the beans about his former lover's pedophilia. Rimbaud spent his final years wandering around Europe and Africa, syphilitic, drug-addled, and alcoholic, in pursuit of various odd jobs. In 1891 at the age of thirty-seven, he returned to France for treatment of a swelling on his knee, which resulted in the amputation of his right leg. He died six months later.

/ 3 / HENRI DE TOULOUSE-LAUTREC

The French artist grew to be only four-feet-six inches tall because he was afflicted by a form of dwarfism, a rare inherited disorder often associated with incest. A family photo shows him with three dwarf cousins, including one who spent her entire life in a wheeled wicker baby basket. At the age of twenty-three he went to live in the red light district of Montmartre, where he became a firm favorite with the working girls, possibly because of his allegedly enormous penis—hence his nickname "Teapot." In between regular Friday night orgies and getting legless with his pal Vincent van Gogh on a cocktail called Earthquake (two parts absinthe, one part red wine, one part cognac), Lautrec spent much of his short life painting and drawing the decadent world of cabaret stars, can-can dancing prostitutes, barmaids, clowns, and actors of Parisian night life. His paintings show that he was obsessed with women's noses, possibly because he was so short that when he looked up at a woman it was the first thing in his line of vision. He also loved the smell of women's armpits and liked to sniff the pits of their elbows and knees; he called them "tobacco shops." One erotic drawing shows the diminutive dipso enjoying a threesome with his friend René and his wife Lily. He was so ravaged by venereal disease that fellow artist Edgar Degas remarked that even his paintings stank of syphilis. He drank heavily to kill the pain, mixing absinthe with cognac. Being short had its benefits, though. "I'm not worried about falling down drunk," he noted. "I am already so near the ground I wouldn't even notice." He died, alcoholic and syphilitic, aged thirty-six.

/ 4 / CHARLES BAUDELAIRE

At the age of twenty-one the kinky French poet and post-romantic debauchee inherited a fortune from his father, a lapsed philandering Catholic priest, but within two years had blown most of it on prostitutes, hashish, and opium. Baudelaire was a member of the Club de Hachichins (Hashish Club), which met in the 1840s and counted Alexandre Dumas and Eugène Delacroix among its numbers. He wrote widely on hash, noting: "Among the drugs most efficient in creating what I call the artificial ideal . . . the most convenient and the most handy are hashish and opium." He spent the rest of his life in semi-poverty, living in fleabag hotels, eking out a meager existence as an art critic and translator of Edgar Allan Poe. To evade his creditors he changed his address six times in a single month. Working with a caged bat on his desk, Baudelaire dyed his hair green and, in between penning begging letters to his mother, wrote poems about prostitution, girl-on-girl sex, fetishism, S&M, drugs, and Satanism. In 1857 he published a collection of sexually explicit poems *Les Fleurs du Mal,* resulting in a famous obscenity trial. His muse was his mistress Jeanne Duval, a drug-addicted bisexual. He contracted the syphilis that would eventually kill him from Jewish prostitute Sarah la Louchette, the "Squint-eyed Sarah" mentioned in some of his works.

/ 5 / WILLIAM S. BURROUGHS

The US "beat generation" author once served in the army before being discharged for psychological reasons: He deliberately cut off the last joint of a finger to impress a friend. In 1951, while living in Mexico and showing off his marksmanship to friends, his wife Joan balanced a glass on her head and dared her husband to shoot it off, à la William Tell. The bullet hit her squarely between the eyes, killing her instantly. The incident was deemed an accident and Burroughs was released without charges. Most of the time Burroughs shot heroin, meanwhile supporting his addiction by writing semi-autobiographical books about drug addiction. In his first novel, *Junkie,* he offered details of his life as a heroin dealer in Greenwich Village. In 1954 Burroughs sold his typewriter to buy heroin. He managed to keep working in longhand but his handwriting was so illegible that his second novel *Naked Lust*—written under the influence of marijuana and an opioid called Eukodol, and which also tackled addiction to heroin and other controlled substances—was misread as *Naked Lunch* and the accidental title was kept. His output was unsurprisingly sporadic. He recalled: "I had not taken a bath in a year nor changed my clothes or removed them except to stick a needle every hour in the fibrous gray wooden flesh of terminal addiction. I did absolutely nothing. I could look at the end of my shoe for eight hours." Burroughs received acclaim through his writings but heroin eventually caught up with him. He was on methadone until the day he died, aged eighty-three.

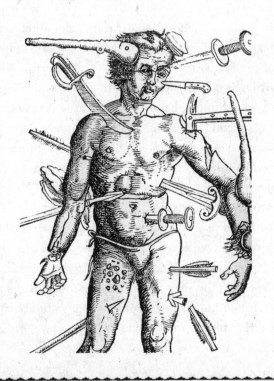

Chapter Six
SAINTS & SINNERS

10 People God Would Like to See Put to Death

Kidnappers (Exodus 21:16)

Homosexuals (Leviticus 20:13)

Anyone who works on Saturday (Numbers 15:32–36)

Any bride who can't prove her virginity on her
wedding night (Deuteronomy 22:20–21)

Anyone who takes God's name in vain (Leviticus 24:16)

Any wife who cheats on her husband and the person
with whom she cheated (Deuteronomy 22:22)

Any woman who loses her virginity to someone she is
not promised to, and the man she loses her virginity
to (Deuteronomy 22:23–24)

Any man who accidentally kills a pregnant woman in
a fight (Exodus 21:22–24)

Any rebellious son, or any person who disrespects his or
her parents (Deuteronomy 21:18–21, Leviticus 20:9)

Anyone not Jewish or Christian and/or worships
another god (Deuteronomy 13:6–11)

12 Saints to Invoke for Medical Conditions

1. February 3 is the feast day of Saint Blaise, patron saint
of throat problems. Saint Blaise, who lived in a cave
with wild animals, once talked a wolf into releasing a
pig that belonged to a poor woman. Blaise was arrested
by persecutors and sentenced to death by starvation,
but the owner of the pig smuggled him some food. He is

the patron saint to invoke if you have a fishbone in your throat, on account of the fact that, on his way to prison, he cured a boy who had one stuck in his.*

2. February 23 is the feast day of Saint Polycarp, patron saint of earache and dysentery. Martyred for his beliefs, he was bound and burned at the stake but the fire didn't burn him, so they stabbed him to death instead.

3. May 11 is the feast day of Saint Gangulphus, the patron saint of eye and skin conditions and knee pains. He married a woman who was frequently unfaithful to him. Disgusted by her infidelity, but not wishing her any harm, he sloped off and became a hermit, but was run through with a spear by his wife's lover as he lay in bed.

4. May 16 is the feast day of Saint Ubald, patron saint of obsessive-compulsive disorders. Saint Ubald was known for his miraculously mild and patient disposition. One day a workman accidentally damaged his vineyard. When Ubald quietly pointed out the damage to him, the workman became quite cross and shoved Ubald so hard that he fell into a pile of wet cement. He got up, cleaned himself off and thought nothing more of it.

5. June 2 is the feast day of Saint Elmo, patron saint of sufferers of stomach cramps and indigestion. This is due to the torture he suffered at the hands of his persecutors, who stuck hot iron hooks into his intestines, a process he miraculously endured.

6. June 8 is the feast day of Saint Medardus, patron saint of toothache. When he was a child an eagle hovered over his head and spread its wings to protect him from the

* In most cases however we recommend the Heimlich Maneuver.

rain. Saint Medardus is usually depicted laughing with his mouth wide open, and so is invoked against toothache. He is also invoked against bad weather and sterility.

7. June 30 is the feast day of Saint Theobald of Provins, patron saint of dry coughs. A renowned hermit, he performed sundry miracles and he died from an unspecified illness in which every inch of his body was covered in pustules and ulcers.

8. August 13 is the feast day of Saint Radegunde, patron saint of scabs. Radegunde was a former virgin queen of France who became a nun. She was on her way to perform an act of kindness when she was attacked and eaten by a pack of wolves.

9. August 30 is the feast day of Saint Fiacre, patron saint of sufferers from hemorrhoids, a medical condition he cured by laying on his hands. His reputed aversion to women is thought to be the reason he is also the patron saint of venereal disease sufferers. He also looks after gardeners, nonspecific venereal disease sufferers, and French taxi drivers.

10. September 2 is the feast day of Saint Nonnosus, patron saint of kidney problems and back pains. Nonnosus once made light work of removing an enormous rock that had occupied land on which he wanted to grow some cabbage, even though fifty pairs of oxen had failed to move it. He also miraculously restored a glass lamp that had fallen on the floor and shattered and filled several vessels with olive oil after a particularly bad olive harvest. Nonnosus is also patron saint of school-related student crises.

11. September 10 is the feast day of Saint Cosmas, patron saint of hernias. Cosmas and his twin brother Damian

were bound hand and foot and thrown into the sea, but were rescued by a passing angel. They were subsequently burned at the stake, racked, crucified, and stoned, but these and various other tortures were ineffectual. Neither twin, however, survived their subsequent beheading.

12. December 15 is the feast day of Saint Christina the Astonishing, patron saint of mental illness. When she was twenty-one she experienced a violent seizure and was thought to have died. During her funeral, she suddenly recovered and levitated to the roof of the church but was ordered down by the priest. She avoided contact with people because she couldn't bear the smell of their sin and would climb trees or buildings, hide in ovens or cupboards, or simply levitate to avoid human contact. She also exhibited a number of other unusual traits, including the ability to handle fire without harm, stand in freezing water in the winter for hours, spend long periods in tombs, or allow herself to be dragged underwater by a mill wheel without sustaining injury.

10 Lost Prophets

∫ 1 ∫ PYTHAGORAS

The Greek introduced the concept of proof into mathematics and with it the concept of deductive reasoning. He also founded his own religion, which was said to have around three hundred followers. Pythagoras issued a long list of pithy precepts to his disciples: "Don't pick anything up that has fallen over"; "Never step over a pole"; "Don't shake hands too eagerly"; "Refrain from handling white cockerels"; "Don't look into a mirror by

the light of a taper"; and "Never eat your own dog." His followers were also forbidden to eat beans on the grounds that a bean,
if placed on a new tomb and then covered with dung for forty
days, will assume human form. After Pythagoras discovered
his famous mathematical theorem he celebrated by feasting on
a roasted ox. It must have come as something of a surprise to
his followers, who were also required to be strictly vegetarian.

/ 2 / JOANNA SOUTHCOTT

In 1814 a spinster and self-styled prophet from Devon announced
that she was the expectant mother of a new Messiah. The fact
that she was a virgin and well into her sixties did not deter a
small army of followers from camping outside her front door to
wait for the impending miracle. Unfortunately the new Son of
God failed to arrive on the predicted date and Miss Southcott
died ten days later. A postmortem, however, revealed that Miss
Southcott was not with child, and that the appearance of preg-
nancy was the result of a large cancerous growth. Despite this
setback she acquired a cult following in the Panacea Society,
a small sect based in Bedford. In the early 1900s cult leader
Helen Exeter announced that the messiah would return in
1914, but didn't live to see her forecast fail, as she was drowned
early that year. The Society pinned its hopes on a large sealed
box, once belonging to Southcott, which it believed would reveal the date of Christ's return. In 1927 the box was opened
and was found to contain sundry items, including a night-
cap, an old purse, and a lottery ticket. Southcott's followers
insisted however that they had simply got the wrong box; the
true box could only be opened in the presence of twenty-four
Bishops of the Church of England, a logistical improbability,

but hope springs eternal. As recently as 1999 the declining membership of the Panacea Society resulted in a series of newspaper advertisements in the UK national press demanding that the bishops assemble to open the box, warning that otherwise "Crime and Banditry, Distress and Perplexity will increase in England." The requisite number of bishops has yet to step forward.

∫ 3 & 4 ∫ JOHN ALEXANDER DOWIE AND WILBUR GLENN VOLIVA

In 1888 Dowie, a faith healer from Scotland, purchased ten square miles of land in Illinois, where he founded the Christian Catholic Apostolic Church in the fundamentalist community of Zion City. It was home to about five thousand followers and an entirely self-supporting community with new factories built for the manufacture of lace, confectionery, and furniture, but short on entertainment, as there were no theaters, cinemas, or dance halls. From his church pulpit Dowie dispensed the law and railed against various earthly sins, including sex, oysters, pork, and life insurance, citing Old Testament injunctions against shellfish and randy insurance salesmen. Dowie also believed that medicine was an instrument of the devil. When his own daughter was severely burned after accidentally knocking over an oil lamp, he banished one of his followers for trying to put Vaseline on her burns. Many others who came to his faith-healing sessions also died of their illnesses without any medical attention. In 1901 Dowie declared that he was the prophet Elijah and embarked on an expensive and ultimately ruinous campaign to spread the word of the Apostolic Church to the rest of America. With his financial problems mounting he turned to a close friend and disciple, the millionaire preacher Wilbur Glenn Voliva, whose $10 million fortune had been made from the manufacture of chocolate biscuits. When Voliva studied Dowie's accounts he found a discrepancy of about $2 million and denounced his old friend as a fraudulent polygamist, banished him from the community, and established himself as the new leader of Zion. Fifty-nine-year-old Dowie, paralyzed by a crippling stroke and evidently insane, died two years later. Voliva continued to rule the sixteen thousand inhabitants of Zion City with an iron hand, banning cigarettes and alcohol and imposing a 10:00 p.m. curfew. No one was allowed to whistle, sing, or even hum on Sundays, or drive a vehicle over 5 mph. In 1922 Voliva became the first religious broadcaster to found a radio station, the 5,000-watt WCBD, to preach his slim grasp of astrophysics to people as far away as New Zealand. Voliva's regular broadcasts taught that the earth was flat and roughly saucer-shaped, that the North Pole was positioned at the center and the South Pole was a crust of ice running surrounding the outer rim. Voliva frequently predicted the world's imminent destruction, but always found new calculations for future Armageddons. When he died in 1934, aged seventy-two, his offer of a $5000 reward to anyone who could disprove "flat earthery" remained uncollected.

/ 5 / ANDRÉ IVANOV

In 1757 the Russian mystic Ivanov formed a sect called Skoptzy—literally, "castrates." The fundamental belief of the cult was the virtue of castration, taking as their tenet Matthew 19:12: "And there be eunuchs which have made themselves eunuchs for the kingdom of heaven's sake." Ivanov declared

that testicles were the "keys of hell" and their amputation conferred upon the initiate "the right to mount the spotted horse
of the apocalypse." Leading by example, he had himself and
his thirteen disciples castrated, an operation carried out with a
red-hot iron. The Skoptzy also wore complementary stigmata—
cruciform cuts and burns of the shoulders, under the arms, on
the belly, pelvis, and thighs. Ivanov was arrested and banished
to Siberia, where he eventually died, but the authorities failed
to halt the spread of the Skoptzy cult. Kondrati Selivanov, one of
the original disciples, was declared "the new Christ descended
among men" and under his leadership the new sect grew in size
and power. As late as 1900 there were still an estimated five
thousand male members of the sect in Russia.

/ 6 / EDGAR CAYCE

Known as the "American Nostradamus" or "the sleeping
prophet" because of his habit of going into a trance to pre-
dict the future or heal the sick. Although Cayce's track record
on the predictions front was generally so erratic that he was
obliged to keep up his day job selling photographic supplies,
he had one notable success just before the 1929 Wall Street
crash when he advised a client against investing in the stock
market because he saw "a downward movement of long duration." Cayce is also said to have foreseen World Wars I and
II, the independence of India, the state of Israel, and the assassination of President Kennedy. He also predicted the fall of
Communism in China, that California would fall into the sea
in 1969, and that Christ would return after World War III in
1999. Cayce predicted that in the year 2000, the earth's axis
would shift and mankind would be destroyed by flooding and

earthquakes. Cayce's followers, the Association for Research and Enlightenment, keep this memory alive from their base at his former home in Virginia.

/ 7 / THE REV. HOMER A. TOMLINSON

Born in Indiana in 1892, Tomlinson was twenty-four when he went to New York to work in an advertising agency but returned to the ministry of his father's church after being "almost hit by lightning." Tomlinson had a flair for self-publicity, first demonstrated in 1940 when he performed the world's first parachute wedding ceremony at the New York World's Fair, when the bride and groom, the minister, the best man, maid of honor, and four musicians were all suspended from parachutes. In 1952, claiming to have been "hailed almost as a new Messiah" during extensive travels abroad, Tomlinson returned to the United States to run for president as the candidate of the Theocratic Party. He advocated the union of church and state, the abolition of taxes, the return of tithing, and the creation of two new cabinet posts: secretary of righteousness and secretary of the Holy Bible. Tomlinson was to run for the presidency again in 1960 and in 1964, but after two more failed campaigns, he topped off his political efforts by declaring himself to be King of the World, an event apparently anticipated by the Bible. He traveled extensively, although probably not the million air miles he claimed, to spread the news of his monarchy, briefly visiting 101 countries for a series of local coronation ceremonies, mostly performed at local airports. During these coronations Tomlinson wore blue silk robes, held an inflatable plastic globe as a symbol of his authority, and, while seated on a folding chair, had a gold-painted iron crown placed on his head. He made extensive claims for the benefits to mankind that resulted from his reign as King of the World: he had fended off revolutions, averted a war between Israel and the Arabs, ended droughts, and launched a period of world peace and harmony. His 1958 "coronation" in Moscow's Red Square, for example, had "melted the iron curtain." The Soviet press, unimpressed by the fact that a king had appeared in its midst and had wrought instant international peace, dismissively referred to Tomlinson as "an American actor." At his peak Tomlinson claimed a worldwide following of somewhere between fifty million and one hundred million people, although a more realistic estimate would put it at under three thousand.

/ 8 / GEORGE KING

In 1954 King, a taxi driver from Shropshire, England, claimed he was visited by aliens who informed him that Jesus was alive and well and living on the planet Venus. Furthermore he had been selected by the "Hidden Masters" to become the "Voice of the Interplanetary Parliament." King's mission on earth was to represent spirituality in its battle with materialism. In his quest he would be assisted by the Hidden Masters, who would occasionally lend support by visiting humanity in their flying saucers. King quit his job as a taxi driver and changed his name to Sir George King, OSP, Ph.D., Th.D., DD, Metropolitan Archbishop of the Aetherius Churches, Prince Grand Master of the Mystical Order of Saint Peter, HRH Prince De George King De Santori, and Founder President of the Aetherius Society. In 1959 the aliens advised him to move to America with his wife, Lady Monique King, Bishop of the American Division, where they opened a temple on Hollywood Boulevard, meanwhile awaiting the arrival of their space brothers. King died in California in 1959 but his organization continues to this day.

/ 9 / THE REV. HENRY PRINCE

In 1835 Prince, a vicar from Somerset, England, alerted the attention of the Anglican authorities when he took to addressing his congregation naked and was defrocked. Prince however continued to preach, and on New Year's Day 1846 he announced that he was the Messiah to a group of people taking tea in a Weymouth café. The incident was brought before the home secretary by Dorset county magistrates who complained that Prince was "impersonating the Almighty." Prince shut himself away in a large mansion in the village of Spaxton, just a mile from his old parish and founded a commune called Church of the Agapemone—Greek for "Abode of Love." It was surrounded by a twelve-foot-high wall and guarded by large dogs, designed to keep prying eyes out, and to keep the faithful in. Prince ruled in despotic style over a cult membership that varied between sixty and two hundred people. His followers, even married ones, were required to live in single-sex quarters, but Prince, now referred to by the faithful as the Beloved, made alternative arrangements for himself with a novel take on "spin the bottle." Once a week his younger female devotees were seated on a giant revolving stage which the men would then rotate. The girl who faced Prince when the stage came to a stop was his "Bride of the Week." Prince funded his community largely by wheedling money out of several well-heeled spinsters, leaving notes under their dinner plates with instructions such as, "The Lord hath need of £50." Prince lived lavishly, surrounded by a bevy of billiard-playing beauties, occasionally driving around Spaxton in a coach attended by liveried outriders who announced his arrival by shouting "Blessed is he who cometh in the name of the Lord," while he ran up large bills with local shopkeepers in the name of "My Lord, the Agapemone." Despite accusations of brainwashing, sex scandals, dramatic rescues of members by their families, and occasional virulent attacks in the popular press, the Abode of Love was allowed to flourish more or less unmolested for the next thirty-odd years. Prince had declared himself and his followers immortal, but the Agapemonites gradually passed away one by one, until Prince himself died in January 1899. His death came as a genuine shock to the faithful and threw the community into a state of panic. They buried him in the front garden in the middle of the night, his body standing upright to facilitate his resurrection. When the expected second coming failed to materialize, instead of arriving at the conclusion that they had been victims of a long and humiliating hoax, Prince's followers stuck together and crowned a new Messiah in the person of his former sidekick, the Rev. John Hugh Smyth-Pigott.

/ 1 0 / THE DUKE OF EDINBURGH

A group of islanders in Southwest Pacific are dedicated to the worship of Prince Philip, the Duke of Edinburgh. The islanders of Tanna believe that Queen Elizabeth II's husband will one day cure all known diseases and grant them eternal youth. The Duke's two hundred followers expect that on his return he will resume his rightful place among them and restore paradise on earth, while wearing the traditional penis gourd. They also believe that Philip secretly runs the Commonwealth and has been able thus far to get away with the tricky business of concealing his true identity from his wife. The islanders of Tanna were last visited by their god in 1971, when they gave him a present, a pig-killing club.

10 Things That Could Get You Hanged in Nineteenth-Century Britain

1. Associating with gypsies
2. Setting fire to a hayrick
3. Writing on Westminster Bridge
4. Impersonating a pensioner of Greenwich Hospital
5. Writing a threatening letter
6. Appearing on the highway with a sooty face
7. Damaging a fish pond
8. Cutting down a tree
9. Secreting notes in a post office
10. Stealing a spoon

History's 11 Most Badly Bungled Executions

1. The most badly executed beheading in history was that endured in 1626 by the French Count Henri de Chalais, condemned to death for his part in a royal assassination plot. When it was time for Chalais to be publicly beheaded with a sword, the regular executioner could not be found and an inexperienced replacement was drafted at the last minute. The Count's head was hacked off by the stand-in on the twenty-ninth stroke: he was still breathing at the twentieth.

2. In accordance with British law, the warm corpses of recently hanged criminals were handed over to medical students for experimentation. In 1740 a sixteen-year-old rapist, William Duell, was hanged for twenty-two minutes at Tyburn, London, but emerged from a deep coma to find that his body had already been donated to science and that a surgeon's knife was already slicing into his stomach. Duell survived, and his death sentence was subsequently commuted to deportation.

3. In 1819 a surgeon in Glasgow, Dr. James Jeffrey, attended a public demonstration of galvanism—the study of the effects of electrical currents passed through the human body. The body was that of a coal miner, Matthew Clydesdale, who had just been hanged for murder. Before a packed audience of students and members of the public, Clydesdale was seated in a chair and his hands were attached to a battery. As the current was switched on, spectators watched in mounting horror as Clydesdale's chest heaved, then he suddenly stood upright. Dr. Jeffrey coolly saved the day by expertly slitting the man's throat with a scalpel. Although Jeffrey had technically committed murder, he was never charged because Clydesdale had already been executed and was therefore legally dead.

4. The public execution of Robert-François Damiens, a mentally defective religious zealot who attacked King Louis XV with a small penknife in 1757, was the most prolonged in history. Damiens was stripped and chained down on a wooden scaffold, where his right hand was to be burned off. A fire was lit, but it kept going out, so one of the executioners improvised by gouging out lumps of flesh from various parts of Damiens's body

with red-hot pincers while boiling oil and melted wax, resin, and lead were poured into the wounds. Between his screams Damiens was heard to cry out "My God, take pity on me" and "Jesus, help me!" The executioners then took long leather straps and wound them up the length of his arms and his legs. Each strap was attached to a rope, which in turn was affixed to four horses. The horses were then whipped, each pulling in a different direction. Damiens was a very large, muscular man, and the horses selected to tear him limb from limb were not quite up the task. For more than an hour the horses were urged on while Damiens screamed in agony. As dusk fell, an attending surgeon suggested that they might want to speed things up by cutting Damiens's sinews; the executioners began hacking at his joints with knives. The horses were again whipped and after several pulls, ripped one arm and leg from Damiens's body. As the second arm was pulled out, Damiens lower jaw was seen to move, as though to speak. He died at 10:30 p.m., five-and-a-half hours after the execution started.

5. James Scott, the Duke of Monmouth and firstborn illegitimate son of Charles II, was victim of Tower Hill's messiest execution on July 15, 1685. The handsome and popular Duke was heard to complain loudly that the axeman's blade appeared to be blunt, but no one paid heed. It was the fifth blow that finally severed his head from his shoulders, just before he had a chance to say "I told you so." The watching crowd was horrified by the axman's incompetence and he narrowly escaped a lynching. It was belatedly discovered that the Duke,

although a person of great historical importance, had never actually had his portrait painted for posterity. His head was duly sewn back on, the stitches covered up, and his portrait taken. He now hangs in the National Portrait Gallery in London.

6. Two men have survived three hangings apiece. The Englishman Joseph Samuels, deported to Australia for robbery in 1801, was sentenced to death in Sydney for murder two years later. He was reprieved after the rope broke twice on the first and second attempts and the trapdoor failed to open on the third. A trapdoor mechanism also saved the life of convicted murderer John "Babbacombe" Lee, a butler sentenced to death in 1884 after hacking to death his elderly employer Emma Keyse in South Devon, England. Even though the trapdoor worked every time it was tested, it failed to open three times in the space of seven minutes. Lee was let off with imprisonment. After serving his sentence he sailed out of Britain for America to settle in Milwaukee, Wisconsin, where he was known as "The Man They Could Not Hang."

7. In 1903 a young American, Frederick Van Wormer, was sent to the electric chair for the murder of his uncle. Van Wormer was duly electrocuted in Clinton prison in New York, and pronounced dead. In the autopsy room, just as he was about to go under the scalpel, his eye was seen to flicker, and he moved a hand. The prison doctor confirmed that two full charges of current had failed to kill the prisoner. Van Wormer was carried back to the chair and several more currents were passed through him until his death was beyond dispute.

8. The American cannibal and child-killer Albert Fish, the oldest man ever executed at Sing Sing Prison, went to the electric chair in 1936. The first electric charge failed, allegedly short-circuited by dozens of needles the old man had inserted in his pelvic region. Doctors later discovered a total of twenty-nine rusty needles in his genitals.

9. In 1983 Jimmy Lee Gray was to be executed in Mississippi's gas chamber. The poisonous gas failed to kill him, and left him gasping and in agony for eight minutes. He eventually died bashing his head against a metal pole behind the chair that he was strapped into. It was later discovered that the executioner was drunk.

10. In 1992 thirty-four-year-old American garbage-truck driver Billy White was executed by lethal injection in Huntsville Prison. It took the medical attendants forty minutes to locate a vein and another nine minutes for him to die.

11. The most badly botched execution by electric chair was that of William Taylor, condemned to death in 1893 for killing a fellow inmate in Auburn Prison in New York. As the first electric charge surged through his body, Taylor's legs went into spasm and tore the chair apart by his ankle strappings. The charge was switched off while repairs were made. The switch was thrown again, but this time there was no current because the generator had burned out. Taylor was removed from the chair and given morphine in an attempt to deaden any pain he may have felt. By the time the power had been restored, Taylor was already dead, but because the law still required an electrocution, the dead man was strapped back into the chair and the current was passed through him for another thirty seconds.

10 Crimes of Passion

1710: To see if he can elicit a reaction from his wife, the Russian Czar Peter the Great has the head of her suspected lover pickled in alcohol and placed in a jar at her bedside.

1895: Robert Buchanan, a Scottish doctor practicing in New York, is charged with the murder of his wife Anna. At his trial the prosecution seeks to prove that Buchanan killed his wife by morphine poisoning so he could pick up her insurance and start a new life with his mistress, the proprietress of a local brothel. Buchanan had disguised the telltale sign of morphine poisoning—contracted pupils—by putting belladonna in her eyes to dilate them. To demonstrate the prosecution's theory, a cat was put to death in the courtroom and the substance was administered to its eyes. The jury was convinced, and Buchanan went to the electric chair at Sing Sing.

1988: France's least competent murderess Patricia Orionno again attempts to kill her husband because of his "excessive sexual demands." Having tried to dispose of him with sleeping tablets (underestimating the dosage, she only made him sleep late), she then slashed his wrists, tried to gas him, then smothered him with a pillow. She was successful in her fifth attempt, stabbing him eight times. She was subsequently freed when the French judge ruled that it was a *crime passionel*.

1993: Texan John Celinski is fined $18 and sentenced to two years probation plus 240 hours of community service after he admits to microwaving two cats belonging to his ex girlfriend.

KARL SHAW

Celinski testified at his trial that he was jealous of her pets Sugar Ray and Bonnie.

1994: The wife of Polish adulterer Boris Paveharik finds a pack of condoms in her husband's pocket and fills them with ground pepper. After the next visit to his mistress, Mr. Paveharik is rushed to the hospital after suffering severe swelling and inflammation.

1994: Jeffrey Watkins, aged twenty-four, is convicted of breaking into a mausoleum and stealing the skull of a woman who had been dead since 1933. Watkins confesses that he had slept with the remains inside coffins: "I feel safe with the dead, and I can trust them. I need their company to make me peaceful inside," he explains.

1995: Baseball lovers Regina Chatien, forty-three, and her partner Melvin Hoffman, fifty-three, are each fined $1,000 for engaging in oral sex during the seventh inning of a game at L.A.'s Dodger Stadium against the visiting New York Mets. The couple were at the game with their four children, aged eight to fourteen.

1995: Sixty-seven-year-old New Yorker Marland Maynard is convicted of the manslaughter of his wife Mabel. Maynard had returned home from work to find his wife in the act of attempting suicide with a handgun. When the gun jammed, Marland helped her to reload it. Mabel, who had a history of mental problems, had already stabbed herself fourteen times before her husband had arrived home from work.

1996: Gail Murphy, aged forty-seven, of Brooklyn, New York, is arrested for shooting her husband to death. She tells the police she did it because he had gone on a six-hour fishing trip while she was recovering from hemorrhoid surgery.

2000: Thai Buddhist monk Sayan Duriyalak, outraged by the discovery that his abbot is violating his vow of chastity by having sex with a fifty-one-year-old nun, sets upon the couple with an ax while they are in bed together, decapitating the abbot and seriously wounded the nun. The monk tells police that his attack was inspired by an execution he had recently seen on TV. He planned to display the abbot's head in the local park as a deterrent to horny monks.

Criminal Justice
15 CONTROVERSIAL COURTROOM CHARACTERS

1. The Persian King Cambyses II was found to have a finely tuned sense of poetic justice when one of his judges was found guilty of corruption. The king had him flayed alive, then had the judge's old seat reupholstered with his skin. As a final touch he appointed the dead judge's son as his successor, thus forcing the son to literally sit in judgment on his father.

2. In 1998 Washington state municipal judge Ralph H. Baldwin resigned from the bench after inviting a lawyer and two jurors back into the jury room to finish off a twelve-pack of beer. Judge Baldwin told them, "Bet you've never met a judge like me before."

3. The seventeenth-century judicial system was inclined to give ugly people a raw deal because ugliness was seen as a sure sign of guilt. The French legal expert Henri Boguet

ruled that the repulsiveness of a man's face was enough to expose him to torture to make him confess his crimes. Some European medieval laws decreed that whenever two people were under suspicion for the same crime, the better looking of the two was always the innocent one.

4. In 1986 a judge in Philadelphia, Bernard J. Avellino, reportedly refused to convict a man for rape on the grounds that the alleged victim was "the ugliest girl I have ever seen in my entire life." He later apologized for calling the victim "coyote ugly" and for remarking that the experience had put him off rape trials for good. He said his remarks had been taken out of context by a newspaper.

5. Judge Roy Bean dispensed justice in Texas for twenty years, presiding from the saloon bar the Jersey Lily in the town of Langtry. Bean was renowned for his erratic methods, often interrupting trials to serve drinks to the court. Whenever he presided over a marriage ceremony he always finished with the line, "May God have mercy on your soul." In 1882 he dismissed a murder charge brought against one of his regulars because "it served the deceased right for getting in front of the gun." The case against another regular drinker at the Jersey Lily was also dropped because the victim was Chinese. According to Bean's version of Texas law, there was "not a damn line here nowheres that makes it illegal to kill a Chinaman."

6. In 1992 the Pennsylvania judge Charles Guyer was fired after a hidden video camera recorded him offering a novel form of plea bargaining. He offered convicted men lighter sentences if they allowed him to shampoo their hair.

7. Sir George "Bloody Jeffreys" was Britain's most sadistic lord chief justice ever. He passed 331 death sentences

and had hundreds more deported to Australia—in the seventeenth century arguably a fate worse than hanging. One of his most notorious sentences was conferred on Lady Alice Lisle, whom he ordered to be roasted alive. There was outrage at the sentence and demands for clemency, so Lady Alice had her sentence commuted on appeal and got away with a beheading. Jeffreys didn't allow a word of self-defense and always drove the prosecution through at high speed. The cause of this behavior was a painful bladder stone: he was compelled to urinate hourly, and had to get through the trials as fast as possible to reach the lavatory.

8. In 1993 California district attorney William Tingle had three members of a jury removed from an attempted murder case because one was "grossly overweight" and wore "a little tiny skirt that doesn't fit her"; another had braided hair, which he regarded as "somewhat radical"; and the third, because of her "braids, obesity, size, and manner of dress."

9. The nineteenth-century Scottish earl Lord Monboddo, reputed to be "the most learned judge of his day," spent his life convinced that babies were born with tails, and that there was a universal conspiracy of silence among midwives who cut them off at birth. Monboddo's faith in his tail theory remained intact even when he witnessed the births of his own children. He concluded that the crafty midwives had tricked him and destroyed the evidence. Monboddo frequently interrupted court proceedings at Edinburgh's Court of Sessions by sending notes of enquiry to witnesses who had recently returned from abroad to ask them if they had seen any foreigners with tails.

KARL SHAW

10. In 1999 Nebraska's Judicial Qualification Commission suspended Omaha judge Richard "Deacon" Jones after seventeen charges were brought against him, including signing official court papers with names "A. Hitler" and "Snow White"; setting eccentric bail amounts, including "13 cents" and "a zillion pengos," "personally and indiscreetly supervising a young male probationer's urine test," and setting off firecrackers in the office of a judge with whom he had an argument.

11. The Irish judge John Toler was described as "fat, podgy, with small gray cunning eyes, which sparkled with good humor and irrepressible fun, especially when he was passing sentence of death." Toler, the First Earl of Norbury, was without mercy and his sentences were usually harsh; on a "good" day he sent ninety-seven men to their deaths. Norbury was famous for a single act of clemency towards an alleged murderer. Although the evidence against the accused was clear and overwhelming he instructed the jury to bring in an acquittal, eliciting a gasp of astonishment around the courtroom. The crown prosecutor interrupted the judge to remind him that the sheer weight of evidence showed the man's guilt was undisputable. Norbury replied, "I realize that, but I hanged six men at last Tipperary assizes [judicial inquiries in County Tipperary] who were innocent, so I'll let this man off now to square matters."

12. Judge Joseph Troisi was a highly regarded member of the West Virginia bench until June 1997, when he actually bit a defendant at a bail hearing. Troisi became annoyed when defendant William Witten mumbled curses at him after just having been refused bail. The judge left the bench,

took off his robes, exchanged words with Witten, then bit his nose severely enough to draw blood.

13. Justice Rayner Goddard was one of the most enthusiastic hangers and floggers ever to have held the post of British lord chief justice, an office he assumed at the age of sixty-nine, elderly even by the standards of the British legal system, and held for thirteen years. The writer and broadcaster Ludovic Kennedy, in his anthology of miscarriages of justice *Thirty-Six Murders and Two Immoral Earnings,* describes the lord chief justice's idiosyncratic approach to sentencing prisoners to hang: "After Goddard's death, his clerk, Arthur Smith, told John Parris . . . that on the last day of a murder trial he would bring a fresh pair of trousers into the robing room, as Goddard was in the habit of ejaculating into his present pair when sentencing a prisoner to death."

14. The British high court judge Justice Michael Argyle (1915–99) was called "the domino judge" because of his habit of handing down sentences of five and seven years, the maximum for most sorts of crime. Argyle was chiefly renowned for his controversial courtroom outbursts. He first came to attention of the British public during the notorious *Oz* magazine "Schoolkids Issue" obscenity trial in 1971, when he told a woman detective, "You are far too attractive to be police woman. You should be an actress." On the subject of the number of British immigrants in Britain, he noted, "I don't have the figures, but just go to Bradford," while a black British defendant was told to "get out and go back to Jamaica." Arygle was a big cricket fan and always kept a TV set in his robing room. In 1986 he told a jury at the Old Bailey that the lack of test-match

cricket on television was "enough to make an Orthodox Jew want to join the Nazi party."

15. In 2007 Judge James Michael Shull was removed from office by the Virginia Supreme Court after he admitted to settling a child visitation dispute by flipping a coin, and to ordering a woman to drop her trousers in court. The Supreme Court noted that Shull had previously been the subject of a judicial inquiry in 2004 for allegedly calling a teenager a "mama's boy" and a "wuss," and for advising a woman in court to marry her abusive boyfriend. Judicial coin-flipping, however, is not unprecedented in the United States. In 1983 the Manhattan criminal court judge Alan Friess was barred from office after deciding the length of a jail sentence on the toss of a coin and asking courtroom spectators to vote on which of two conflicting witnesses was telling the truth.

No Second Helpings
10 LAST MEALS ON DEATH ROW

1. Ham, eggs, toast, and coffee—Gee Jon, Chinese murderer, the first man ever to be executed in the United States by lethal gas, at Carson City State Prison, Nevada, in 1924.
2. Hot fudge sundae—Barbara Graham, convicted murderess, executed by lethal gas at San Quentin, California, in 1955.
3. Steak and fries followed by peach cobbler desert—murderer Charlie Brooks, executed by lethal injection at Huntsville, Texas, in 1982.
4. Cheez Doodles and Coca-Cola—mass poisoner Margaret Velma Barfield, a fifty-two-year-old grandmother and the

first woman ever to die by lethal injection, at Central Prison, North Carolina in 1962.

5. Hamburger, eggs, and potatoes—Texan killer Gary Gilmore, the first man to be executed in the United States for a decade; shot dead by firing squad at the Utah State Prison in 1977.

6. Candy—Chauncey Millard, the youngest person ever executed in the state of Utah, killed by firing squad in 1869. The eighteen-year-old was still finishing his candy bar as he was being shot.

7. A large steak salad, potato pancakes, and two helpings of jelly and ice cream—Isidore Zimmerman, a twenty-six-year-old convicted of murder, at Sing Sing in 1939. Zimmerman continued to protest his innocence to the last mouthful.

8. A one dollar bill sandwich—Joshua Jones, hanged in Pennsylvania in 1839 for the murder of his wife. While Jones was awaiting execution he sold his body to the prison doctors for ten dollars. He spent nine dollars on delicacies to vary his prison diet. Upon realizing that he still had a dollar bill in his pocket just minutes before his execution, he requested two slices of bread.

9. Two hamburgers and Coca-Cola—Leslie B. Gireth, executed at San Quentin in 1943 for the murder of his girlfriend. Gireth had lost his nerve halfway through a suicide pact with her. His last meal was an exact replica of what she had eaten just before he shot her.

10. Garlic bread, shrimp, French fries, ice cream, strawberries, and whipped cream—the heroic last order of Perry Smith and Richard Eugene Hickock, before their double hanging at Kansas in 1965. They lost their appetites, however, at the last minute and the meal was untouched.

CHAPTER SEVEN
MAD, BAD &
DANGEROUS TO KNOW

11 People Who Didn't Like Their Nicknames

/ 1 / CONSTANTINE "THE COPRONYMUS"

The eighth-century Byzantine emperor was so named because, according to his enemies, at his christening in 718 the baby Constantine defecated in the baptismal font (*kopros*—Greek for dung).

/ 2 / WILLIAM "THE BASTARD"

Or "William the Conqueror" as he was known within earshot, was born illegitimate then became King of England in 1066. William survived a lifetime of almost endless warring and bloodletting to die at the ripe old age of sixty, when his horse stumbled on some hot cinders, throwing him against the iron pommel of his saddle, mashing his left testicle, and causing fatal internal injuries.

/ 3 / HENRY "THE IMPOTENT"

The fifteenth-century King of Castile's nickname was unfair, according to local prostitutes who testified that the king was more than sexually capable. He unfairly acquired the "impotent" thing because his wife Queen Isabella had several children, none of which were his.

/ 4 / SELIM "THE GRIM"

The sixteenth-century Sultan of Turkey was so named after his less than liberal sentencing policy and his penchant for wholesale slaughter of sibling rivals to the throne. He also offered to remove the tongues and testicles of anyone who called him "grim."

/ 5 / ADOLF "CARPET BITER" HITLER

Hitler was prone to temper tantrums, prompting his subordinates to nickname him "carpet biter." His personal physician Dr. Theodor Morell recorded that the Führer would turn white with his jaws tightly clenched and his eyes dilated; a sign for everyone in his entourage to make themselves scarce because the fits were usually followed by an order to dismiss or execute someone.

/ 6 / THOMAS "BUTTERFINGERS" MORAN

The legendary pickpocket got his nickname because he got caught so often. Moran picked his first pocket after the 1906 earthquake in San Francisco, and by the time of his death at age seventy-eight in 1970 had been arrested in almost every US state and Canada. Shortly before he died, he said: "I've never forgiven that smart-alecky reporter who named me 'Butterfingers.' "

/ 7 / GEORGE "BABY FACE" NELSON

Born Lester Gillis, America's "Public Enemy No. 1" in the 1930s had a youthful, almost angelic face, which belied the fact that he killed more FBI agents than anyone in history. He despised his nickname and told everyone he wanted to be known as "Big George" Nelson. It never really caught on, mostly because he was only five-feet-four-inches tall.

∫ 8 ∫ BENJAMIN "BUGSY" SIEGEL

Siegel, who was charged by the New York mafia to run their gambling rackets in Las Vegas, was put on trial in 1939 for the murder of Harry "Big Greenie" Greenberg, but was acquitted. During the trial the press picked up on his allegedly psychotic temper and began referring to him as "Bugsy," from the gangland slang "bugs," meaning "crazy." Any mention of the nickname in his presence, however, was enough to land you in the hospital, or the morgue.

∫ 9 ∫ AL "SCARFACE" CAPONE

Capone acquired the three scars that gave him the nickname on the left side of his face, in a fight over a woman while he was working as a bouncer on the door of a Brooklyn nightclub. He was touchy about his injuries, and often lied about how he got them, claiming they were war wounds, although he never served in the armed forces. Although the nickname served him well, close associates knew better than to call him "Scarface" and always called him "Snorky"—meaning "high class."

∫ 1 0 ∫ GIUSEPPE "JOE BANANAS" BONANNO

The Sicilian-born American mafioso and head of the Bonanno crime family in New York was naturally resentful of his nickname because it implied he was one olive short of a pizza. He fell from grace during the 1960s, allegedly for trying to become the boss of bosses in what came to be known as "the Banana War," when he plotted to assassinate other family bosses including Carlo Gambino and Thomas Lucchese.

⌠1 1⌡ CHARLES "PRETTY BOY" FLOYD

There is disagreement on how the legendary bank robber Charles Arthur Floyd acquired his "Pretty Boy" tag. According to one version it was given to him by grateful prostitutes, or it could have been a newspaper story after his first major robbery, recording an eyewitness description of him as "a pretty boy with apple cheeks." Either way, the mere mention of "Pretty Boy" drove him into a literally murderous rage. According to legend, when he was gunned down by the FBI his dying words were, "I'm Charles Arthur Floyd!"

10 Vain Leaders

1. During the Second Punic War the great Carthaginian commander Hannibal wore a wig into battle, but kept a second on hand for special occasions.

2. Hadrian was the first Roman emperor to make beards fashionable, apparently to hide a disfiguring skin complaint. The big talking point of his reign, however, was his Greek boyfriend, Antinous. They were inseparable for six years, until a freak boating accident in A.D. 130 when they were sailing down the Nile and Antinous mysteriously fell overboard and drowned. The death of

Antinous may not have been entirely accidental. Hadrian was seriously ill with tuberculosis at time, and believed in the myth of the resurrection of the underworld god Osiris, who was also drowned in the Nile. It was rumored that in an attempt to rejuvenate himself, he had persuaded Antinous to sacrifice himself, or had helped him make his mind up with a firm shove.

3. The Russian Czar Paul, who was both snub-nosed and bald, had a soldier scourged to death for referring to him as "Baldy." The Czar later has the words "snub-nosed" and "bald" banned on pain of death.

4. The Prussian Kaiser Wilhelm II wore so many medals that his chest was described as "a declaration of war," and had a fetish for military uniforms. He owned over four hundred of them and in the first seventeen years of his reign "Kaiser Bill" had his own uniform as chief commander of the Prussian armed forces redesigned thirty-seven times and had a squad of tailors in his palace on permanent standby. There were uniforms for every occasion: uniforms for attending galas, uniforms to greet every one of his regiments, uniforms with which to greet other uniforms, uniforms for eating out, even "informal" uniforms for staying in. When he attended military parades there was little danger of mistaking the Kaiser among all the other brightly uniformed Prussian automatons: he was the only one wearing a solid gold helmet. The Kaiser also liked to hand out photographs of himself to his friends, always taking care not to show his withered left arm, the result of a bungled breach-birth.

5. Saparmurat Niyazov, president "for life" of Turkmenistan (1990–2006) was omnipresent even by the standards of

cult dictatorship. Towns, mosques, factories, power plants, universities, airports, brands of aftershave, vodka, yogurt, tea, and even a meteor are named in his honor. His image also adorns the nation's stamps and currency, causing a costly recall when his dyed black hair turned permanently white after a quadruple heart bypass operation in 2001.

6. Benito Mussolini's busy sex life was an important part of the appeal of the Italian fascist movement. According to his propagandists, Il Duce thought pajamas were "effete," and always slept in his underwear. Mussolini was very careful to portray himself as a man of virile, robust health. He shaved his head so no one could see that his hair was turning gray, and although his eyesight was poor, was never seen wearing spectacles in public. Secretly he suffered from a variety of health problems, including a crippling gastric ulcer, which caused him to roll on the carpet in agony. Although Mussolini's doctors were generally reticent in their public pronouncements, Dr. Aldo Castellani, an expert in tropical diseases, revealed that Mussolini in fact suffered from intestinal worms. According to Castellani, the roundworm which eventually emerged from an unspecified orifice of Il Duce was enormous: "A real hypertrophic fascist ascaris."

7. The North Korean leader Kim Jong-il is always shown in pictures viewed from his left—propaganda management to hide a large unsightly growth on the right side of his neck. US intelligence experts "analyzed" the Dear Leader's mole and pronounced that it was a cancerous tumor. Predicting his imminent death, they forecast that North Korea would soon collapse or at least suffer mass riots.

Against all odds, Kim survived to become the subject of another rumor, this time that he had been run over by a truck and was suffering brain damage. In 1986 intelligence experts confidently announced the "assassination of Kim Il-sung," a story that occupied headlines for several days. The episode was quietly forgotten when Kim showed up to meet the Mongolian president a couple of weeks later.

8. The Romanian dictator Nicolae Ceausescu was very short, not that it was ever apparent from the photographic evidence of his time in office. Pictures of the tyrant meeting foreign dignitaries were always taken at a foreshortened angle so that he looked as tall, or even taller, than his guests. No such measures were necessary for domestic photo opportunities, however, as appointments to his government were made on the basis of height. Ceausescu insisted that his ministers had to look up to him; consequently two of his most senior ministers, Postelnicu and Bobu, were near-dwarfs. The stock photos of Ceausescu in the 1980s also showed him looking twenty years younger and wrinkle-free, the result of a great deal of retouching, with occasionally bizarre results. In 1989 he was photographed meeting the Bulgarian dictator Todor Zhivkov, who was wearing a hat. As Ceausescu was hatless in the original photo, the retouchers were required to paint in a hand holding a hat. Unfortunately they forgot to remove one of his real hands; Ceausescu appeared in the newspapers the following morning with three arms. Ceausescu was also a fussy dresser. Convinced that foreign agents were trying to poison his clothes, he had the state police make everything he wore for him—including his favorite German-style hunting outfits—under surveillance

in a specially constructed warehouse. Each garment was worn once then burned.

9. The short, misshapen Soviet leader Joseph Stalin was born with webbed toes on his left foot and was scarred by smallpox. Soviet artists and photographers were warned to favor his right profile because it bore fewer pockmarks. His height also rankled him, and he regularly wore platform heels in an effort to appear taller. Stalin chain-smoked cigarettes but liked to be seen in photographs pulling pensively on a pipe. The pipe, an important part of his image, was a prop to disguise another deformity. When he was a child he was run over by a horse and cart, and as a result of his injuries, suffered septicemia, leaving him with a permanently crooked left arm.

10. Adolf Hitler had a half brother, Alois, and a sister-in-law, Bridget, who lived in Liverpool, England. Bridget Hitler tried to cash in on her family connection by writing a book, *My Brother-in-Law Adolf,* but couldn't find a publisher. The most surprising and unprovable claim in the 225-page typescript was that Adolf spent six months with them at their home at 102 Upper Stanhope Street, beginning in November 1912. Hitler never once mentioned his visit to England, according to Bridget, because he was avoiding compulsory service in the Austrian army. The trip however had a lasting impression on the Führer. Before adopting his famous toothbrush moustache, he experimented with a variety of facial hairstyles from a "full set" to a pointed goatee; at the time of his trip to England he was sporting a large handlebar mustache. Before he took leave of his sister-in-law in May 1913, Bridget advised him to trim it. Years later, when she saw his picture in

a newspaper, she saw that he had taken her advice, but noted in her book: "Adolf had gone too far." The Führer also required reading glasses but was too vain to wear them. At his insistence, all of his memoranda were printed out in banner headlines, requiring the invention of a special "Führer typewriter," equipped with very large keys.

10 Milestones in Juvenile Bad Behavior

323 B.C.: Alexander the Great conquers most of the known world then drops dead after a marathon drinking contest, aged thirty-two.

A.D. 211: The young Roman emperor Elagabalus has a couple of palace dinner guests suffocated in rose petals for a laugh.

1544: The young Ivan "the Terrible" kills time by throwing live dogs off the Kremlin roof.

1561: King Philip II of Spain's son and heir Don Carlos has young girls whipped and animals roasted alive while he watches. Dissatisfied with a pair of new boots, he has them cut into pieces and force-fed to the cobbler. When some water is inadvertently emptied from a house balcony and splashed near him, he has the occupants executed.

1712: Peter the Great's son Alexis travels to Dresden to marry a German princess but upsets the in-laws by shitting on his bedroom carpet and wiping his backside on the curtains.

1741: The Comte de Charolais, cousin of France's King Louis XV, orders his coachman to run over any monks he encounters on the road and shoots a man he sees working on a roof, just for the hell of it. The king pardons his naughty cousin but warns "let it be understood I will similarly pardon anyone who shoots you."

1793: Russian Grand Duke Constantine, a grandson of Catherine the Great, amuses himself by kicking Hussars to death and firing live rats from a cannon.

1828: King Miguel of Portugal enjoys tossing live piglets into the air and catching them on the point of his sword.

1909: After a night out that went too far, Prince George of Serbia, eldest son and heir of King Peter I, is removed from the line of succession for kicking his valet to death.

1931: The German serial killer Peter Kurten, dubbed "the Vampire of Dusseldorf," goes on trial charged with nine murders and seven attempted murders. During his marathon confession Kurten admits that he has been enjoying sex with farmyard animals, including sheep, goats, and pigs since he was thirteen years old.

Doing One's Bit for Race Relations
12 NATIONALITIES AND ETHNIC GROUPS INSULTED BY QUEEN ELIZABETH II'S HUSBAND*

/ 1 / CHINESE

In Beijing in 1986 Prince Philip, the Duke of Edinburgh, advised a British student, "Don't stay here too long or you'll go back with slitty eyes." He later described Peking as "ghastly." Ten years earlier, on tour in Hong Kong and unaware that he was on an open microphone, he told a Chinese photographer, "Fuck off or I'll have you shot."

/ 2 / CHILEANS

At an official function in Chile, Prince Philip was introduced to Dr. Allende, soon to become the country's president, and criticized Allende's choice of clothing. (He was wearing an ordinary suit instead of the required white tie and tails.) Allende explained that his people were very poor and that as their representative it would be inappropriate of him to dress expensively. Philip replied: "And if they told you to wear a bathing costume, I suppose you'd have come dressed in one."

/ 3 / PARAGUAYANS

On a tour of South America he told General Alfredo Stroessner, the fascist dictator of Paraguay and protector of Nazi war

* Prince Philip, the Duke of Edinburgh is evenhanded. In 1966 he reminded his wife's loyal subjects, "You know, British women can't cook."

criminals, "It's a pleasant change to be in a country that isn't ruled by its people."

∫ 4 ∫ CANADIANS

On a tour of Canada Philip reminded his British Commonwealth hosts: "We don't come here for our health, you know."

∫ 5 ∫ AUSTRALIANS

While visiting an Aboriginal cultural park in Queensland, Australia, Prince Philip demanded to know, "What's it all about? Do you still throw spears at each other?"

∫ 6 ∫ DUTCH

"What a po-faced lot the Dutch are."

∫ 7 ∫ FRENCH

"Isn't it a pity Louis XVI was sent to the guillotine?"

∫ 8 ∫ PANAMANIANS

On a trip to Panama he shouted at his official police escort who had sounded a siren, "Switch that bloody thing off you silly fucker."

∫ 9 ∫ HUNGARIANS

"Most of them are pot-bellied."

∫ 1 0 ∫ SCOTS

"They drink too much." In 1995 he asked a Scottish driving instructor: "How do you keep the natives off the booze long enough to pass the test?"

∫ 1 1 ∫ KENYANS

"You are a woman, aren't you?" To a Kenyan woman, after accepting a small gift from her in 1984.

∫ 1 2 ∫ PAPUA NEW GUINEANS

"You managed not to get eaten, then?" In 1998, to a student who had been trekking in Papua, New Guinea.

10 Visitors to Buckingham Palace

1873: The Shah of Persia Nasir ud-din cut a striking figure on his trip to London with his huge, wax-tipped mustache. It was noted that throughout his stay at the palace the Shah repeatedly failed to use the royal lavatories and went wherever the spirit moved him. Eschewing the formal dinner laid out for him, he also barbecued a pig in his suite and organized a boxing match in the palace gardens. It was widely rumored that during the Shah's visit he had one of his staff executed with a bowstring and that the body was buried somewhere in the palace grounds, where it probably remains to this day.

1886: Leopold II, king of the Belgians, also known as "the Butcher of the Congo" after killing around ten million Africans.

He brought with him a gift for Queen Victoria, a pair of racing pigeons. He stayed in the palace's Belgian Suite, so-called because they were first decorated in honor of Victoria's uncle Leopold, the first King of the Belgians.

1972: Idi Amin, president of Uganda. When he came to power Britain sent out a Foreign Office minister, Lord Boyd, to congratulate him. Amin requested a signed portrait of the Queen and a royal visit as soon as possible—he assured Boyd that he had already written Her Majesty "a very nice letter." In July 1972 Amin got his wish and went to Buckingham Palace to have lunch with the Queen and her husband, the Duke of Edinburgh, whom he addressed throughout as "Mr. Philip." Affronted that he was never asked back, Amin wrote to the Queen again three years later: "I would like you to arrange for me to visit Scotland, Ireland, and Wales, to meet the heads of revolutionary movements fighting against your imperialist oppression."

1973: Joseph Mobutu, president of Zaire. A kleptocrat ranked the seventh richest man in the world when his country was among the poorest, he chartered the Concorde to pick up his groceries in Paris and Brussels, and slept with a bottle of patent medicine by his bedside for "rheumatism and syphilis." What was described in the press as "nearly a diplomatic incident" occurred when British customs officials refused to give a visa to Mobutu's pet terrier.

1978: Romanian dictator Nicolae Ceausescu and his wife Elena. Following a telephoned warning from the wife of their immediate previous host, the president of France, small valuable works of art were temporarily removed from their suite in order to prevent them from disappearing. Her Majesty was baffled by the discovery that her guests had brought with them their own bedsheets and a host of minders, including a personal food taster. She was also alarmed by Ceaucescu's habit of washing his hands every time he shook hands with anyone, a trick he repeated after shaking hands with the Queen herself. He was seen at 6:00 a.m. the following morning, walking in the palace gardens with his minders. The dictator naturally assumed that his host had bugged his room and the garden was the safest place for him to talk. Inappropriately, the Queen presented him with the gift of a rifle and telescopic sight.

1982: An unemployed Irishman Michael Fagan wandered into the grounds of Buckingham Palace unchallenged, shimmied up a drainpipe, and walked into the Queen's bedroom as she slept. When the Queen woke to find a strange man sitting on her bed, she rang two "panic buttons" to summon help, but both failed. Fagan spent half an hour chatting to the Queen, occasionally threatening to slash his wrists with a glass ashtray, until a maid intervened. He was to spend two months at a high-security mental hospital. In spite of the supposedly heightened state of alert following this incident, three months later a group of German tourists was found camping in the Queen's garden.

1985: Hastings Banda, president of Malawi. An Anglophile with a taste for three-piece Savile Row suits and homburg hats, Banda liked to boast that he fed his political opponents to the crocodiles, but he was not always to be taken literally. In 1983 three of his cabinet ministers and a member of the Malawi parliament died in a mysterious "car accident." Only several years later did it emerge that the victims had had their heads smashed in with tent-peg hammers.

1987: King Fahd of Saudi Arabia. While his security services back at home were busy flogging dissidents, during his visit to London, Fahd lost millions of dollars in casinos and circumvented the curfew imposed by British gaming laws by hiring his own blackjack and roulette dealers to continue gambling through the night in his hotel suite.

1989: President Ibrahim Babangida of Nigeria, whose idea of a good political debate was to lock up his opponents, is conferred with the Knight Grand Cross of the Bath (GCB) by the Queen.

1994: Zimbabwe's Robert Mugabe, who in his spare time tortures by electric shocks and clubbings organized by his right-hand man, Chenjerai Hunzvi (affectionately known as "Hitler") and locking up opponents for "discussing politics without a permit," is entertained at a state banquet and awarded an honorary GCB. In 2003 Britain asks for her medal back.

8 Sporting Dictators

1. According to the North Korean media, their Dear Leader Kim Jong-il is the world's best golfer ever. Although Mr. Kim came to the sport late in 1994, on his very first outing at the Pyongyang course he eagled the opening hole then went on to register five holes in one (or possibly eleven, according to some reports) on the way to shooting a 34 (or

38) under par. The previous lowest recorded score in PGA history was 59, attained only three times by Al Geiberger (1977), Chip Beck (1991), and David Duval (1999).

2. The Dominican leader Rafael Trujillo ruled as an ironfisted dictator, in control of the army and placing family members in high political office. The only thing he couldn't completely control was baseball, his country's national obsession. Trujillo decided to form his own baseball team, but there was more than sporting pride at stake. As his political opponents already owned a share in two other major teams in the Dominican League, for the dictator not to have the best baseball team in the country would have been an unacceptable loss of face. Trujillo took over two of the existing biggest rival teams and merged them to form one squad, the Ciudad Trujillo Dragons, then improved it by raiding the Negro American League for their most talented players. The climax of a tense season came when Trujillo's all-star team was forced into a dramatic seventh and deciding game of the championship series against a Cuban squad, Estrellas de Oriente. On the eve of the big game Trujillo tipped the odds in his favor by having some of the opposing team thrown in jail, then hinted to his own all-stars that their lives depended on a favorable result. When Trujillo's team entered the stadium the next day they found their employer's troops lined up with rifles and bayonets near the first-base. The Dragons took the hint, won the series, and Trujillo was comfortably reelected by his baseball-mad countrymen.

3. Idi Amin was heavyweight boxing champion of Uganda from 1951–1960. When his country was being overrun by Tanzanian troops in 1978, he suggested that he and

Tanzanian president Julius Nyerere settle the war between them in the ring with Muhammad Ali as referee. Amin once phoned the Egyptian president Anwar Sadat to tell him that he wanted to become the world's first head of state to swim across the Suez Canal. He also organized basketball games in which he alone was allowed to score: he had a palace guard killed for blocking his shot.

4. Chairman Mao was a swimming fanatic who he liked to be filmed taking the plunge in the heavily polluted rivers of southern China, despite the best advice of his guards and doctors, breast-stroking his way through chunks of gently bobbing human ordure. When rumors of Mao's declining health began to circulate in the 1970s, the Chinese Communist Party published clumsily doctored photographs showing Mao's disembodied head bobbing on the waves, purporting to show him swimming in the ocean. Mao's oceanic dips were always strictly for propaganda purposes however: the Great Helmsman had heated swimming pools built into every one of his fifty-five homes. In 1971 Mao allowed a team to go to Japan to compete in the World Table Tennis Championships, the first Chinese sportsmen to be allowed to travel abroad since the Cultural Revolution. They were given precise instructions on how to behave: They were not to fraternize with Americans, nor shake their hands. To give them an even chance of winning, however, Mao personally excused them from having to brandish his Little Red Book during actual play.

5. The Italian fascist leader Benito Mussolini claimed he had the biggest thighs in Italy. He liked to show off by jogging down the lines when he was reviewing his troops,

and enjoyed humiliating out of shape visitors by making them run up to his desk and then run out again on the double, before saluting him from the door. He was also an enthusiastic but poor tennis player, which presented certain problems for his opponents. The Italian foreign minister Count Galeazzo Ciano noted that it took more skill and stamina to lose to Il Duce than it did to defeat most men.

6. The Romanian dictator Nicolae Ceausescu loved hunting but was a poor shot and nearly always bagged less than anyone else in his shooting party. To compensate, his aides brought supplies of dead game and hung it outside his hunting lodge. Ceausescu mostly enjoyed shooting bears. Teams of forest rangers would spend hours preparing an area for a bear hunt, tying down half of a dead horse near a watering hole. When a large, hungry bear arrived on the scene, the rangers would notify their president. Ceausescu would arrive by helicopter and depart with a bearskin a couple of hours later.

7. During a soccer match in Tripoli in 1997, a team sponsored by Libyan president Muammar Gaddafi's son Al Saadi was at the receiving end of a questionable refereeing decision, and sparked a mass brawl between players. When fans jeered, Gaddafi's bodyguards opened fire on them. Some spectators returned fire, resulting in a death toll by some estimates as high as fifty. Gaddafi declared a period of mourning, during which time all TV broadcasts had to be transmitted in black and white only. The gesture went largely unnoticed as no one in Libya owned a color TV.

8. Saddam Hussein appointed his son Uday as head of both Iraq's Olympic committee and the Iraqi soccer federation,

an inspired choice designed to give his nation's top athletes an extra incentive to do well—underperformance was rewarded with beatings with iron bars or canings on the soles of feet, followed by dunkings in raw sewage to ensure the wounds became infected. Motivational soccer team talks included threats to cut off players' legs and throw them to ravenous dogs. A missed training session was punishable by imprisonment. A loss or a draw brought flogging with electric cable, or a bath in raw sewage. A penalty miss carried the certainty of imprisonment and torture. During a World Cup qualifying match in Jordan, Iraq played the United Arab Emirates to a 3–3 draw, calling for a penalty shootout, which Iraq lost. Two days after the team returned to Baghdad their captain was summoned to Uday's headquarters, then blindfolded and taken away to a prison camp for three weeks. A red card penalty was particularly dangerous. Yasser Abdul Latif, accused of thumping the referee during a heated club match in Baghdad, was confined to a prison cell two meters square, where he was stripped to the waist, then ordered to perform push-ups for two hours while guards flogged him with lengths of electric cable. When Iraq lost 4–1 to Japan in the Asian Cup, goalkeeper Hashim Hassan, defender Abdul Jaber and striker Qahtan Chither were fingered as the main culprits and were whipped for three days by Uday's bodyguards. When Iraq failed to reach the 1994 World Cup finals, Uday recalled the squad for extra training—with a concrete football. (Saddam himself was a keen fisherman, but with little time for the subtleties of angling; he preferred to lob hand grenades into the water then have a diver pick up the dead fish.)

Stand by Your Mao
10 FIRST LADIES

1. Messalina, the third wife of Roman Emperor Claudius, claimed an all-time record for marital infidelity when she slept with twenty-five men in twenty-four hours for a bet. When news of Messalina's strumpetry was revealed to Claudius he had her executed, and then promptly forgot about it: he went to dinner and asked one of the guests, "Anyone seen my wife?"

2. Eva Braun, wife of Adolf Hitler, eventually married her boyfriend fifteen years after they first met, then celebrated by swallowing poison the following day; the Führer took his own life two minutes later. Generally regarded as not the brightest of dictator's consorts, Eva dreamed of a postwar career as a film actress. The part she wanted to play was Hitler's lover in a big Hollywood movie. After Germany conquered the United States, that is.

3. Eva, wife of Juan Perón, president of Argentina from 1946–1955 and 1973–74, was said to have kept a glass jar on her desk containing the pickled genitals of her husband's political enemies.

4. Imelda, wife of Ferdinand Marcos, president of the Philippines from 1965–86, was a former beauty queen (Miss Manila 1958) and so high maintenance that according to one US senator, she "made Marie Antoinette look like a bag lady." In addition to the three thousand pairs of shoes that the Philippine government eventually confiscated from Imelda, including a pair of battery-powered sling-backs that twinkled when she danced and

the pair of canvas espadrilles she was wearing at the time
she had to flee from the palace to escape a revolt, they also
took away her only bulletproof bra. When she and her
husband fled the Philippines for exile in 1986 they also left
behind a house on the palace grounds with every room
crammed to the ceiling with boxes of Heinz Sandwich
Spread.

5. Female news presenters on Romanian TV were not
    allowed to wear jewelery in case they appeared more
    glamorous than their First Lady Elena, wife of Nicolae
    Ceausescu. She once ordered a TV blackout after 10:00
    p.m. so that the workers of Romania could wake up early
    in the morning, fresh to start a new day's work in order to
    complete the president's five-year plan. Elena employed
    her husband's secret police to film the sexual liaisons of
    foreign diplomats and used the tapes for blackmail. She
    abandoned the practice when her daughter Zoia showed
    up on one of the tapes.

6. The Ugandan dictator Idi Amin was a persistent suitor.
    He married four times, after murdering then consigning
    to his fridge the partners of women he liked the look of.
    He met Sarah Kyolaba Amin, known as Suicide Sarah, in
    1974 when she was serving as a teenage go-go dancer with
    his army's Revolutionary Suicide Mechanized Regiment
    Band; the head of her then fiancé Jesse Gitta became one
    of many stored in the refrigerator of Amin's "Botanical
    Room." Sarah left Amin in 1982 and sought political
    asylum in Germany, where she spent time as a lingerie
    model, then moved to London, running a café serving
    African dishes including goat stew and cow hoof in gravy.
    In 1999 environmental health officers closed her down

when they found a "gray furry thing" in her kitchen. It was later identified as a decomposing mouse.

7. While her husband was killing off 95 percent of the male population of Paraguay by waging a pointless war of attrition against his neighbors, Eliza Lynch, wife of the Paraguayan dictator Francisco López, bled the country dry in her quest for fairytale palaces and marble baths. While Paraguay's demoralized, ill-equipped soldiers bled or starved to death, she tried to raise morale by touring the army camps in a coach, followed by several carriage-loads of her luggage, including her wardrobe of gowns and a grand piano. She once turned up in the middle of a battlefield dressed in white crinolines.

8. President Joseph Mobutu of Zaire slept with a bottle of patent medicine by his bedside for "rheumatism and syphilis." He also slept with the wives of his government ministers and officials, both to humiliate his underlings and "to keep an eye on things." After the death of his first wife, Marie Antoinette, Mobutu married his mistress, Boby, with whom he already had several children, then took her identical twin sister, Kossia, as his new mistress. No one could tell them apart, except possibly Mobutu. He said he kept twins as lovers to ward off malignant influences from his first wife's spirit.

9. Nigeria's military dictator Sani Abacha enjoyed hanging his critics while videotaping the executions for his personal viewing pleasure, and stole more than $4 billion during his five-year reign. Abacha died of a heart attack in 1998, aged fifty-four, during a Viagra-fueled romp with two, or possibly three, Indian prostitutes. A few weeks after his death police at Kano Airport became suspicious

when his widow, Maryam, tried to leave the country with thirty-eight pieces of luggage. Each was found to be stuffed with US dollars. Mrs. Abacha explained she was not stealing the money, just "putting away the funds in some foreign accounts for safe keeping."

10. Madame Mao, the fourth bride of Chairman Mao Zedong, was highly paranoid and terrified of sudden, loud noises. Her staff was warned to speak softly and never to cough, sneeze, or wear shoes around her, and had to walk with their legs apart to prevent their clothes from rustling. She was also extremely vain and thought she could retain her looks and youthful vigor by regular blood transfusions from young "volunteers" selected from her husband's Praetorian Guards. Despite her best efforts, Madame Mao could not hold back time. One night she was in need of a bathroom and attempted to squat on a spittoon, having mistaken it for a commode. She fell off, breaking her collarbone. She later insisted that the embarrassing incident had been part of an assassination plot.

10 Spectacular Sadists

⎰1⎰ ROMAN EMPEROR TIBERIUS (42 B.C.–A.D. 37)

He was such a well-respected torturer that many of his prisoners committed suicide as soon as they were accused, rather than bother to wait for the trial. Bored with the array of techniques in fashion at the time, he invented a few of his own; one favorite was to force the victim to drink vast quantities of wine until the bladder was at maximum pressure, then tie up his genitalia with a lute string.

/2/ ROMAN EMPEROR DOMITIAN (A.D. 51–96)

Infamous for murdering thousands of Christians, he extracted confessions from his enemies by holding a blazing torch under their genitals. Courtiers guilty of even the mildest of criticism were crucified upside down. His inevitable assassination in A.D. 96 was almost a carbon copy of the death of one of his predecessors, Emperor Caligula—he was stabbed in the genitals.

/3/ GENGHIS KHAN (1162–1227)

His conquests were marked by acts of breathtaking cruelty: he once stormed a town called Termez and slaughtered all of the inhabitants. One old woman was about to be killed but she begged for mercy in return for a pearl, which she said she had swallowed for safekeeping. The old woman was promptly disemboweled and several pearls were discovered inside her. Khan heard about it and ordered that all of the dead should be opened up and their stomachs inspected. He was not, however, entirely without compassion: he once decided that a defeated foe, who turned out to be an old childhood friend, should be spared the expected bloody execution; he had him rolled in a carpet and kicked to death instead.

/4/ TAMERLANE (1336–1405)

A descendant of Genghis Khan, considered the most violent of all the Mongol leaders. He celebrated his conquest of Sabzawar in 1383 by having two thousand prisoners buried alive and he had five thousand people beheaded at Zirih, using their heads to build a pyramid. In India he massacred about one hundred thousand prisoners and had thousands of Christians buried alive. Tamerlane was not known for his sense of humor: he had anyone who told a joke put to death.

/ 5 / VLAD III "THE IMPALER" (1431–76)

The historical Count Dracula and ruler of Wallachia, now part of Romania, had about twenty thousand of his enemies impaled on wooden stakes and often drank the blood of his victims. He forced wives to eat the cooked flesh of their husbands, and parents to eat their own children. When a large troop of Tartars strayed into his territory he selected three of them, had them fried, and force-fed to the others. When Turkish envoys arrived at his palace to sue for peace, he had their hats and coats nailed to their bodies.

/ 6 / CZAR IVAN IV "THE TERRIBLE" (1530–84)

In a bad mood aggravated by tertiary syphilis, Ivan rampaged through his homeland, slaughtering thousands of peasants. It earned him the epithet *Grozny*, mistranslated as "the Terrible," but which in Russian merely means "the Awesome." Given to bouts of random and spectacular brutality and tearing clumps of his hair out until his scalp bled, Ivan also specialized in ingenious deaths for his enemies. When the archbishop of Novgorod was suspected of organizing an uprising against him, Ivan had the entire population, about fifty thousand people, massacred by tossing them in a freezing river, then had the archbishop sewn into bearskin and hunted to death by a pack of hounds. When he conquered Wittenstein he had the defeated Finnish leader roasted alive on a spit. On his deathbed Ivan repented and became a monk.

∫ 7 ∫ SULTAN MAHOMET III (1566–1603)

To eliminate the threat of sibling rivalry when he came to the throne the Ottoman leader murdered his nineteen brothers, all of them under age eleven, then almost clogged up the river Bosphorus with the bodies of his father's pregnant mistresses. In his spare time he enjoyed watching women's breasts being scorched off with hot irons.

∫ 8 ∫ FAUSTIN SOULOUQUE (1782–1867)

A nineteenth-century Haitian dictator, the self-styled Emperor Faustin I took part in cannibalistic rites, drinking the blood of his late rivals and keeping their skulls on his desk to use as drinking cups. Faustin once had a suspected enemy arrested and shackled to a dungeon wall. Later a report came to Faustin that the man's legs were turning gangrenous from the pressure of his irons. Faustin sent word back: "Tell him not to worry. When his legs drop off I'll chain him by the neck."

∫ 9 ∫ RAFAEL TRUJILLO (1891–1961)

The Dominican Republic's longest-serving president was a torturer par excellence in whose name a variety of methods were employed, including slow-shocking electric chairs, an electrified rod known as "the cane"—especially effective on genitals—nail extractors, whips, tanks of bloodsucking leaches, and "the octopus," a multi-armed electrical appliance strapped to the head. Trujillo's most respected torturer was a dwarf known as "Snowball" who specialized in biting off men's genitals.

SADDAM HUSSEIN (1937–2006)

The president of Iraq's chastisements followed a clearly defined scale of barbarity. Deserters had an ear cut off; thieves
had fingers or hands cut off, depending on the source and
value of stolen goods. Liars had their backs broken; offend-
ers were tied facedown on a wooden plank between two cement blocks and another block was dropped on the victim's
spine. Informants who supplied the state police with tips that
proved false had a piece of red-hot iron placed on their tongues.
Homosexuals were often bound then pushed off the roof of
a building. Traitors, spies, smugglers, and, occasionally, prostitutes paid the ultimate price: beheading with a five-foot broad-
sword known as al-Bashar. Saddam also executed underlings
himself by shooting them on the spot, sometimes by giving his
gun to someone else and ordering them to shoot, thereby making them his accomplices.

12 Megalomaniacs

1. François "Papa Doc" Duvalier, president of Haiti (1957–71),
    liked to terrorize his people by posing as the incarnation of
    a malevolent voodoo deity called Baron Samedi, guardian
    of the graveyard, but liked to keep all bases covered
    by comparing himself to Jesus Christ. His best-known
    propaganda image showed a picture of Papa Doc sitting
    down with Christ standing behind him, his right hand
    on the president's shoulder; it bore the caption, "I have
    chosen him." A flashing neon sign outside the presidential
    palace meanwhile proclaimed: "I am the Haitian flag: I am

indivisible." Later he had the Lord's Prayer rewritten for use in Haitian schools: "Our Doc, who art in the National Palace for life, hallowed be Thy name by present and future generations. Thy will be done in Port-au-Prince as it is in the provinces. Give us this day our new Haiti, and forgive not the trespasses of those antipatriots who daily spit upon our country . . ."

2. In 2007 Yahya Jammeh, president of Gambia, disclosed that he was personally able to cure HIV, AIDS, and asthma via a combination of charms, charisma, and magic. The president promised that the "cure" takes about three days, after which, "I can tell you that he/she will be negative." Jammeh did not disclose what the treatment involved exactly, other than that patients are not allowed to eat seafood or peppers, but advises that "they should be kept at a place that has adequate toilet facilities because they can be going to the toilet every five minutes." Official Gambian news sources reported that the president's astonishing curative resources had left medical staff "mesmerized and stunned." Gambian bloggers report the treatments leaving patients vomiting and in agony.

3. Macias Nguema, president for life of Equatorial Guinea (1968–79) underwent several confusing changes of title and by the end of his rule was known as Unique Miracle and Grand Master of Education, Science and Culture. Nguema was prone to making rash pronouncements while under the influence of marijuana and iboga, a traditional hallucinogen with effects similar to LSD. In one speech he claimed that Adolf Hitler "was the savior of Africa," and ordered workers at the power plant of Malabo, the capital city, to stop using lubricating oil; he promised he would

keep the machinery going with magic. The plant exploded, plunging the capital permanently into darkness. In 1974 Nguema ordered Catholic priests in Equatorial Guinea to hang his portrait on the church altar, above the message: "Only and unceasing miracle of Equatorial Guinea. God created Equatorial Guinea thanks to Macias. Without Macias, Equatorial Guinea would not exist." A priest who refused to cooperate was later found frozen to death in a refrigeration truck.

4. The Philippines' President Ferdinand Marcos liked to portray himself as the living personification of the best qualities of Napoleon and Julius Caesar. While his wife Imelda was busy shopping for shoes, however, Ferdinand's vanity was of the more monumental variety. He had his face carved into a mountainside, à la Mount Rushmore.

5. Mao Zedong, the totalitarian ruler of one quarter of the world's population, considered getting rid of people's names and replacing them with numbers. Chairman Mao (or "No.1" as he could have been known had things turned out differently) thought it would make China's 550 million peasants more obedient workers. More than 90 percent of the Chinese people wore Chairman Mao badges, each embossed with the Great Helmsman's image; estimates of the total number produced range between 2.5 billion and 5 billion. Most carried the left profile of Mao's head, some showed full frontal views of his head or his body from the waist up, and on rare occasions his whole body. In deference to the prevailing political mood, badges featuring Mao's right profile were taboo. Each badge had a safety pin with which it could be affixed to clothing, or, for the more zealous, directly through the skin.

6. Maximiliano Hernández Martínez, president of El Salvador (1931–1944) was known as *El Brujo*—the wizard—thanks to his habit of making decisions in consultation with occult powers rather than his cabinet. He held séances in the presidential palace, during which it was revealed to him that there are an additional five human senses—hunger, thirst, procreation, urination, and bowel movements. Martinez also believed that color had magical healing qualities: He once tried to cure a smallpox epidemic by covering all of the streetlights with red cellophane.

7. The Romanian dictator Nicolae Ceausescu (1974–89) bulldozed the center of Bucharest, sweeping aside historic boulevards to straighten the streets so that the sights of his machine guns could get a clear line of fire at the approaches to his new residence, The People's Palace—a one-thousand-room eyesore incorporating the work of around seven hundred interior designers, second in size only to the Pentagon and featuring a marble-lined nuclear bunker. During construction of the palace the designers ran out of gold for the door handles and used so much marble that they had to invent a synthetic substitute. The palace required the destruction of dozens of historic buildings, forcing about forty thousand people to give up their homes in exchange for small apartments in grim, concrete tower blocks where bugging devices were standard, but heating and drainage was not. In 1978 Ceausescu planned a welcome speech to new students of Bucharest's polytechnic. His chosen venue was the local park, but he was annoyed to find that where open parkland had once lain, a huge hole had been excavated to make way for Bucharest's new underground station. He

ordered the hole to be "removed" until after his speech. Throughout the night, hundreds of laborers toiled to fill in the hole, covering it with grass and trees uprooted from other parts of the city.

8. Idi Amin, military dictator of Uganda (full title: Lord Of All The Beasts Of The Earth And Fishes Of The Sea And Conqueror Of The British Empire In Africa In General And Uganda In Particular) patented the word "president" and banned anyone else in Uganda, including heads of companies, unions, and other organizations, from using the title. Fickle in international relations, Amin was once allied to Israel, a country that awarded him the wings of a parachute commando, which "Big Daddy" wore with pride on his military uniform. Amin, however, soon shifted his allegiance to Libya and Palestine, claiming that Israelis had deliberately poisoned the waters of the Nile and were planning to invade Uganda and declare it a Zionist state. In 1972 he rang Jordan's King Hussein, his cabinet, and military commanders in the middle of the night to tell them he had a plan to conquer Israel. His enemies were puzzled when, a year later, he was shown still sporting his coveted Israeli paratrooper wings in his likeness on Uganda's new banknotes.

9. Saddam Hussein's official title was "His Excellency, President Saddam Hussein, Servant of God, Believer, Leader of All Muslims," but he was also variously known as Great Uncle, Anointed One, Glorious Leader, Direct Descendant of the Prophet, and, courtesy of George W. Bush, "the World's Most Evil Man." To celebrate his "victory" in the first Gulf War—"the Mother of All Battles"—he commissioned a court calligrapher to

reproduce a copy of Islam's holy book, the Koran, written entirely with Saddam's blood. The book is 605 pages long and took three years and fifty pints of blood, donated one pint at a time. The Iraqi people were looked down upon by thousands of giant portraits of Saddam striking various poses: in the countryside he was depicted as a farmer, in the factory as a laborer, and in the barracks he wore military fatigues. Baath party commissars, however, faced a dilemma over how to portray their leader in Baghdad's newly opened showpiece gynecology clinic.

10. The North Korean president Kim Il-sung had around seventy bronze statues and over twenty thouand plaster busts made in his image and the entire population of North Korea was also compelled to wear lapel badges bearing the face of their Eternal Leader. He also had every road in the country built with an extra lane for his sole private use. According to his propagandists, over a period of fifteen years he participated in more than one hundred thousand battles against the Japanese in the 1930s, an unlikely average of over twenty battles a day. The biggest box-office hit in North Korea is *Sea of Blood,* a "war musical" depicting Kim Il-sung, with some artistic license, as a heroic guerrilla leader owed most of the credit for the victories over Japan. It also has a hit song, "My Heart Will Remain Faithful." The long deceased Kim Il-sung now holds the post of "Eternal Leader," which is but one of his many accomplishments. He once turned sand into rice and could cross rivers on a leaflet.

11. North Korea's Dear Leader Kim Jong-il enjoys a personality cult beyond his late father's wildest dreams, lauded as an all-around great soldier, peerless filmmaker,

movie critic, philosopher, scientist, and "brilliant and industrious scholar imbued with great wisdom." Kim's birth was allegedly foretold by a swallow from heaven and attended by a bright star and double rainbows. According to Pyongyang media reports Kim has learned how to "expand space and shrink time"—a rare gift in a man who is afraid to board a plane. From 1992–94 the North Korean authorities published over three hundred poems and over four hundred hymns in praise of their Dear Leader Kim Jong-il. Many paid tribute to Kim's skills as a cutting-edge gardener. He is said to have grown and nurtured a new flower, a hybrid orchid called Kimjongilia. According to the North Korean press, on Kim's birthday Kimjongilia has been known to miraculously bloom in the dead of winter. Both Kims are said to be descended from Tangun, a divine "bear-man" who founded their country more than five thousand years ago.

12. Although he has been dead for several years, Saparmurat Niyazov, the king of post-Soviet bling and former president of Turkmenistan (1990–2006) known to his countrymen as Turkmenbashi—Father of all the Turkmen—is omnipresent even by the standards of cult dictatorship. Towns, mosques, factories, power plants, universities, airports, brands of aftershave, vodka, yogurt, tea, and even a meteor are named in his honor. Among the hundreds of monuments to Turkmenbashi, most conspicuous is a 120-foot golden statue in the capital, Ashgabat, erected on a motorized plinth. The monument rotates a full 360 degrees every twenty-four hours, so that the president's arm always points to the sun. Every town in Turkmenistan has a Turkmenbashi Street; confusingly, Ashgabat has

several. Niyazov was obsessed with his deceased mother Gurbansoltan, who was killed by an earthquake in 1948 when he was eight. He officially renamed the month of April and the word for "bread" after her.

10 Autocrats

1. Adolf Hitler never learned to drive, but he was the driving force behind the development of Professor Ferdinand Porsche's KdF-wagen—the "Strength Through Joy" car, or Volkswagen Beetle as it came to be known. He sketched the original Beetle design on a napkin at a restaurant table in Munich in 1932. Adolf preferred to be driven along his new autobahn in a big, powerful, bombproof Mercedes-Benz. His preference was for eight-cylinder, open-topped models, such as the six-wheeled Mercedes G-4. Hitler was so proud of his country's automobile industry that in 1939, when Nazi Germany and the Soviet Union signed their pact of nonaggression, he gave a supercharged sports Mercedes roadster to his good friend, Joe Stalin.

2. The Soviet Union's home-grown ZIS—Zavod Imeni Stalina—was originally named after Stalin, but later renamed ZIL. Stalin's personal favorite, a special 1949 ZIS eight-cylinder limousine, was a twenty-foot-long, seven-ton behemoth with three-inch thick bulletproof glass. It did about 4 mph on a good run.

3. Stalin once presented Chairman Mao with five ZIS bulletproof stretch limousines with art deco–style red flags on their crest. Mao was so impressed that he commissioned a homemade, ten-meter-long, luxury

six-door stretch "Red Flag" limousine, complete with fridge, telephone, TV, double bed, desk, and sofa. He died in 1976 before he could use what would become the first, and last, limo produced by China's First Automobile Works.

4. Vladimir Ilyich Lenin, the father of the Russian revolution, liked to travel in style, and owned nine Rolls-Royces. One, a Silver Ghost open tourer, is exhibited at the Lenin Museum in Moscow. His was not the first Rolls-Royce in Russia; Czar Nicholas II had two Silver Ghosts, Joseph Stalin also had a Roller, as did Leonid Brezhnev, as part of his extensive car collection.

5. The Haitian dictator "Papa Doc" Duvalier traveled in a Mercedes 600, throwing wads of banknotes out of the window as he went. The Mercedes stretch limo is so popular among African despots (President Mobutu of Zaire owned fifty-one of them) that the political elite are known in Swahili as *wabenzi*—"men of Mercedes-Benz."

6. Among the revolutionary memorabilia on view in a museum in Tripoli, Libya, pride of place goes to a turquoise Volkswagen Beetle, circa 1967, registration number 23398 LB: the car that Colonel Gaddafi used while plotting his coup against the Libyan ruler King Idris in 1979. In 1991 Gaddafi announced that he had invented the world's safest vehicle, a revolutionary "Rocket car" featuring all-around air bags, an inbuilt electronic defense system, and a collapsible front bumper to protect passengers in head-on collisions. A Libyan government official described the car as proof that Gaddafi was "thinking of ways to preserve human life all over the world," and predicted that Libya would turn out fifty

thousand cars a year. Nothing more was ever heard of mass production of the "Rocket."

7. In 1948 the Paraguayan dictator Alfredo Stroessner found himself on the wrong side of a failed coup attempt and was forced to escape to the Brazilian embassy hidden in the trunk of a car. The experience earned him an embarrassing nickname: "Colonel Trunk."

8. Before being shot, kicked, spat upon, and hanged upside down from a lamppost on meat hooks, the Italian fascist Benito Mussolini had a soft spot for Alfa Romeos. Il Duce's favorite sports car, a 1937 Alfa Romeo 2300 MM, was once raced in the notorious Mille Miglia by Mussolini's own racing team, led by his personal chauffeur Ercole Boratto.

9. Because of his anti-Soviet stance, the Romanian leader Nicolae Ceausescu was courted by the West and regularly showered with gifts by visiting dignitaries, including such cars as a '74 Hillman from the Shah of Iran and a customized '71 Volkswagen from the West German chancellor, complete with gun-port facilities. In 1974 President Nixon gifted him with a Buick Electra 225, equipped with air conditioning and leather upholstery. The car did less than 6 mpg, but fuel consumption isn't a problem when you're a dictator.

10. The extent of Saddam Hussein's car pool is not known but is conservatively estimated at sixty luxury vehicles, ranging from London taxis to Rolls Royce Silver Shadows. Most were destroyed by war or Iraqi looters.

CHAPTER EIGHT

AD NAUSEUM

12 Golden Showers

1. Rock and roll's most celebrated three pints of urine, released against a garage wall on March 18, 1965, cast the Rolling Stones as Britain's public enemy No. 1. The notorious leak took place at a service station in Stratford, East London, after a garage attendant refused them admission to the toilets. Mick Jagger explained, "We piss anywhere, man." Jagger, Bill Wyman, and Brian Jones, described in court as "shaggy-haired monsters," were charged with insulting behavior and fined £5 each.

2. According to the *National Enquirer,* the actor Jack Nicholson routinely asks male guests at his Hollywood Hills home to urinate freely in his garden because it helps keep wild raccoons away.

3. Madonna once confided to the TV talk show host David Letterman that she urinates on her feet to help cure her athlete's foot problem.

4. When nature called the Spanish soccer player David Villabona during a game between his club Bilbao and Cadiz, he decided he couldn't make it to halftime and discreetly urinated behind a goalpost. Unfortunately he wasn't discreet enough to escape the attention of a crowd of twenty thousand and a local photographer who splashed a picture of the leaking Spaniard all over Spanish newspapers. Villabona was fined £2,000.

5. The first space flights were so brief that astronauts could usually wait until they had returned to Earth before having to pee. In 1961, however, Gus Grissom, anticipating a possible bathroom emergency, asked NASA

to find a solution before his next mission. NASA's answer was an off-the-rack ready-made absorbent undergarment. Consequently on July 21, 1961, Grissom became the first man in space wearing a woman's panty girdle.

6. On February 28, 1983, at precisely 11:03 p.m., water usage in New York City rose by an unprecedented three hundred million gallons. It coincided with the ending of the final episode of *M*A*S*H,* as an estimated one million New Yorkers flushed their toilets in unison.

7. The Ethiopian Emperor Haile Selassie employed a man whose job it was to attend official functions and keep an eye on the Emperor's dog, which was in the habit of pissing on the shoes of visiting dignitaries. Whenever this happened, the servant was on hand to wipe off the urine with a satin cloth.

8. Paul Burrell, former butler to Princess Diana, published his memoirs in 2002. He revealed that during a hospital visit one day, Prince Charles was asked for a urine sample. Charles complied and had his valet hold the specimen bottle while he peed.

9. The comic actor W. C. Fields once spent several days of serious drinking in a hotel in Mexico during production of a film he was starring in. One morning W. C. was rudely awakened by a loud brass band. Still inebriated, he staggered onto the balcony outside his hotel room and relieved himself over the rail. In the square directly below stood a Mexican politician in full dress army uniform about to launch into a speech. W. C. was thrown out of the country.

10. Howard Hughes's pathological fear of germs obliged him to spend the last years of his life clad in Kleenex tissues.

He also had an obsession about his own urine, which he had sealed in glass jars, numbered, dated, and cataloged. He employed an assistant whose sole responsibility was to count and watch over them.

11. In 1956 Elvis Presley appeared on the *Steve Allen Show* wearing a tuxedo, singing "Hound Dog" to a basset hound sitting on a stool. The show went well until the basset hound started peeing all over the studio floor.

12. When Andy Warhol finally got to meet his idol Salvador Dali, he gave him a gift, one of his famous Marilyn Monroe screen prints. Dali promptly whipped out his penis and pissed all over it.

16 Jobs Badly in Need of a Union

1. In eighteenth-century London, long before the invention of public restrooms, it was possible to make an honest living from ownership of a long cloak and a bucket. You simply walked the streets until you found a desperate client, then for an agreed fee wrapped the cloak around him and looked the other way while your client relieved himself.

2. British monarchs employed "purple makers," whose job it was to create the purple dye for coronation robes. The only way to make it was by jumping up and down on rotting shellfish, which had been soaked in human urine.

3. In the nineteenth century, alcoholism was reckoned to be more commonplace among English gravediggers than in any other occupation. Churchyards were in a terrible state, overcrowded and clogged up with bones and rotting

corpses. Gravediggers found their work so difficult that most felt it necessary to get blind drunk before they could do their job.

4. Tormented by the prospect of something deadly being slipped into their meals, royals used "disposable staff," usually slaves, to sample their food. King Henry VIII was famed for never being far from his royal food taster. In France the job was known by the title Officer of the Goblet. The Japanese Emperor Hirohito had a food-poisoning phobia and so every scrap of his food had to be first laboratory tested by scientists for signs of contamination, then served on sterilized plates. Even the royal feces and urine had to be chemically analyzed afterward.

5. Jack Black was Queen Victoria's longest serving Royal Rat and Mole Destroyer. Although he was nearly killed three times by rats and once found that a rat had bitten clean through a bone in his finger, snapping it in two, Black didn't mind because he got to eat as many rats as he could take home with him. Rats, he said, were "moist as rabbits and twice as nice."

6. The collection of dog feces was once a lucrative business. "Pure Finders" sold the dung to tanners, who rubbed it into animal skins to help "purify" them. Not surprisingly, the tanners were nearly as far down on the social scale as their suppliers. According to experts the very best tanning dung was the imported Turkish variety.

7. The position of poet laureate to Queen Victoria was worse paid than that of the royal rat-catcher.

8. When the Russian Empress Catherine the Great found out that she was suffering from dandruff, she had her

hairdresser locked in an iron cage for three years to prevent him from telling anyone else about it.

9. In 1911 the Japanese Emperor was delayed for twenty minutes when his train jumped the rails. A station master accepted responsibility and disemboweled himself.

10. In seventeenth-century England, human ordure was known as "gong": professional cesspit emptiers were called "gongfarmers."

11. When one of Louis XI's courtiers drew attention to the fact that the king had a flea on his lace collar and removed it for him, the king rewarded him with gold. When another of his courtiers tried to ingratiate himself by repeating the same trick the following day, Louis had him flogged.

12. Anne Boleyn, the second wife of King Henry VIII, was in the habit throwing up between courses. She employed a "royal vomit collector"—a lady-in-waiting whose job was to hold a bowl and catch the royal spew whenever the Queen looked like she was about to retch.

13. King Henry II of England kept a court jester named Roland who was required to fart for the amusement of his guests at the annual Christmas Day banquet.

14. Patent screw manufacturers Nettlefold and Chamberlain, the firm behind British Prime Minister Neville Chamberlain's personal fortune, pioneered an unorthodox approach to health and safety regulations in the 1930s. None of the company's dangerous factory machinery was fitted with safety guards, and serious injuries occurred often. Noting that the cries of wounded workers tended to distract other employees from their jobs, the management slapped a big fine on anyone who screamed when injured.

15. Before Austria's Emperor Franz Josef climbed into his lederhosen (leather shorts), his valet had to wear them first to break them in. More recently, Charles, the Prince of Wales, still employs a man to apply paste to his Royal Highness's toothbrush.

16. From 1956 to 1963 between one quarter and half a million US military personnel were deliberately exposed to radiation from atomic test bombs, mostly without any form of protective clothing or equipment, so that could experience fallout "for troop training purposes." The US air force brigadier general A. R. Luedecke once complained that his men weren't allowed to stand close enough to the blast.

12 Ingenious Uses for Ordure

1. The seventeenth-century beautician Hannah Wolley wrote several books offering tips on household management, cosmetics, and cookery. In *The Accomplish't Lady's Delight in Preserving, Physick, Beautifying & Cookery,* she recommends hare dung as a remedy for sagging breasts and washing hair with goat dung to make it grow thicker.

2. Some of the most sought after varieties of Virginian tobacco acquired their distinctive flavor by being left to cure in lavatories to absorb the fumes of human ordure and urine.

3. Class-conscious German farmers traditionally stacked piles of feces, animal and human, in front of their farms and dwellings. The size of the pile was a status symbol, their way of showing off to the neighbors that they had loads of livestock and could afford a big family.

4. In A.D. 100, the ancient Germanic tribe, the Teutons, would punish anyone caught as a prostitute by suffocating them in excrement.

5. Bedouin tribesmen recommend fresh, warm camel feces as a cure for dysentery. Camel shit was similarly used by German soldiers in Africa during World War II.

6. Dried white dog turds and pigeon droppings were stocked by the druggists of the 1600s and were used to "draw the humors out." Pleurisy was cured by a drink made from stallion manure.

7. Human feces, in a dried powdered form called *poudrette*, was sniffed like snuff by ladies of the eighteenth-century French court.

8. Cakes of animal excrement, especially pig manure, which contains ammonia, were commonly used in some parts of Britain as an alternative to soap, right up until World War II. Women became so immune to the stench of dung on wash days that when soap became popular they often complained that the suds made them nauseous.

9. An edition of *Lamery's Dictionnaire Universelle des Drogues*, published in 1759, contains a list of remedies under the heading "Homo." The book recommends the drinking of two or three glasses of urine each morning to cure gout, to relieve obstructions of the bowels, and to dispel hysterical vapors. It also prescribes human dung, eaten after it is dried out, as a cure for epilepsy. It adds that dung can also be eaten fresh as a cure for quinsies or anthrax.

10. An Alabama mail-order company once sold paperweights made from fossilized animal droppings, marketed as Endangered Feces. Each of the sixty-five-million-year-old, four-ounce turds came with a signed and numbered

certificate of authenticity and cost $25 apiece, packaged with a logo depicting a brontosaurus with a turd under its tail. The company motto was, "if you package it right, you can sell shit." In 2003, a Japanese businessman Koji Fujii began selling "lucky charms" made from three-inch gold-plated lumps of human excrement, many with funny faces painted on them. His inspiration was the realization that the words for "luck" (koun) and "poo" (unko) are similar in Japanese. Fujii said that his countrymen would be happy to receive a "little piece of poo" as a gift. "People like products that are humorous and look nice." More than two million charms have been sold to date.

11. A salad, fashionable in eighteenth-century Britain, consisted of horse dung with mustard and watercress.

12. In 2009, sixty-six-year-old James Orr, on trial in Cincinnati, Ohio, for aggravated robbery and kidnapping, complained to his defense team that he hadn't eaten and was hungry. When his lawyer ignored him, Orr pulled out his colostomy bag, emptied the contents out on the table, and began eating them. Prosecuting attorney David Prem said Orr was not insane; he was just trying to avoid a possible sixty-year sentence. The courtroom was closed off and declared a biohazard area by Judge Ethna Cooper.

10 Celebrity Pets

ʃ ˈiː ʃ TYCHO BRAHE'S MOOSE

Apart from being recognized for making some of the most accurate astronomical observations of his day, the great Dane is chiefly famous for his gold and silver artificial nose (he lost his real nose in a sword fight) and for his controversial manner of death (via a burst bladder at a banquet, or, alternatively, mercury poisoning by a rival astronomer). There was also some unfortunate business concerning Brahe's pet moose, which apparently got drunk during the night, fell down some stairs, broke a leg, and had to be shot. What it was doing upstairs drunk in the first place is of course nobody's business but Brahe's.

/ 2 / FLORENCE NIGHTINGALE'S OWL

The "Lady with the Lamp" had a miniature owl called Athena that she took with her everywhere, in her pocket. While she was getting ready to depart for the Crimea for war nursing duties, Florence locked the owl in her attic and then forgot all about it, thinking it would be safe and could live on mice. Sadly the domesticated owl, due to its inability to function without its owner, quickly starved to death. Brokenhearted, she arranged for the services of a taxidermist and the mounted Athena was put on display at the family residence until her own death. The owl is the subject of a book written by her sister Parthenope, *Florence Nightingale's Pet Owl, Athena: A Sentimental History.*

/ 3 / ALEXANDER GRAHAM BELL'S CAT

Bell and his older brother Melville began researching the mechanics of speech in their teens when they made a model skull and fitted it with a voice box that was operated via bellows. Eventually they were able to make their model cry "Ma-ma" in such a lifelike manner that the neighbors thought it was a child in distress. Flushed with this success, they tried to teach their family dog to talk by manipulating its mouth and vocal cords. They claimed that they had persuaded the dog to growl, "How are you, grandmother," although to impartial listeners it sounded a bit very much like "Bow-wow-wow-grrrr." Eventually they gave up on this idea and decided instead to dissect their pet cat to study its vocal cords in more detail, much to the relief of their dog.*

/4/ NIKOLA TESLA'S PIGEON

Although the great Serbian American inventor and electrical engineer struggled to form relationships with people, he was an obsessive pigeon fancier. Almost every day and night for several years he could be seen in Bryant Park, a small green square behind New York's public library, carrying a brown paper bag full of breadcrumbs, covered in a carpet of pigeons. Surprisingly, for someone with a phobia for germs, he kept a flock of sick and wounded pigeons in his hotel room, where he nursed them back to health. Tesla took pigeon fancying to a new level when he fell in love with a favorite white pigeon with brown-tipped wings. "I loved her as a man loves a woman and she loved me," Tesla confessed. "When that pigeon died, something went out of my life . . . I knew my life's work was finished."

/5/ ALGERNON CHARLES SWINBURNE'S MONKEY

The nineteenth-century poet Charles Swinburne kept a monkey called Nip at his home in Kent. Swinburne claimed he once had sex with the monkey, which was dressed in women's clothing,

---

* "That was a fucking relief I don't mind telling you," a Skye terrier was heard to comment later.

then ate it. According to another version, the monkey was hanged by one of Swinburne's servants after it bit him.

/ 6 / ADOLF HITLER'S DOG

After a hard day at the office the Führer would come home and give his German Shepherd dog Blondi and his blond mistress Eva a little pat on the head. Of the two, it was said, Hitler liked the dog more, because unlike Eva, it didn't smoke. When Adolf decided to commit suicide he tested a lethal dose of cyanide on Blondi by crushing a capsule between her teeth. The death of his dog caused him more distress than proposing the suicide of his recent bride, whom he had married thirty-six hours earlier.

/ 7 / ERIC GILL'S DOG

Eric Gill was not only the best known British artist and sculptor of the 1930s, he was also a very religious man and a pillar of Roman Catholic community, known as "the married monk" because of his choice of work wear: a habit and a girdle of chastity of the order of Saint Dominic. So it caused something of a furor in the Catholic Church when, forty years after his death, his diaries revealed a highly deviant sex life, chronicled with perverse precision across forty volumes, including details of sex sessions with the family dog. His diary entry for December 8, 1929, reads: *"Bath. Continued experiment with dog after and discovered that a dog will join with a man."* His name lives on in the popular typeface, Gill Sans.

/ 8 / CLARA BOW'S KOALA BEAR/GREAT DANE

Bow's trademark short skirts and cupid-bow lips made her America's most popular female movie star of the late 1920s, but her career was destroyed by one of the biggest sex scandals of the age, forcing the greatest flapper of them all into premature retirement at the age of twenty-eight. In 1930 Bow sacked her personal assistant Daisy DeVoe, who retaliated by demanding $125,000 for the return of some of Clara's love letters. The police were called in and DeVoe was charged with thirty-five counts of extortion, but her defense lawyers took their client's court appearance as an opportunity to reveal unflattering details about Bow's sex life, which ran to marathon drug-fueled bedroom romps with a list of her lovers, including her chauffeur, her cousin Billy, a string of leading ladies, and, allegedly, her pet koala bear. It was rumored that Bow was about to be fired by her studio for getting involved in some heavy petting with her dog, a Great Dane called Duke. Her "comeback" film, *Call Her Savage,* featured Bow wrestling with an enormous Great Dane; the camera appears to linger unnecessarily on the dog's testicles throughout the tussle.

/ 9 / JACK PARSONS'S DOG

Parsons was a brilliant scientist whose innovations in solid rocket fuel technology made him one of the most important figures in the history of the US space program, and is honored with an eponymous crater on the dark side of the Moon. Sadly, he didn't live to see his greatest invention take man to the Moon. While working with explosives at home in his backyard laboratory, he left a small crater of his own when he accidentally blew himself up. There was one interesting item found by police investigators on the Parsons property after his death, a small box. It contained a film, showing Jack Parsons having sex with his dog, and with his mother Ruth.

∫ 1 0 ∫ DOROTHY PARKER'S CANARY

The US writer, critic, and wit had a pet canary named Onan. She explained that, like the Biblical son of Judah, he often spilled his seed.

12 Monarchs Who Were Shot At

∫ 1 ∫ PRINCE WILLIAM I "THE SILENT" OF HOLLAND

On July 10, 1584, the Protestant Dutch monarch was talking to a group of friends in the hallway of his home in Delft when a Catholic cabinet-maker's apprentice, Balthasar Gerard, walked up to him and shot him at close range with two pistols. The bullets passed straight through William's stomach into the wall beyond—the first ever successful assassination of a head of state with a handgun.

∫ 2 ∫ KING GUSTAV III OF SWEDEN

On March 15, 1792, the king was shot in the back by guards officer Johan Anckarstrom while attending a masked ball. The murder weapon was loaded with two balls, five shot, and six bent nails. The forty-six-year-old king lingered on in agony for twelve days with fragments of the lead bullet in his hip, and died of gangrene.

/ 3 / KING GEORGE III OF GREAT BRITAIN

On the evening of May 15, 1800, as the king was taking his seat in his royal box at Drury Lane Theatre, he was shot at from the stalls below by a mentally ill former soldier, James Hadfield. The bullet struck a wooden pillar only fourteen inches above his head. The king was apparently so unfazed by the assault that he followed his usual practice of having a short nap at the end of the play.

/ 4 / QUEEN VICTORIA

On June 10, 1840, as she and her new husband Prince Albert were riding in the carriage near Constitution Hill in London, they were shot at by eighteen-year-old Edward Oxford, later described in court as "an undersized, feeble-minded youth." He was found "guilty but insane," and sent to Bedlam Lunatic Asylum where he spent the next twenty-seven years. It was the first of several* attempts to kill the Queen, and greatly improved her popularity. "It is worth being shot at," she wrote to her daughter, "to see how much one is loved."

/ 5 / EMPEROR LOUIS-NAPOLEON III OF FRANCE

One of the premier bullet-dodgers of the era, he came to consider himself something of an expert on the subject, having survived at least five direct attempts on his life. Louis-Napoleon survived another one indirectly on June 6, 1867, while sitting

---

* Sometimes estimated at seven; two of the eight "attempts" on the Queen's life were by the same person on different days.

next to the accident-prone Russian Czar Alexander II in an open landau in Bois de Bologne, Paris, when a Pole called Antoni Berezowski shouted, "Long live Poland!" and opened fire twice at the carriage. The first bullet hit an equerry's horse, the second jammed in the pistol's barrel. Eyewitnesses reported that the Czar remained calm but Louis-Napoleon fainted.

∫ 6 ∫ EMPEROR WILHELM I OF GERMANY

On June 2, 1879, Wilhelm was riding in his carriage through Berlin when from the upper window of an inn, the Three Ravens, a double-barreled shotgun discharged two rounds of buckshot into the Emperor's head and shoulders. Wilhelm, who was waving to the crowd, slumped back in his seat, blood pouring from his face. Everyone around him was convinced he was dead, but in fact his steel helmet had deflected most of the shot. Police stormed the building and found the would-be assassin Karl Eduard Nobiling, but as they charged toward him, Nobiling put the revolver to his own head and pulled the trigger. The bullet penetrated his skull, but did not kill him outright. As the would-be assassin was sped away to a prison hospital in an open-topped police van, the driver, keen to get his passenger to his destination before he bled to death, drove his van under a low bridge, breaking his own neck and killing him instantly.

∫ 7 ∫ KING ALPHONSE XII OF SPAIN

On October 25, 1878, the reclusive Spanish monarch made a rare trip outside his palace in Madrid when a twenty-three-year-old anarchist Juan Oliva Moncasi fired two pistol shots at his carriage from a range of about twelve feet, missing his target with both bullets. The gunman was brought to trial in January 1879, was found guilty, and died by the Spanish mode of execution, the garrotte, watched by a crowd of about fifty thousand people. King Alphonse died peacefully in his own bed from syphilis.

∫ 8 ∫ KING EDWARD VII OF GREAT BRITAIN

On April 4, 1900, the then prince of Wales was on a train leaving a railway station in Brussels when a sixteen-year-old Belgian anarchist, Jean-Baptiste Sipido, fired two shots into his carriage, missing his target's head by inches. As the Prince ducked he was heard to cry, "Fuck it, I've taken a bullet!"

∫ 9 ∫ KING UMBERTO I OF ITALY

On July 29, 1900, while attending the prize-giving at a gymnastics display in Monza, the king was shot three times and killed by Italian American Gaetano Bresci. The gunman and several anarchist colleagues had drawn lots to see who should kill the king. Umberto had survived one earlier attempt to stab him to death, dismissing it as "one of the little risks of our profession."

∫ 1 0 ∫ KING CARLOS I OF PORTUGAL

On February 1, 1908 the Portuguese royal family was in a horse-drawn open carriage driving through Lisbon's main public square when expert marksman Manuel Buica jumped onto the carriage running board and shot at the king three times, hitting him in the left side of his neck. Carlos's two sons, Crown Princes Luis Filipe and Manuel, drew their own pistols and returned fire. Buica turned his gun on twenty-one-year-old Luis, and discharged several more bullets. Several onlookers threw themselves at the gunman who fell to the ground, firing as he fell, and a policeman shot him dead as he lay there. The fatally wounded Crown Prince Luis Filipe had the shortest reign of any monarch, surviving his dead father by just twenty minutes.

ʃ 1 1 ʃ KING ZOG I OF ALBANIA

He was the subject of an estimated fifty-five assassination attempts. On February 21, 1931, as Zog was leaving a performance of *Pagliacci* at the Vienna Opera House, two gunman opened fire at him as he was climbing into the car. The bullets meant for him were stopped by an aide and an Albanian government minister. Zog drew a gun and returned fire, thus sealing his undeserved reputation in the European press as a dashing, royal hero. At their trial, his two Albanian assailants, Noloc Gjeloshi and Aziz Cemi, said they had acted alone, on impulse. Gjeloshi was eager to explain an ethic of Albanian manhood: "When an Albanian has not got himself in hand, he has a revolver in it."

ʃ 1 2 ʃ KING ALEXANDER I OF YUGOSLAVIA

On October 9, 1934, while being driven in an open-topped car on a state visit to France, Vlado Chernozemski, aka "Vlado the Chauffeur," a thirty-six-year-old Bulgarian professional hit man, jumped on the car's running board and opened fire at the king with a twenty-round Mauser machine pistol and continued until the gun was empty. He was shot dead on the spot by a policeman. The murder of King Alexander was the first ever political assassination captured on film. The six-minute newsreel, showing the death of a king close up was in its day as sensational as the famous Zapruder film of bullets striking President Kennedy in Dallas in 1963.

Building a Better Mouse Trap
10 INVENTIONS THAT NEARLY TOOK THE WORLD BY STORM

1786: The German S. G. Vogel invents a cagelike contraption to prevent masturbation.*

1852: One of the first ever inventions lodged at the British Patent Office is a device for flushing out the Loch Ness monster with a series of electric shocks.

1854: Indiana doctor Alpheus Myers patents his Trap for Removing Tapeworms from the Stomach and Intestines. Myers's invention comprises a trap that is baited, attached to a string, and swallowed by the patient after a fast of suitable duration, to make the worm hungry. The worm seizes the bait and its head is caught in the trap, which is then withdrawn from the patient's stomach by the string, which has been left hanging from the mouth, dragging after it the whole length of the worm.

1862: The British Patent Office receives a patent for a toilet shooting stick, "to assist persons of short stature in personal evacuation."

---

* The US Patent Office currently has the registration on thirty-three similar devices, registered between 1856 and 1932, to prevent male masturbation, including handcuffs, chains, and armored codpieces.

1914: Natalie Stolp from Philadelphia patents a device to discourage men from rubbing their thighs up against ladies in crowded trains. Her spring-loaded undergarment responds to unwanted male pressure by releasing a metal spike into the offender's thigh.*

1959: Bertha Dlugi of Milwaukee is the first person to realize the commercial possibilities of a bird diaper, which would allow pet birds to fly freely around the house without depositing droppings.

1977: Charles Barlow of Arizona patents a device designed to be inserted into a woman, containing three spears with harpoon-like barbs which would mutilate the penis of would-be rapist.

1994: The US-based Kimberly-Clark Corporation patents a chemically realistic synthetic feces for testing diapers and incontinence garments. The company concluded that previously

---

* The US Patent Office has since received plans for several more antirape devices. Anna Pennystone's antirape invention, patented in 1983, also involved a rigid sheath inserted into the woman: the inside of the device was coated with adhesive and contained chemicals that would burn the flesh. Others included Alston Levasque's "Penis Locking and Lacerating Vaginal Insert" and George Vogel's "Female Protective Device"—a large lump of metal with a solid spear in the center. A creation devised by Joel Rumph and Lynda Warren promises to inject the assailant's penis with a fast-working sedative thus rendering him unconscious. None of these or similar devices are ever likely to get off the drawing board because of a basic design flaw—each device would have to be large enough to house an erect penis and would make wearing them uncomfortable, not to mention dangerous, if any of them suddenly "went off" by themselves.

used substitute concoctions made from mashed potatoes, peanut butter, and canned pumpkin pie mix were inadequate because they separate into liquids and solids more quickly than the real thing.

1995: The Italian inventor Lino Missio patents a condom that plays Beethoven whenever it ruptures during use. The prophylactic is coated with a substance that changes electrical conductivity upon rupture, setting off a microchip that produces a sound.

2002: The Museum of Questionable Medical Devices, the world's largest display of quackery, relocates to the Science Museum of Minnesota. Gadgets on view include a machine that increases virility and cures prostrate problems by electric shock treatment; a nose straightener; a foot-powered breast enlarger; weight-reducing soap; weight-reducing spectacles; and an X-ray shoe-fitting device.

10 Heroic Business Opportunists

1904: The Russian psychologist Petrovich Pavlov, known for his experiments proving that dogs can be conditioned to salivate by ringing a bell, attempts to cash in on his discovery by collecting large quantities of doggy phlegm and selling it bottled as an appetite stimulant. There are few takers.

1911: A mail-order con in the United States nets hundreds of thousands of dollars with the promise of a miracle cure that could turn black people into white people.

1914: Long before he dreams of world domination, Adolf Hitler hopes to make his fortune from a miracle baldness cure.

1946: William Johnson, a semiliterate miner from Kentucky, cashes in on a rumor sweeping America that Adolf Hitler has been smuggled out of Europe after World War II and is alive and well and living in North America. Johnson poses as Hitler, supposedly now settled in Kentucky with some of his Nazi chiefs of staff and planning to take over the United States. Johnson's "Hitler" makes a public appeal for cash to help his cause and right-wing Americans and fascists of German extraction send him a steady stream of postal orders as he elaborates on his plans for space ships, "invisible ships." and underground hordes of ammunition. The fact that he often signs as his name as "the Furrier" instead of "the Führer" doesn't stop the American public from sending him tens of thousand of dollars.

1986: A couple from Winnipeg, Manitoba, open the world's one and only toilet-themed restaurant, The Outhouse. It is closed down by health inspectors within a few weeks.

1992: A Swedish court convicts a thirty-four-year-old taxi driver of overcharging a forty-nine-year-old woman after he left the meter running while he had sex with her. According to the *Aftonbladet* newspaper, the driver billed the woman the equivalent of about £5,000 for 25 occasions of "sexual services." The bill included 25 percent sales tax, plus charges for trips, hotel, and telephone calls.

1993: A morgue in Brisbane, Australia, is caught selling organs from corpses without seeking permission from the families of the deceased. A former morgue attendant confesses that the facility sold pituitary glands for about fifty cents each in order to fund the staff Christmas party.

1994: Three hospital workers in Zimbabwe are arrested and charged with stealing human hearts from the mortuary and selling them to witch doctors. The hearts, worth around £90 each, or four times the local average monthly wage, were made into fashionable good luck charms for wealthy businessmen.

1996: The US cult ringleader and accessory to murder Charles Manson releases his first exercise video. Manson's promoter Fred Zalemond explains: "Charles regrets the lives he took. Now he's saving lives by protecting people from heart attacks and strokes."

1996: While serving a life sentence for the rape and murder of eight girls and three boys, one of Canada's biggest ever serial killers, Clifford Olson, registers a copyright for his proposed video offering psychological insights into murder. It is snappily entitled "Motivational Sexual Homicide Patterns of Serial Child Killer Clifford Robert Olson."

10 Awesome Insights

1776: On July 4, thirteen American colonies declare their independence from Great Britain. King George III writes in his diary, "nothing of importance happened today."

1886: Prospector Sors Hariezon decides to cut his losses and sell his South African gold claim for $20. Since that day, mines dug on or near his claim have produced over a million kilograms of gold a year, about 70 percent of the Western world's gold supply.

1899: Charles H. Duell, commissioner of US Patent Office declares: "Everything that can be invented, has been invented."

1917: Ernest Rutherford proves that the atom can be split. Although his work is the basis of all modern understanding of nuclear energy, Rutherford never considered it to be of any useful significance.

1928: MGM boss Louis B. Mayer refuses to give a contract to the young cartoon maker Walt Disney and his creation, Mickey Mouse, because a ten-foot-tall rodent on the screen was an appalling idea and bound to frighten pregnant women.

1938: Joe Shuster and Jerry Siegel sell all rights to the comic strip character Superman to their publishers—for $65 each.

1943: Thomas Watson, chairman of IBM, predicts, "I think there is a world market for maybe five computers."

1955: Sam Phillips, owner of a small recording company in Memphis, sells to RCA Records for the sum of $35,000 the exclusive contract he has with a young performer named Elvis Presley. Phillips thereby forfeits royalties on over a billion records.

1963: A BBC radio producer takes aside Andrew Loog Oldham, manager of failed auditionists the Rolling Stones, and advises him: "The band's okay, but If I were you I'd get rid of the singer with the tire tread lips."

1994: A Chinese TV crew in Hong Kong films a documentary on the first open-heart surgery ever performed at the Weifang Medical University in Shandong. The crew is later informed that they would have to reshoot. Hospital officials had belatedly discovered that the open-heart patient was in fact a boy who had been admitted for a tonsillectomy.

10 Golf Hazards

1951: Edward Harrison is playing a round at Inglewood in Kenmore, Washington, when the shaft of his driver breaks and pierces his groin, severing the femoral artery. He staggers 100 yards down the course before collapsing and bleeding to death.

1987: A caddie at the Cameron Highlands golf club, Malaysia, unwisely laughs when his employer King Mahmood Iskandar misses a putt. The king beats the man to death with his putter. The news is suppressed because all Malaysian royals enjoy legal immunity.

1994: Emil Kijek of Massachusetts achieves his first ever hole in one at the age of seventy-nine at the Sun Valley Golf Club. He is unable to stand the traditional round of drinks at the "19th Hole," however, as the shock kills him several minutes later.

1994: Whitney McIntosh from Edinburgh drowns while attempting to retrieve his ball from a water hazard.

1994: Sixteen-year-old Jeremy Brenno, annoyed at missing a shot on the sixth hole at the Kingsboro Golf Club, New York, vents his frustration by whacking a nearby bench with his golf club. The shaft on the No. 3 wood breaks and bounces back at him, fatally piercing his heart.

1994: Golf widow Diana Nagy files a lawsuit in Charleston, West Virginia, against the manufacturer of the golf cart from which her husband fell to his death during a tournament at the Berry Hills Country Club. She accepts that her husband had been drinking heavily but maintains that the cart should have been fitted with seat belts and doors.

1995: Frenchman Jean Potevan throws his golf bag into a lake in disgust after a poor game at a course near Lyon. Realizing, however, that his car keys are still in the bag, Potevan dives in after it and drowns when he becomes entangled in weeds. His golf partner Henri Levereau said his last words were, "I'm going for the keys, but the clubs stay down there."

1995: Japanese golfer Takeo Niyama is arrested after beating his playing partner to death with a 5 iron. Niyama, aged forty-three, reacted when Aioa Sakajiri laughed at his slice into the lake at a Tokyo course. He had only two previous convictions for golf-course assaults, including a six-month prison sentence for a links assault.

2009: A thirty-eight-year-old Japanese woman, Takae Gassho, is playing golf at the Le Petaw Golf Club when the turf under her feet collapsed and she plunged into a five-meter-deep hole, causing her to drown in a puddle of water at the bottom of a cavern.

2009: Seventy-seven-year-old Bruce James Wiencek reaches into a water hazard on the 11th hole of a South Carolina course to retrieve his ball and has his arm ripped off by a ten-foot-long alligator. The severed arm is recovered from the alligator's stomach an hour later.

12 Uninspiring US Presidents

∫ 1 ∫ JOHN QUINCY ADAMS (PRESIDENT, 1825–29)

"A disgusting man to do business with. Coarse and dirty and clownish in his address and stiff and abstracted in his opinions, which are drawn from books exclusively."
—William Henry Harrison

∫ 2 ∫ ANDREW JACKSON (1829–37)

"A barbarian who could not write a sentence of grammar and hardly could spell his own name."
—John Quincy Adams

∫ 3 ∫ RUTHERFORD BIRCHARD HAYES (1877–81)

"A third-rate nonentity, whose only recommendation is that he is obnoxious to no one."
—Henry Adams

∫ 4 ∫ CHESTER A. ARTHUR (1881–85)

"A nonentity with side whiskers."
—Woodrow Wilson

/ 5 / WARREN G. HARDING (1921–23)

"He writes the worst English I have ever encountered. It reminds me of a string of wet sponges . . . of tattered washing on the line . . . of stale bean soup, of college yells, of dogs barking idiotically through endless nights. It is so bad that a sort of grandeur creeps into it. It drags itself out of a dark abyss of pish, and crawls insanely up the topmost pinnacle of posh. It is rumble and bumble. It is flap and doodle. It is balder and dash."
—H. L. Mencken

/ 6 / CALVIN COOLIDGE (1923–29)

"He slept more than any other president, whether by day or night. Nero fiddled, but Coolidge only snored."
—H. L. Mencken

/ 7 / FRANKLIN D. ROOSEVELT (1933–45)

"Had every quality that morons esteem in their heroes. He was the first American to penetrate the real depths of vulgar stupidity."
—H. L. Mencken

/ 8 / DWIGHT D. EISENHOWER (1953–61)

"This fellow don't know any more about politics than a pig knows about Sunday."
—Harry S. Truman

/ 9 / LYNDON BAINES JOHNSON (1963–69)

"How does one tell the president of the United States to stop picking his nose and lifting a leg to fart in front of the camera and using 'chickenshit' in every other sentence?"
—Stuart Rosenberg, TV director

/ 1 0 / GERALD FORD (1974–77)

"In the Bob Hope Golf Classic the participation of President Gerald Ford was more than enough to remind you that the nuclear button was at one stage at the disposal of a man who might have either pressed it by mistake or else pressed it deliberately to obtain room service."
—Clive James, Australian writer

/ 1 1 / RONALD REAGAN (1981–89)

"In a disastrous fire in Ronald Reagan's library, both books were destroyed. And the real tragedy is that he hadn't finished coloring them."
—Jonathan Hunt, US journalist

/ 1 2 / GEORGE W. BUSH (2001–2009)

"Apparently Arnold (Schwarzenegger) was inspired by President Bush, who proved you can be a successful politician in this country even if English is your second language."
—Conan O'Brien, US TV host

10 Unsung Siblings

1. Bleda the Hun, elder brother of Attila
2. Pierre d'Arc, flameproof younger brother of Joan
3. Feodor the not remotely Terrible, younger brother of Ivan
4. Saloth Neap, the nongenocidal brother of Pol Pot
5. Amule Amin Dada, big brother of Idi
6. Maria Ulyanova, younger sister of Lenin
7. Paula Hitler, younger sister of Adolf
8. Gebhard Himmler, elder brother of Heinrich
9. Mao Zemin, little brother of Mao Zedong
10. Omm Omar Hussein, half-sister of Saddam

Send in the Clones
5 PEOPLE WHO EMPLOYED BODY DOUBLES

/ 1 / ENVER HOXHA

The Albanian dictator had a village dentist abducted by his secret police, the Sigurimi, and surgically enhanced to make him appear to be the president's identical twin. Hoxha's plan was to keep his lookalike close at hand in case of an invasion; the double would be sacrificed to enemy soldiers while the president escaped to the mountains. The double spent ten years in relative luxury in a small compound within the presidential palace and was brought out to stand in for his president at official events every now and then. When Hoxha died and the communists were overthrown, the double was attacked by a mob who thought he was the former dictator's ghost.

KARL SHAW

/ 2 / ADOLF HITLER

The Führer was rumored to have employed as many as six doubles. His regular driver Julius Schreck often acted as the Führer's double because of their close natural physical resemblance. According to some reports, Schreck died in a traffic accident in 1936; according to other reports he died from an abscessed tooth. *Time* magazine once named a second Hitler double, Heinrich Bergner, who was killed in July 1944, by a bomb intended for the Führer.

/ 3 / JOSEPH STALIN

The Soviet leader used several doubles, including a man identified only as Rashid who closely resembled the dictator even down to his deep facial pockmarks. After Uncle Joe's death in 1953 Rashid shaved off his mustache and gradually went bald, but even then the resemblance was so striking that people stopped and stared at him on the street. Some people actually believed that Stalin had faked his death and gone into hiding among them. Another Stalin lookalike, an actor called Alexei Dikiy was hired to live in the dictator's dacha outside of Moscow in the late 1950s when Stalin was seriously ill, to fool visitors into thinking that their leader was still in control of his faculties. A third Stalin double, Felix Dadaev, worked as Stalin's body double at public functions, even meeting party officials, and once stood in for Stalin before a parade in Red Square. Dadaev kept quiet about his work for more than half a century, fearing a death sentence if he told anyone about his old job.

/ 4 / BERNARD MONTGOMERY "OF ALAMEIN"

Britain's World War II military commander employed a looka-like called M. E. Clifton James, a soldier who was hired for his natural resemblance to "Monty" as a decoy, and sent to Gibraltar and Algiers to confuse the Germans about Allied invasion plans. James studied Montgomery's mannerisms and voice and had to give up smoking; he also had to wear a false middle finger on his right hand because he lost his own in the First World War. James later starred in a film *I Was Monty's Double* in which he played himself and Monty. A second double, Keith Banwell, was also dressed up in appropriate "Monty" clothing, includ-ing his insignia and general's badges, and sent on trips around the Middle East to confuse enemy spies. As he was much taller than Montgomery, he was told that on no account should he get out of the car. Banwell found the assignment so tedious that he begged to be allowed to go back to killing Germans.

/ 5 / KIM JONG-IL

The North Korean dictator routinely hires doubles to carry out some of his more mundane duties, including regular visits to farms and tractor factories. According to South Korean intel-ligence sources, the two stand-ins are the same height as Kim and have had plastic surgery to enhance the resemblance to their chubby leader, right down to his bouffant hairstyle and pot belly. Some US analysts were convinced that when former president Bill Clinton traveled to North Korea in August 2009 to meet Kim Jong-il, he actually met with a Mr. Kim lookalike.

Beard Bias
10 FAMOUS POGONOPHOBICS

/ 1 / PETER "THE GREAT"

In 1705 the Russian Czar passed a law banning beards because he wanted his hairy countrymen to look more like the prosperous, whiskerless Western Europeans. Peter would rip a beard out by the roots if he came across anyone wearing one.

/ 2 / ARTHUR SCHOPENHAUER

The gloomy German philosopher hated beards and thought they should be outlawed because they shielded the inherently sinister features of a criminal's face, but he hated shaving with razors even more. It made him so miserable that one day he tried to burn off his facial hair. The attempt landed him in the hospital.

/ 3 / BENITO MUSSOLINI

The clean-shaved Italian fascist dictator declared in the 1920s, "whiskers are a sign of decadence."

/ 4 / WALT DISNEY

Although, ironically, he wore a mustache himself, he forbade his employees on pain of dismissal to wear facial hair.

/ 5 / MARGARET THATCHER

Male politicians in the Iron Lady's cabinet were slaves to the daily shave after she announced, "I would not tolerate any minister of mine wearing a beard."

/ 6 / ROSS PEROT

In 1983 a federal judge found that the billionaire Texas businessman and twice failed US presidential candidate, while head of Electronic Data Systems, fired one of his employees for no other reason than his refusal to shave his beard.

/ 7 / ROALD DAHL

The famous children's author thought that facial hair was "disgusting." It inspired him to write *The Twits,* featuring Mr. Twit and his revolting food-encrusted beard.

/ 8 / ENVER HOXHA

The Albanian dictator banned beards even on visiting foreigners. Albanian border barbers were employed to snip excess hair from all foreigners entering the country; the degree of hairiness was then noted in police files. Enver Hoxha spent his last few years as a total recluse, dictating dense, rambling books that lambasted his communist allies for betraying the Marxist cause. His final book, *The Dangers of Anglo-Americans in Albania,* warned his countrymen to watch out for men with beards— which were apparently cunning devices used to disguise British and American spies.

∫ 9 ∫ SAPARMURAT NIYAZOV

The president of Turkmenistan banned beards, having already banned ballet, theater, circuses, loud mobile phone conversations, music in cars, math tuition in schools, gold teeth, and makeup on female newscasters. In 2002 Niyazov showed he still had a few surprises up his sleeve when he abolished the calendar.

∫ 1 0 ∫ CAPTAIN SENSIBLE

Rebelling against "hairy hippies," the cofounder of the punk rock band the Damned said: "I had a thing about beards. I hated beards. I didn't want to see anyone with a guitar around their necks and a bloody beard going on."

10 Lavatorial Euphemisms

1. House of the morning—ancient Egypt
2. Jakes—England, sixteenth century
3. Cackatorium—England, eighteenth century
4. Boghouse—England, nineteenth century
5. Quincy—United States, nineteenth century*
6. Dunny, diddy, toot, brasco—Australia, twentieth century
7. Bagno (bath), cabinetto (cabinet)—Italy, twentieth century
8. Ubornaya (adornment place)—Russia, twentieth century
9. Abort (away place); stilles örtchen (silent little place); donnerbalken (thunder board); plumsklo (plop closet)—Germany, twentieth century
10. Pissoir—France, twentieth century

* So named after the sixth US president, John Quincy Adams, who was the first to have a convenience installed in the White House.

CHAPTER NINE
LAST RITES

10 Ways to Recycle a Corpse

1. A company in Jönköping, Sweden, offers an environmentally friendly method of burying the dead by transforming corpses into organic compost and giving people the chance to come back as flowers, or possibly a salad. The dearly departed are first supercooled in liquid nitrogen to about minus 196°C, then broken down into very small pieces by mechanical vibration. The remains are then dehydrated and cleared of any amalgam fillings, crowns, titanium hip joints, etc., reducing a body weighing 165 pounds in life to 55 pounds of pinkish powder. The whole process takes about two hours, as opposed to a corpse buried in a coffin, which takes several years to decompose completely. The innovation is the work of Swedish biologist Suzanne Wiigh, whose freeze-dried late cat currently feeds a rhododendron bush in her front garden.

2. In 1891 the French surgeon Dr. Varlot developed a method of preserving corpses by covering them with a thin layer of metal—in effect, he was electroplating the dead. Dr. Varlot's technique involved making the body conductive by exposing it to silver nitrate, followed by immersion in a galvanic bath of copper sulfate, producing a one-millimeter-thick coating of copper—"a brilliant red copper finish of exceptional strength and durability." Why he wanted to do it in the first place however is unclear.

3. In ancient Rome, where human blood was prescribed as a cure for epilepsy, epileptics hung around near the exit gates of the public arenas so they could drink the blood

of slain gladiators as they were dragged out. Elizabethan medical textbooks recommended an alternative remedy— powdered human skull dissolved in red wine.

4. According to a centuries-old European tradition, a "hand of glory" was a human candelabra made from body parts of a man executed for murder. The dried or pickled hand of the offender was used as a candleholder for a candle made from the fat of the dead man's body—and often hair from the same body was used as a wick. The hand of glory was attributed with magical powers; it could help its possessor carry out robberies by making him invisible or by unlocking any door he came across (in *Harry Potter and the Half-Blood Prince* by J. K. Rowling, Draco Malfoy uses a hand of glory during the invasion of Hogwarts School). There are several hands of glory in museums and private collections today but they are almost certainly fakes made from medical cadavers in the nineteenth century to satisfy a craze for collecting occult artifacts, especially death relics.

5. A church in the Czech town of Sedlec has a chandelier made entirely of human skulls and bones.

6. British farmers were "processing" human corpses long before the Nazis thought of it. In 1822 the British newspaper the *Observer* reported that the Napoleonic battlefields of Leipzig, Austerlitz, and Waterloo had been "swept alike of the bones of the hero and of the horse which he rode," and hundreds of tons of the bones had been shipped to Yorkshire bone-grinders to make fertilizers for farmers. After the siege of Plevna in 1877, a local newspaper farming column casually reported that "thirty tons of human bones, comprising thirty thousand skeletons, have just landed at Bristol from Plevna."

7. Until 2003 German and Austrian scientists involved in car safety research routinely used human crash dummies, including the cadavers of children. Researchers in other European countries condemned the practice of smashing human cadavers into brick walls as abhorrent, but it didn't prevent many from paying to see the data.

8. The practice of binding books in human skin dates back to at least the seventeenth century. First edition copies of Dale Carnegie's 1932 biography of Abraham Lincoln, *Lincoln the Unknown,* had a patch of African American skin on its cover, onto which the title had been embossed. An edition of Milton's complete works published in 1852 was bound in the skin of the murderer George Cudmore, executed in 1830, and was described as "white and looks something like pig-skin in grain and texture." When the mistress of the nineteenth-century French novelist Eugène Sue died, she willed him her skin with instructions that he should bind a book with it. He did. In 1951 a copy of Sue's *Vignettes: les Mystères de Paris,* bound in his mistress's skin, sold at auction in London for $29.

9. Dr. Gunther von Hagens, the German anatomist who made his fortune by preserving corpses of humans with a special plastic solution, has a mail-order business offering human body parts. Von Hagens, inventor of a system known as plastination, in which fluids are removed from dead humans or animals and replaced with hardened silicone, allowing body parts to be preserved indefinitely, offers body parts priced from around $1,800 for a sliver of human head or $18,000 for a section of the entire length of a human body. Smokers' lungs are available for $4,300 and a slice of human hand for as little as $225.

10. According to the most recent estimates (2010) your body is worth anything from $10,000 to $100,000 on today's open market—that is, if sold to companies legitimately trading in body parts sourced from willing donors and sold to recognized medical facilities. Your most valuable body parts, generally used by surgeons practicing new techniques, include the spine ($900); hands, forearms, and shoulders (from $385–$500 per item); heart ($500); corneas ($6,000 per pair); knees ($650 each); tendons ($1,000 each); kidneys ($300–$500); intact head including brain, used by trauma doctors and plastic surgeons to practice new techniques ($600). The human body also contains about $1.50 worth of chemicals, while human body fat is thought to be regularly sold on the black market by illegal "body brokers" to cosmetic companies.

Causes of Death of the Last 10 British Monarchs

1. George I—paralytic stroke, probably brought on by indigestion after binging on melons while suffering the aftereffects of seasickness, near Osnabrück, Germany, aged sixty-seven.
2. George II—burst a coronary blood vessel while on the toilet at Kensington Palace, straining to overcome the effects of constipation, aged seventy-six.
3. George III—senile decay, aged eighty-one, at Windsor.
4. George IV—heart disease and alcoholic cirrhosis of the liver, aged sixty-seven, at Windsor.

5. William IV—arteriosclerosis and alcoholic cirrhosis of the liver, aged seventy-one, at Windsor.

6. Victoria—cerebral hemorrhage, aged eighty-one, at Osborne, Isle of Wight.

7. Edward VII—pneumonia and heart failure, aged sixty-eight, at Buckingham Palace.

8. George V—iatrogenic regicide (a lethal injection of cocaine and morphine in his jugular vein) aged seventy, at Sandringham.

9. Edward VIII—throat cancer, aged seventy-eight, in Paris.

10. George VI—lung cancer, aged fifty-six, at Sandringham.

II Notable Suicides

1860: Thomas Addison, a lecturer at Guy's Hospital, London, described a blood-gland disorder resulting in such symptoms as general weakness, vomiting, increased skin pigmentation, and diseased adrenal gland. Unfortunately the disease that bears his name, Addison's disease, was also the last he ever described. On June 29, 1860, for no apparent reason he jumped headfirst through the dining room window on the ground floor of his family home in Wellington Villas. Although he fell only a few feet he landed directly on his head and suffered a fatal trauma.

1930: William Kogut, an inmate awaiting the executioner at San Quentin, elects to take his own life in his prison cell using the only materials available to him—several packs of playing cards. He tore the cards into small pieces and stuffed them into the hollow metal leg of his bunk bed. He then poured water into the leg and sealed it with a wooden broom handle. The ink in the red playing cards contained nitrocellulose, a highly flammable and unstable substance which, when wet, can create an explosive mixture. Placing the leg on top of a paraffin heater, Kogut lay his head on top of the device and waited. The warmth from the heater accelerated the reactions taking place within his improvised pipe bomb and soon the concoction reached a critical state and exploded, killing Kogut instantly.

1932: MGM film director Paul Bern, the husband of actress Jean Harlow, tried to commit suicide on a number of occasions, once by attempting to drown himself in his toilet. He changed his mind at the last minute but found that his head was stuck in the bowl and a plumber had to rescue him by unscrewing the toilet seat. A few months after their honeymoon he put a gun to his head and pulled the trigger. At the time he was said to be wearing an enormous rubber codpiece and large water-filled false testicles. According to the official explanation, Bern shot himself because he was impotent.

1933: Kiyoko Matsumoto, nineteen-year-old Japanese student, starts a craze by jumping into the thousand-foot crater of a volcano on the island of Oshima, Japan. In the ensuing months three hundred other young people do the same thing.

1963: Thich Quang Duc, a Buddhist monk demonstrating against government corruption in Vietnam, sat down in the middle of a busy road junction in Saigon and committed suicide by pouring gasoline over his head and setting fire to himself. In reply, the Vietnamese government offers to supply all of the country's Buddhist monks with free gas.

KARL SHAW

1975: West German Heinze Isecke cures his hiccups by throwing himself from a hospital window. He had become depressed after being afflicted by nonstop hiccups over a period of about two years. It was estimated that approximately his thirty-six millionth hiccup was the last straw.

1995: The Medical Journal of Australia reports that an unnamed thirty-nine-year-old man took his life in Canberra by shooting himself three times with a pump-action shotgun. The first bullet passed straight through his chest and went out the other side. He reloaded and shot away his throat and part of his jaw. Breathing through the wound in his throat, he reloaded, held the gun against his chest with his hands, and operated the trigger with his toes, shooting himself fatally through the heart.

2007: Kevin Whitrick, a forty-two-year-old man from Wellington, UK, hangs himself live on a webcam during an Internet chat room session, after being egged on by other chat room users. One chatter said, "Fucking do it, get on with it, get it around your neck. For fuck's sake he can't even do this properly."

2008: Fifty-eight-year-old David Phyall, the last resident in a block of apartments due to be demolished in Southampton, UK, cut his own head off with a chainsaw, by tying it to the leg of a snooker table with string and plugging it into a timer. He did this to highlight the injustice of being forcibly evicted from his home.

2008: Gerald Mellin, a fifty-four-year-old UK businessman, tied one end of a rope around his neck and the other to a tree, then jumped into his open-topped Aston Martin DB7 and drove down a main road in Swansea until the rope decapitated him. Police found his headless body on the driver's seat with his head in the back. He did it to spite his wife for leaving him.

2009: Jonathan Campos, a US sailor charged with murder, took his own life in his prison cell by stuffing toilet paper in his mouth until he choked to death.

10 People Who Feared Being Buried Alive

/ 1 / FYODOR DOSTOEVSKY

The Russian novelist and short-story writer had a morbid fear of premature burial, and whenever he was sleeping away from home he left a bedside note begging anyone who found him "dead" to check thoroughly that he actually was.

/ 2 / HANS CHRISTIAN ANDERSEN

Andersen was afflicted with an impressive list of phobias, including a fear of animals, germs, eating pork, arriving late, and hotel room fires, which caused him to carry a coil of rope with him at all times. Phobic to the very end, he left written instructions for one of his main arteries be severed before he was placed in his coffin.

/ 3 / GIACOMO MEYERBEER

The German composer arranged to have bells tied to his extremities so that any movement in his coffin would make a noise. To date, Meyerbeer has continued to decompose quietly without any outward sign of life.

〔 4 〕 GEORGE WASHINGTON

He ordered his servants to lay him out for a full two days after he died—just in case.

〔 5 〕 EDMUND YATES

The British novelist and dramatist and friend of Charles Dickens left a fee for any surgeon kind enough to slit his jugular vein before interment.

〔 6 〕 WILKIE COLLINS

The British novelist always carried a letter with him, imploring anyone finding him "dead" to contact the nearest doctor for a second opinion.

〔 7 〕 HARRIET MARTINEAU

She took extreme measures to make sure she was well and truly deceased before her burial by leaving her doctor $35 with instructions that he should cut her head off.

〔 8 〕 FRÉDÉRIC CHOPIN

As he lay dying in 1849, the composer said: "The earth is suffocating. Swear to make them cut me open, so that I won't be buried alive."

/ 9 / GEORGE BATESON

The Victorian inventor patented an "escape-coffin" known as "Bateson's Belfry." It consisted of a bell on the end of a rope above ground, connected to the buried casket with the other end of the rope attached to the deceased's hand. Bateson was so personally afraid of being buried alive that in 1886, driven mad by his dread, he committed suicide by dousing himself with linseed oil and setting himself on fire.

/ 1 0 / JOHN DACKENEY

In 1969 the Arizona multimillionaire was buried in a huge security vault he had built for himself. It contained an alarm and steel doors that opened for three hours every night for the first twelve weeks after he died.

10 Stressful Funeral Experiences

1852: The Tenth Duke of Hamilton, Alexander Douglas outbids the British Museum when he pays £11,000 for a magnificent ancient tomb originally made for an Egyptian princess. Douglas puts it in a fabulous mausoleum at his ancestral home, Hamilton Palace, where it awaits his death. When death arrives, however, it is discovered that he is much too tall to fit inside it and the only way they can get him in is by sawing his feet off.

1927: King George V's wife, Queen Mary, attends the funeral of her brother Adolphus. The funeral procession is interrupted by the sound of her brother's body exploding noisily inside his coffin.

1979: Sid Vicious's mother Anne Beverley carries the late Sex Pistol's cremated remains to scatter on girlfriend Nancy Spungen's Philadelphia grave. Several eyewitnesses report however that she drops Sid's urn in a busy Heathrow terminal, sending most of her son's ashes into the airport ventilation system.

1988: In the Ukrainian village of Zabolotye, a funeral wake is held for a man who has died of poisoning from drinking black market industrial spirit. Unwisely, the very same drink is served at the wake, resulting in ten more deaths.

1993: Frederick Armstrong is convicted of stabbing an eighty-one-year-old preacher to death and cutting off his head before stunned onlookers, including a few police officers, at a funeral home in Baton Rouge, Louisiana. Armstrong's defense attorney appeals against the verdict on the grounds that his client was obviously insane at the time. "A rational man," reasoned Armstrong's lawyer, "does not decapitate a man's head in the presence of a police officer."

1994: A Croatian, Stanislav Kovac, is knocked down and killed by a car on a business trip to Bottrop, Germany. Local undertaker Rudolf Dauer subsequently completes a 560-mile trip from Bottrop to his funeral in Zagreb, only to have to explain to bereaved relatives that he had forgotten to bring the corpse with him.

1995: The crematorium at the Meadow Lawn Memorial Park in San Antonio, Texas, is partially destroyed by fire. It broke out when staff began cremating a body that weighed over three hundred pounds. The owner of the crematorium explained that the fat in the body caused an unusually high temperature, which caused the regular crematorium fire to rage out of control.

2006: A sixty-seven-year-old woman from Houston is killed when she loses control of her car, swerves across the road, and slams into the lead car of a funeral procession leaving the Guadalupe Funeral Home for the local cemetery.

2006: In Milwaukee, relatives of the late Robert Senz demand that his body be dug up when they realize that his wallet is missing. The body is exhumed, along with the wallet containing $64 and credit cards still in Senz's pocket. The funeral home sends the family a reburial bill for $2,149.

2007: Iowa TV station cameraman Gerry Edwards is fired for unprofessional conduct after covering a funeral. It went on for so long that the desperate Edwards had to urinate in front of the mourners.

10 Ethnic Exits

1. In some Inuit cultures, if an elderly or infirm person tells his family he is ready to die they will oblige by either killing him on the spot or abandoning him in the cold and letting nature take its course.
2. The ancient Britons practiced euthanasia by throwing themselves off overhanging rocks: if they were too old to jump, someone would give them a helpful shove.
3. In ancient Athens the local magistrate would keep a supply of poison handy for any elderly, depressed, or

terminally ill person who wanted to commit suicide. All you had to do to was ask.

4. In nineteenth-century Britain, failed suicides were hanged.

5. Scandinavians practiced euthanasia by putting their old people in big earthenware jars and leaving them to die.

6. The Hottentot tribe of Africa used to give their senior citizens a huge farewell party before abandoning them to die in a hut in the wilderness.

7. In Ceos, in ancient Greece, it was obligatory for people over the age of sixty to commit suicide.

8. Elderly Ethiopians who wanted to die allowed themselves to be tied to wild bulls.

9. Congolese natives used to jump up and down on their elderly or terminally ill relatives until they had finished them off.

10. The suicide method most commonly used by Western men is carbon monoxide poisoning in cars. Among women the most common method is drug overdose. The greatest mass suicide in Western history was committed by the seventeenth-century Russian Orthodox cult called the Old Believers in protest against reforms in their religion. It was estimated that about twenty thousand cult members burned themselves alive.

The World's 10 Favorite Tourist Destinations for the Depressed

1. Niagara Falls—2,780 known suicides from 1856 to 1995

2. Golden Gate Bridge, San Francisco, California—1,500+ suicides

3. Colorado School of Mines, Golden, Colorado—678+ suicides
4. Beachy Head, East Sussex, England—500+ suicides
5. West Gate Bridge, Melbourne, Australia—500+ suicides
6. Eiffel Tower, Paris, France—350+ suicides
7. Coronado Bridge, San Diego, California—200+ suicides
8. Aurora Bridge, Seattle, Washington—230+ suicides
9. Aokigahara, Mount Fuji, Japan—averages 70 suicides annually
10. The Gap, New South Wales, Sydney, Australia—averages 50 suicides annually

To Die For
10 LAST SUPPERS

1. Buddha: died at the age of eighty in 483 B.C. from an intestinal hemorrhage after eating a very hot curry.
2. King John: fell dead after gorging on peaches and cider, one year after signing the Magna Carta.
3. Robert Greene, sixteenth-century English dramatist: expired after consuming too much Rhenish wine and pickled herring at an authors' gala luncheon.
4. Bonnie Parker and Clyde Barrow: enjoyed bacon and tomato sandwiches in their car before dying of multiple gunshot wounds.
5. Adolf Hitler: vegetarian ravioli, washed down with arsenic.
6. James Dean: crashed on a glass of milk and an apple.
7. Ernest Hemingway: cleansed his palate by applying a shotgun to his head after dining on New York strip steak, baked potato, Caesar salad, and Bordeaux wine.

8. Jimi Hendrix: choked to death on his own vomit after enjoying a tuna fish sandwich.

9. Diana, Princess of Wales: asparagus and mushroom omelette, Dover sole with vegetable tempura, and Champagne.

10. *First Course;* Hors D'Oeuvres/Oysters. *Second Course:* Consommé Olga/Cream of Barley. *Third Course:* Poached Salmon with Mousseline Sauce, Cucumbers. *Fourth Course:* Filet Mignons Lili/Saute of Chicken, Lyonnaise/ Vegetable Marrow Farci. *Fifth Course:* Lamb, Mint Sauce/ Roast Duckling, Apple Sauce/Sirloin of Beef, Chateau Potatoes, Green Peas, Creamed Carrots, Boiled Rice, Parmentier & Boiled New Potatoes. *Sixth Course:* Punch Romaine. *Seventh Course:* Roast Squab & Cress. *Eighth Course*: Cold Asparagus Vinaigrette. *Ninth Course:* Pâté de Foie Gras/Celery. *Tenth Course:* Waldorf Pudding/Peaches in Chartreuse Jelly/Chocolate & Vanilla Eclairs/French Ice Cream
—First Class menu, RMS *Titanic,* April 14, 1912

10 Profane Last Words

1. "Get these fucking nuns away from me!"
   —Norman Douglas, British author

2. "Oh shit."
   —Gangland figure Des "Tuppence" Moran, after he was gunned down in a café

3. "Goddamn the whole fucking world and everyone in it except you, Carlotta!"
   —W. C. Fields to his mistress Carlotta Monti

4. "Shit, why did I not think of that earlier?"
   —Robert Sullivan, US writer

5. "Hold me up, I want to shit."
   —Walt Whitman, US poet

6. "You sons of bitches, give my love to Mother!"
   —US gangster Francis "Two Gun" Crowley

7. "I knew it. I knew it. Born in a hotel room and, God damn it, died in a hotel room."
   —Eugene O'Neill, US playwright

8. "God damn you!"
   —King George of the United Kingdom, to a nurse as she administered a painful injection of a sedative

9. "Channel 5 is all shit, isn't it? Christ, the crap they put on there. It's a waste of space."
   —Adam Faith, British actor and singer

10. "That's all guys. Fuck."
    —The captain of Vladivostok Avia Airlines flight 352, which crashed and exploded in flames in the Siberian woodlands near the village of Burdakovka, about twenty-one miles from Irkutsk, on July 4, 2001, killing all 145 people on board

FURTHER READING

A Cow Is Too Much Trouble in Los Angeles by Joseph Foster
  (Duell, Sloan & Pearce, 1952)

A History of Orgies by Burgo Partridge (Prion, 2002)

Advances in Potato Chemistry and Technology by Jaspreet
  Singh & Lovedeep Kaur (Academic Press, 2009)

Afterthoughts of a Worm Hunter by David Crompton
  (Glenstrae Press, 2009)

An Incomplete History of the Art of the Funerary Violins
by Rohan Kriwaczek (Gerald Duckworth & Co., 2006)

An Intellectual History of Cannibalism by Catalin Avramescu
(Princeton University Press, 2009)

Baboon Metaphysics by Dorothy L. Cheney & Robert M. Seyfarth
(University of Chicago Press, 2007)

Bacon: A Love Story by Heather Lauer (William Morrow, 2009)

Be Bold with Bananas (author unknown—Crescent Books, 1972)

Bombproof Your Horse by Rick Pelicano & Laufren Tjaden (J. A.
Allen, 2004)

Budgeting for Infertility by Evelina W. Sterling & Angie Best-Boss
(Fireside, 2009)

Cheese Problems Solved by P. L. H. McSweeney (Woodhead
Publishing, 2007)

Collectible Spoons of the Third Reich by James A. Yannes
(Trafford Publishing, 2009)

Crocheting Adventures with Hyperbolic Planes by Daina
Taimina (A K Peters, 2009)

Curbside Consultation of the Colon by Brooks & D. Cash
(SLACK Incorporated, 2009)

Dental Management of Sleep Disorders by Donald Attanasio
& Dennis R. Bailey (Wiley Blackwell, 2009)

Fancy Coffins to Make Yourself by Dale L. Power (Schiffer
Publishing, 2000)

Fifty Sad Chairs by Bill Keaggy (Blue Q, 2008)

Flow: The Cultural Story of Menstruation by Elissa Stein and
Susan Kim (St. Martin's Griffin, 2009)

Food Digestion and Thermal Preference of Toad by Hsin-Lin
Wei (VDM Verlag Dr. Muller Aktiengesellschaft & Co., 2009)

Highlights in the History of Concrete by C. C. Stanley (British
Cement Association, 1979)

History of Shit by Dominique Laporte (MIT Press, 2002)

How Green Were the Nazis? by Franz-Josef Bruggemeier, Mark Cioc & Thomas Zeller (Ohio University Press, 2005)

How to Be Pope: What to Do and Where to Go Once You're in the Vatican by Piers Marchant (Chronicle Books, 2005)

How to Defend Yourself Against Alien Abduction by Ann Druffel (Crown Publications, 1999)

How To Make Love While Conscious by Guy Kettlehack (HarperCollins, 1993)

How to Shit in the Woods: An Environmentally Sound Approach to a Lost Art by Kathleen Meyer (Ten Speed Press, 1989)

If You Want Closure in Your Relationship, Start with Your Legs by B. Boom (Simon & Schuster, 2006)

I'm Not Hanging Noodles on Your Ears by Jhag Bhalla (National Geographic, 2009)

Is the Rectum a Grave? by Leo Bersani (University of Chicago Press, 2009)

Is Your Dog Gay? by Charles Kreloff, Patty Brown, Victoria Roberts (Simon & Schuster Ltd., 2005)

I Was Tortured by the Pygmy Love Queen by Jasper McCutcheon (The Nazca Plains Corporation, 2007)

Knitting with Dog Hair: Better a Sweater from a Dog You Know and Love Than from a Sheep You'll Never Meet by Kendall Crolius & Anne Montgomery (St. Martin's Griffin, 1997)

Living with Crazy Buttocks by Kaz Cooke (Penguin, 2001)

Masturbation: The History of a Great Terror by Jean Stengers, Anne Van Neck & Kathryn Hoffmann (Palgrave Macmillan, 2001)

Old Tractors and the Men Who Love Them: How to Keep Your Tractors Happy and Your Family Running by Roger Welsch (MBI, 1995)

Oral Sadism and the Vegetarian Personality by Glenn Ellenbogen (Routledge, 1996)

People Who Don't Know They're Dead: How They Attach Themselves to Unsuspecting Bystanders and What to Do About It by Gary Leon Hill (Red Wheel/Weiser, 2005)

Proceedings of the Second International Workshop on Nude Mice (University of Tokyo Press, 1978)

Remember Your Rubbers: Collectible Condom Containers by G. K. Elliott, Dennis O'Brien & George Goehring (Schiffer Publishing, 1998)

Reusing Old Graves: A Report on Popular British Attitudes by Douglas Davies and Alastair Shaw (Shaw & Son, 1995)

Sodomy and the Pirate Tradition: English Sea Rovers in the Seventeenth Century Caribbean by B. R. Burg (New York University Press, 1995)

Superfluous Hair and Its Removal by A. F. Niemueller (NYC: Harvest House, 1940)

Tattooed Mountain Women and Spoon Boxes of Daghestan by Robert Chenciner, Gabib Ismailov, Magomedkhan Magomedkhanov & Alex Binnie (Bennett & Bloom, 2006)

Teddy Bear Cannibal Massacre by Tim Lieder (Dybbuk Press, 2005)

The Amputee's Guide to Sex by Jillian Weise (Soft Skull Press, 2007)

The Baby Jesus Butt Plug by Carlton Mellick (Eraserhed Press, 2004)

The Big Book of Lesbian Horse Stories by Alisa Surkis & Monica Nolan (Kensington Publishing, 2002)

The Great Pantyhose Crafts Book by Edward A. Baldwin & Stevie Baldwin (Western Publishing, 1982)

The Haunted Vagina by Carlton Mellick III (Eraserhead Press, 2006)

The Lesbian S/M Safety Manual by Pat Califia (Alyson Books, 1988)

The Madam as Entrepreneur: Career Management in House Prostitution by Barbara Sherman Heyl (Transaction Press, 1979)

The Origin of Feces by Mark Bown (Baker Street Publishing, 2009)

The Romance of Proctology by Charles Elton Blanchard (AMS Press, 1978)

The Stray Shopping Carts of Eastern North America: A Guide to Field Identification by Julian Montague (Abrams Image, 2006)

The Waterless Toilet—Is It Right for You? by Ron Poitras (Prairee City Books, 2002)

Walled Up Nuns and Nuns Walled In by W. Lancelot Holland (Holland, 1895)

What Kind of Bean Is This Chihuahua? by Tara Jansen-Meyer (Mirror Publishing, 2009)

What to Say When You Talk to Yourself by Shad Helmsetter (Thorsons, 1991)

Why Do I Vomit? by Angela Royston (Heinemann Library, 2003)

Karl Shaw wrote and illustrated for UK newspapers and magazines for several years before working in advertising and marketing. He now lives in Staffordshire, England, where he has channeled a misdirected education into several books, including *Royal Babylon: The Alarming History of European Royalty; 5 People Who Died During Sex; Curing Hiccups with Small Fires: A Miscellany of Great British Eccentrics;* and *10 Ways to Recycle a Corpse.*